THE ABSURD HERO IN AMERICAN FICTION

THE *Absurd Hero*

IN AMERICAN FICTION

UPDIKE • STYRON • BELLOW • SALINGER

REVISED EDITION

BY DAVID D. GALLOWAY

UNIVERSITY OF TEXAS PRESS, AUSTIN & LONDON

*Published with the assistance of a grant from the
Ford Foundation under its program for the support of
publications in the humanities and social sciences.*

Printed in the United States of America
by the Printing Division of The University of Texas, Austin
Bound by Universal Bookbindery, Inc., San Antonio
Second Printing, 1971

For Lyle Glazier

PREFACE TO THE FIRST EDITION

In popular badinage, as in serious literary criticism, "absurdity" is the *bon mot* if not always the *mot juste* of this decade. I should therefore point out in the beginning that the concept of the absurd treated in these pages differs considerably from its use with respect to the contemporary theatre—especially the theatre of Beckett and Ionesco. The most obvious differences are in terms of style: the surfaces, at least, of the work of John Updike, William Styron, Saul Bellow, and J. D. Salinger are far more conventionally "realistic" than anything found in avant-garde drama. And as style is above all the writer's method of expressing his point of view, there are also, therefore, fundamental divergences in attitudes. The initial assumptions of absurd literature are, however, compatible: the belief that human experience is fragmented, irritating, *apparently* unredeemable. The ubiquitousness of the absurd arises from the individual artist's vision of the ultimate consequences of this life-denying experience. Albert Camus repeatedly suggested that man could, despite the hostility of an absurd environment, establish a new and viable basis for heroism and thus for human dignity; the "non-hero" who populates so much contemporary drama and fiction is thus not the sole or unavoidable product of such a milieu. In short, absurd literature can be either optimistic or pessimistic; the fundamental and determining issue is whether, in the conflict between man and his "absurd" environment, man or environment will emerge victorious; whether, in terms of the individual, humanistic or nihilistic impulses will dominate; whether, denied conventional social and religious consolation, man is capable of producing adequate spiritual antibodies to resist despair. Thus, when we deal with absurd literature, we are confronted as we are in all styles (but particularly, as an historical precedent, in naturalism) not solely with the immediate image of life which the artist presents, but with the ultimate conclusions to which his work leads us: is absurdity both our birthright and our inevitable doom, or is it merely another vigil through which man must pass in advancing to a new level of human consciousness and new standards of responsibility? Is it senescence or puberty?

Like Camus, the four contemporary novelists discussed in this book share a belief in man's ability to establish a new secular humanism in a world not only postlapsarian, but also post-Freudian and collectivist. If such a man goes beyond the absurd, he does so only by coming directly to grips with his absurd environment; he is thus an absurd hero. The fruits of his labor may also seem absurd in comparison with traditional notions of heroic conflict and reward (or redemption); but they bring a believable promise of rain to the fashionable wasteland, and because they transcend (or promise to transcend) the absurd in terms of the absurd, the challenge which they offer to the choristers of anti-literature possesses vital integrity.

Because the novelists whom I have considered are optimistic chroniclers of the absurd experience, their work is stylistically less extreme than that of Beckett or Ionesco, less preposterously discontinuous and fragmented than a novel like William Gaddis's *The Recognitions* or Lawrence Ferlinghetti's *Her*. For however unconventional the environments and "heroes" of whom they treat, their work is part of a recognizable humanistic tradition; indeed, the only term which seems to me at all satisfactory in describing the redeeming life-stance which they suggest, is "post-existential humanism," a phrase offered by Wylie Sypher in his provocative study of *The Loss of the Self*.

A number of reasons encourage me to investigate the optimistic literature of the absurd rather than the pessimistic. First of all, the angry, pessimistic, even nihilistic literature of the postwar decades, in its extremes of attitude and form, has been vigorously self-advertising—however unclearly it may have been understood; the wasteland theory of literature has thus become something of a popular as well as a critical cliché, meaninglessness has often characterized both theme and style (most extremely, perhaps, in William Burroughs), and alienation has become the hallmark of the "serious" novel and the "serious" novelist. This book does not attempt to deny the significance or the richness of the work produced by exponents of the pessimistic concept of absurdity, but merely to suggest that this view is countered by a weight of optimism, and indeed one represented by some of the most skilled writers of our time: writers who grant the absurd premises, but who deny, even decry, the somewhat conventional absurd conclusions. Merely to chronicle the horrors and hazards of a meaningless world may be a significant achievement (and one in which the American gift for gab can be a great asset), and some of these contemporary chronicles—most notably Thomas Pynchon's V—have employed exciting and perhaps crucial new narrative techniques; but an obsession with the meaningless can result in art that is puerile, or merely prurient, as contrived and predictable and fashionable as the "mass," selfless world which it purports to reject. Pynchon avoids these pitfalls through his acute comic vision as well as sheer stylistic dexterity, as do a large company of younger humorists—Terry Southern, J. P. Donleavy, Thomas Berger, Bruce Jay Friedman, Donald Barthelme, John Barth, Warren Miller, James Purdy, Ken Kesey, and Richard G. Stern—who promise to usher in a vital new phase in American fiction. And despite the frequent "blackness" of their humor, it serves to maintain a crucial balance, to avoid the pitfalls of preciousness and chic despair.

In our devoted mourning of the giants of the older generation, the flurry of lionizing and then denigrating the Beat Generation, the typically American fascination with cultivating and appropriating such new writers as the black humorists, and in merchandising the hitherto unpublishable like Henry Miller, we have perhaps slighted what may well be the most important development in contemporary American fiction, represented by those writers who have grappled

with the meaningless and with great integrity have suggested paths
through the modern wasteland, even if they have not always been
able to chart those paths with complete precision. Recognizing the
discontinuity of much modern experience, they nonetheless have
seen man's plight in terms of a continuous humanistic tradition, and
not as some uniquely soured modern pottage. They can express despair without succumbing to it, and they can question and deny the
validity of traditional consolations without denying the traditions
of the human spirit.

I have turned to the work of Albert Camus because his essays—
particularly those in *The Myth of Sisyphus*—seem to me most consistently and fruitfully to present the optimistic potential of the absurd experience, and to offer useful terminology for an analysis of
that experience in fiction. I have nowhere maintained that he has
exercised a direct influence on the four novelists whom I have analyzed, but only that they share impressions of the modern environment and hopes for it which are mutually illuminating. I have consciously avoided any discussion of Camus's own ambiguous relationship to the existentialist movement, which is itself continuously recruiting new founding fathers (or grandfathers—as in Paul Tillich's
tracing of the movement to Pascal) and claiming an almost mean-
inglessly wide circle of progeny. The most fundamental question
raised by these novelists is, to be sure, *existenz*, and the choice between being and nothingness is always with us; nonetheless, my primary interest in Camus has been his vivid evocation of what so often
seems the dominant mood of our literary time, and his description
of the alternatives which man can choose during the dark night of
the besieged soul.

In electing to discuss the work of Updike, Styron, Bellow, and
Salinger in light of these theories, I have excluded, of course, other
writers who might have been considered with equal fruitfulness.
John Hawkes and Edward Lewis Wallant seem to me the most significant contemporary omissions, and I particularly regret that Wallant

receives only brief reference in *The Absurd Hero*; but his four brilliant and moving novels surely qualify him for a book in his own right. In the final analysis, I can only resist hiding behind the idea that selection entails omission, for my choice of these particular novelists is also the result of a personal conviction that each has made a major and distinct contribution to our understanding of the contemporary milieu, and that each now presents us with an adequate "critical mass" to warrant such detailed analysis. Nonetheless, it is to be hoped that this book will not contribute to that instant canonization which literary criticism all too often produces in America. Of the four writers presented here, only Saul Bellow has fulfilled what is patronizingly termed a writer's "promise," though all of them have produced works of social and intellectual significance. Updike may still fall prey to his precocious sense of technique (though this seems to me unlikely), and Styron is yet to demonstrate that he can successfully combine in a mature work the compressed metaphysical style of *The Long March* with the more epic and frequently diffuse point of view which characterizes his two long novels. And if Seymour Glass succumbed to the mystical banana fever, J. D. Salinger may never himself recover from Seymour fever; that, in any event, is what most of his recent fiction suggests—in particular, the charmingly inconsequential "Hapworth 16, 1924," published too recently to be discussed in *The Absurd Hero*. But if the final literary merits of these writers must await the verdict of future generations, the value of their diverse examinations of the absurd modern environment is nonetheless of acute significance to this generation, and it is to analyze the significance of their novels, not to canonize the novelists, that *The Absurd Hero* was written.

The University of Sussex
Brighton, England

PREFACE TO THE REVISED EDITION

Several years have elapsed since the following study was completed, and I look back on it now with something of that surprised recognition one experiences when discovering himself staring out from a forgotten photograph. The face is familiar, but time has wrought changes, and my first impulse was to make sweeping alterations in order to reflect these changes more thoroughly than the brief scope of a preface will permit. In the end, I have had to content myself with some selective retouching: these introductory remarks, the correction of errors in the original text, and the updating of the four checklists. Criticism of contemporary literature must always lag behind the dynamic fact of that literature, and it would be "absurd" to presume otherwise; but the four writers considered here still represent a vital part of the modern American literary experience—which will hopefully argue the relevance of repeating this description of the post-existential tradition to which Updike, Styron, Bellow, and Salinger seem to me to belong.

My own more recent interests have carried me toward the more extreme philosophical and stylistic aspects of "absurd" thought—into the *nouveau roman,* the modern theater and cinema, and the fine arts.[1] Nevertheless, I continue to believe that there is a recognizable tradition in Western literature whereby the absurd becomes a way of affirming the resources of the human spirit, of exalting sacrifice and suffering, of ennobling the man capable of sustaining the vital opposition between intention and reality. That American writers

[1] See my article "Absurd Art, Absurd Men, Absurd Heroes," in *The Literature of the Western World,* vol. VI, ed. David Daiches and A. J. Thorlby.

should so frequently illustrate these more affirmative aspects of absurd experience is hardly surprising. The writer in America has traditionally had a strong resistance to despair, and although there are now signs that an absurd tradition, in something like the purer "French" sense, is emerging in America, absurd art in its most extreme forms will no doubt continue to be tempered by the essential optimism and the concern for practical solutions that so strongly color American thinking and that serve as a barrier to the exploitation of those darker and more grotesque absurdities encountered in Beckett or Genet or Kosinski.

Since the initial publication of *The Absurd Hero in American Fiction,* two large and complex novels have appeared that call for special attention. Both John Updike's *Couples* and William Styron's *The Confessions of Nat Turner* are impressive achievements, although neither, perhaps, is the novel for which Updike's or Styron's followers have hoped for so many years; both have obvious flaws, but any balanced critical appraisal of their virtues has been obscured by the highly topical controversies that they provoked, and that the novels themselves seemed to invite. In narrative manner, structure, and symbolism, both are rather "old fashioned": they are intricately plotted, densely populated (although dominated by a single male character), historically allusive, and constructed with a craftsmanlike pride in neat, tight joints and well-mitred corners that accommodate their carpenter heroes with symbolic appropriateness. Both works suffer at times from a top-heavy weight of symbolic innuendo, and both raise more questions about the experience of the hero than they are able to answer. While *Couples* seems to me more totally realized than *The Confessions of Nat Turner,* both are engrossing studies of the insidious mechanisms by which society creates its victims, asks them to make public their agony, and then purges itself through their ritual sacrifice.

In *Couples,* John Updike moved from the miniaturist tradition in which he had consistently worked, to the creation of a vast and

variously populated fictional world. The contrast between this sprawling novel and his earlier, simple, lyric works seems at first improbable
—as though Jane Austen had decided to write *Middlemarch*. (There
are real parallels between this novel and George Eliot's work, not
merely in Updike's creation of a macrocosmic environment, but also
in his use of contemporary history and his overt treatment of a
sexuality that is strongly present in the symbols of *Middlemarch*.)
Nonetheless, the break with his own creative past is not so great as
it first appears. First of all, Updike has always sung the praises of
heterosexual love; no American writer has described the physical act
itself with more rapturous or voluptuous language. Furthermore, Updike's central preoccupation is still, as it has always been, with the
prerequisites, the privileges, the scope, and the terror of individual
freedom; his hero is still a pilgrim in search of that world where his
soul can give its best.

Structurally, *Couples* represents a new departure; thematically, it
carries forward the quest motif reiterated by Updike in all his major
work; stylistically, it furthers the argument that even his most hostile
critics grudgingly allow—that for sheer technical mastery of the
English language, Updike has few contemporary equals. In *Couples*,
that mastery is most readily apparent in the descriptions of sexual
encounters—never marred by the face of the giggling schoolboy who
sometimes emerges in Lawrence. But Updike can shower on inani-
mate objects, or on fleeting sensations, the same wealth of language,
endowing them not so much with symbolic import (when he does, the
symbols are often too obtrusive) as with an enrichment of their own
significant reality, their "thingness." The following brief passage,
casual and entirely representational in manner, illustrates well the
distinctive magic of such a style: "He would spend most of each day
on Indian Hill with the three ranch houses, which rose in quick
frames from the concrete foundations: an alphabet of two-by-fours,
N and T and M and H, interlocked footings and girders and joists
and studs and plates and sills. Piet, hammer in hand, liked to feel
the bite taken into gravity."

Updike's hero, Piet Hanema, finds "all his fate in the letters of his name: *me, a man, amen ah.*" His role as modern everyman and the religious implications of his quest are thus carefully suggested. The jacket design for *Couples,* a detail from William Blake's watercolor drawing *Adam and Eve Sleeping,* selected by Updike himself, is hardly (as some reviewers suggested) a gratuitous attempt to give the novel's frank sexual scenes a respectable context. The drawing is related to the novel in a variety of ways, but most significantly through the numerous references to Eden and to the prelapsarian, "overheated warmth" of the greenhouse where Piet played as a boy; through his own obsession with his parents' death; and through the name Piet, with its suggestions of piety and Pietà.

In one sense, Piet's "sacrifice" is a redemption of the fallen world of Tarbox: "The couples, though they had quickly sealed themselves off from Piet's company, from contamination by his failure, were yet haunted and chastened, as if his fall had been sacrificial." And Piet, with his reverence for past civilizations (arrowheads and unearthed Indian bones), the simple joy he takes in carpentry, his compassion and his acute awareness of death, is appropriately compared to both Christ and Noah, as well as to Adam. But Updike's novel is hardly a simple allegory, and it is ultimately through the flesh that Piet finds his way out of the maze of gossip and adultery and cynicism that is Tarbox. He leaves behind the angel Angela to love a woman of the earth, Foxy, and the church that had once promised some other consolation stands in ruins.

Thus, Updike has once more celebrated the communion of love—more fully and more hopefully than in any of his previous novels. Piet's roguish quest is more than an exceptionally energetic example of the fashionable couplings of a fashionable New England town; it is an earnest, often harrowing search for something to still the voice of death that rings in his ears. In celebrating the body, he also celebrates life itself. That he does so singlemindedly, without regard for custom and convention, and, most significantly, in a world that speaks repeatedly in terms of death (his parents, a hamster, Indian bones,

the Kennedy baby, Kennedy himself, Foxy's aborted child, John
Ong), is sufficient, I believe, for him to represent the absurd tradition
as defined by Camus—the tradition in which a man consistently opposes his inmost intention to even the most hostile reality. Piet
Hanema is as intriguing, as whole, as real, and as "heroic" a character
as we have had in American literature for a great many years; and
Couples, despite occasional repetitiveness and a creaking Victorian
conclusion, is a novel whose interest will not soon be exhausted.

There are moments when the conjuring act on which *The Confessions of Nat Turner* depends is unquestionably successful, but ultimately Styron's own rich prose style betrays him. Perhaps the choice
of a first-person narrator was a mistake, although equally improbable
but imaginatively far more successful experiments with first-person
narration have been made in a number of recent novels, including
Romulus Linney's *Slowly, By Thy Hand Unfurled* and Brian Moore's
I Am Mary Donne. At times Nat Turner tells us too much, in a
language far too subtle, too literary and polished; at other moments
he tells us too little, as though there were areas of his experience that
Styron himself was incapable of penetrating—for the vagueness cannot be Nat's alone. There are even instances when the novel assumes
an almost journalistic anonymity, when the speaking voice seems to
belong neither to Styron nor to Nat, as in the description of Miss
Sarah: ". . . a fat, silly, sweet woman with small intelligence but with
an amplitude of good cheer that enabled her to disgorge without
effort peals of jolly, senseless laughter." The style here is surely closer
to Fielding than to Styron, and at any rate wholly inappropriate for a
Negro slave who has learned to write chiefly by his own reading of
the Bible.

That clouds melodramatically fill the sky on days of ill fortune or
that the sun conveniently spotlights moments of joy seems to me
appropriate to the novel's tone and intentions. Nat would seek just
such supernatural confirmation and perhaps imagine it if it were not
present, but there is no such organic justification for his description

of the approach of cavalrymen as "a plunging of hoofbeats in erratic muffled tattoo." It is perhaps true that the fictional narrator must be more aware and more articulate than his real-life counterpart, but the reader, expecting at least an illusion of reality, too often finds an overzealous imitation of high romantic prose; that Nat, gazing from his prison window, would describe a steaming chamber pot as a "crucible" asks more suspension of disbelief than the image itself can possibly merit.

There are, to be sure, scenes in which the monologue rings true, particularly when Nat harrangues his followers in the simultaneously wheedling, chiding, flattering language they best understand. Clearly, too, Styron has a fine ear for drawing verbal distinctions between poor whites and "aristocracy" as well as between master and slave. Nat's story is arresting, touching, and disturbing, but a great deal of the enigma shrouding his extraordinary life originates not so much in his tormented and complex impulses as in the ironically genteel style he uses to recount it—a style described by one of the novel's black critics as "a sterile and leaden prose that not even massive transfusions of Old Testament rhetoric can vitalize, a strange fusion of Latinate classicism, a kind of New England Episcopalian prissiness."[2] While some of the objections raised by the ten black writers who "responded" to *The Confessions of Nat Turner* have little to do with the novel's literary merits, most of these critics comment directly or indirectly on the inappropriateness of Styron's language, and the point is well taken.

In a brief preface to *The Confessions of Nat Turner*, Styron describes the novel as "a meditation on history," thereby asking that it be understood in terms of a contemporary literary phenomenon that has nothing to do with the irritated racial nerves the novel initially touched. Various contemporary novelists have questioned the arbitrary lines once thought to make a neat division between fact and

---

[2] Mike Thelwell, "Back with the Wind: Mr. Styron and the Reverend Turner," *William Styron's Nat Turner: Ten Black Writers Respond,* ed. John Henrik Clarke, p. 81.

fiction, between "truth" and "imagination." John Barth's *The Sot-Weed Factor*, Truman Capote's *In Cold Blood*, and Norman Mailer's *Armies of the Night* question both the relevance of such literary gerrymandering and the uses to which "reality" (including the reality of so-called history) can be put in the novel. Like Capote and Mailer, Styron discovered a "real" situation whose imaginative possibilities were strikingly apparent, unquestionably relevant to our times, and symbolically suggestive (a black prophet, a carpenter by training, whose immediate vengeance was directed at the town of Jerusalem).[3] Nonetheless, in *The Confessions of Nat Turner* Styron never presses the question of relevant form as do Barth, Capote, and Mailer. *Armies of the Night* is truly "a meditation on history"; *The Confessions of Nat Turner* is at best a skilled, if forced, "imitation" of history.

The character of Nat Turner, however unsatisfactorily developed, has interesting parallels with a kind of absurd man who has figured more prominently in European than in American fiction. In his attempt to overthrow the white order that has suppressed him, Nat becomes a cousin, at least, to a type I have found of increasing interest and relevance—the absurd man as criminal. The type was richly explored in Camus's *Caligula*, where the young emperor's growing awareness of the absurdity of existence provoked him to

---

[3] There are interesting antecedents to Styron's work in Herman Melville's densely structured, enigmatic novella *Benito Cereno*. Melville found the germ of his story in Captain Amasa Delano's *Narrative of Voyages and Travels* (1817), and responded deeply to the imaginative implications of Delano's turgid account of a slave uprising at sea. Symbolically, the domination of the effete Spanish nobleman by the vengeful slaves would have appealed to Melville; so, too, would the captain's name, Benito Cereno. Babo, the mastermind of the bloody revolt, takes no lives himself, but leaves most of the violence to a savage giant who is his second-in-command—an interesting parallel to the relationship between Nat and Will; and Babo is seen, in the conclusion of the story, as a kind of black Christ. A comparison of Melville's novella with Delano's own narration offers a unique insight into the functioning of the creative imagination. Unhappily, a comparison of Styron's *Confessions* with Nat's own is a far less rewarding exercise.

force a similar awareness on his complacent patricians; to do so he challenged a hostile and destructive universe through the sheer force of his own most despotic powers. While Caligula's actions are hostile to the reverence for life that Camus found at the heart of the absurd, criminal activity is clearly one way of sustaining the disproportion between intention and reality.

No more powerful expression of a criminal response to the absurd is to be found than in the work of Jean Genet. Genet's intention is to unseat bourgeois values, to make us accept our own darkest selves, and to create a morality of drugs, thievery, imposture, homosexuality, and murder that is the precise inverse of the conventional (and, for Genet, life-denying) bourgeois morality to which his characters are denied admission. In a world where all men of feeling are outsiders, the criminal and the convict, bathed in improbably elegant imagery, stand for and suffer from the universal human plight; hence, the criminal in Genet's work is often metamorphosed into a saint, and in *Notre-Dame-des-Fleurs*, Our Lady achieves his moment of greatest glory when he ascends the scaffold. Similar conceptions of the hero as criminal are to be found in Melville's *Confidence Man*, Dostoevski's underground men, Thomas Mann's Felix Krull, and Joyce Cary's Gully Jimson. No artist in our own day, however, has carried the sense of the necessity of criminal response so far as Genet.

The concept of rebellion is fundamental to the absurd, and in the violence of his protest against the white "reality" of tidewater Virginia, Nat Turner joins with other absurd characters who sustain the disproportion between intention and reality through criminal activity; he also shares with them a characteristic lack of remorse. But Styron himself seems uncertain that we should accept his character on these terms, and in the concluding paragraphs of the novel Nat vanishes into Baldwinesque romanticism. *The Confessions of Nat Turner* is an important work because of the vital questions it raises concerning the form and function of the novel; it is compelling because at moments something like a realized vision of Nat Turner emerges from beneath the rhetoric; and it is memorable in its painstakingly detailed portrait of plantation life. Styron is still clearly one of our most talented writers, but the ultimate significance of Nat Turner's experience seems to elude him. Nonetheless, there are sufficient hints of that significance to demonstrate a link between Nat and numerous other contemporary heroes (including Piet Hanema) who pit their wills against an indifferent world and who are exalted, not by their "victories," but by the very fierceness of their striving.

Case Western Reserve University
Cleveland, Ohio

ACKNOWLEDGMENTS

So many persons have given me their generous advice and assistance in the preparation of this book that it would be difficult to name them all and to express the proper gratitude in only a few paragraphs. Though I am not able to cite all of the thoughtful friends and colleagues who gave me encouragement and stimulation through their conversation and letters, my gratitude to them is nonetheless real, and in an equally real sense, this book is addressed to them.

The ideas which are presented here first took shape under the guidance of Lyle Glazier, Professor of English at the State University of New York, at Buffalo; his generous interest has been my constant and invaluable mainstay through every stage in the preparation of this book, which is dedicated to him with affectionate gratitude. Like the many students who have benefitted from his example and encouragement, I owe him an immense debt of personal and professional thanks; for his sake and for theirs, I wish that this could be a far better book.

Mrs. Shirley Stout, of the State University of New York, read the first draft of *The Absurd Hero* and made numerous detailed and enlightening suggestions for revision. John Updike graciously consented to read the chapter devoted to his work, commented most helpfully on the concept of the new, secular "saint" in his novels, corrected misprints which had appeared in his early work, and offered well-timed encouragement for my study of the absurd. Although he has formally posted his work against "symbol-hunters," Saul Bellow sympathetically discussed with me the concept of absurdity in contemporary literature, and the possible role which it plays in his own fiction.

In my introduction to the four checklists which conclude this book I acknowledge some of the more important sources of technical assistance which I received in their preparation. Here also, however, I should like to thank the State University of New York and the University of Sussex for research funds which permitted me to keep these checklists up to date.

Portions of an earlier draft of this book have appeared in journals, and I am grateful to their editors for permission to use some of that material here: to *Critique* for "The Love Stance: Richard Kim's *The Martyred*" (Winter, 1964–1965) and "Clown and Saint: The Hero in Current American Fiction" (Spring–Summer, 1965); to *Modern Fiction Studies* for "The Absurd Man as Saint: The Novels of John Updike" (Summer, 1964); to *The Southern Review* for "Moses-Bloom-Herzog: Saul Bellow's Everyman" (Winter, 1966); and to *Texas Studies in Literature and Language* for "The Absurd Man as Picaro: The Novels of Saul Bellow" (Summer, 1964) and "The Absurd Man as Tragic Hero: The Novels of William Styron" (Winter, 1965).

I am also grateful to the following publishers for permitting me to quote from copyrighted editions: The Bobbs-Merrill Company for William Styron's *Lie Down in Darkness*, copyrighted, 1961, by William Styron; Harcourt, Brace and World for T. S. Eliot's *The Cocktail Party*, copyrighted, 1950, by T. S. Eliot, and for "The Function of Criticism," from *Selected Essays*, copyrighted, 1932, 1936, 1950 by the publisher, and 1960, 1964, by T. S. Eliot; Alfred A. Knopf for Albert Camus's *The Myth of Sisyphus* and *The Rebel*, and for John Updike's *The Centaur, The Poorhouse Fair, Rabbit, Run, Pigeon Feathers*, and *The Same Door*; McIntosh, McKee and Dodds, Inc. for William Styron's *The Long March*, copyrighted, 1951, by William Styron; Random House for William Styron's *Set This House on Fire*; Vanguard Press for Saul Bellow's *Dangling Man* and *The Victim*; and to Viking Press for Saul Bellow's *The Adventures of Augie March, Seize the Day, Henderson the Rain King*, and *Herzog*, and for the interview with William Styron in *Writers at Work* by Peter Matthiessen and George Plimpton.

CONTENTS

THE ABSURD HERO IN AMERICAN FICTION

I thought of literature then, and I think of it now, of the literature of the world, of the literature of Europe, of the literature of a single country, not as a collection of the writings of individuals, but as "organic wholes," as systems in relation to which, and only in relation to which, individual works of literary art, and the works of individual artists, have their significance. There is accordingly something outside of the artist to which he owes his allegiance, a devotion to which he must surrender and sacrifice himself in order to earn and obtain his unique position. A common inheritance and a common cause unite artists consciously or unconsciously: it must be admitted that the union is mostly unconscious. Between the true artists of any time there is, I believe, an unconscious community.

T. S. Eliot, "The Function of Criticism" (1923)

THE MYTH OF THE *Absurd*

The decay of traditional Christianity as a unifying force in the life of Western man, whether it be mourned, celebrated, or merely acquiesced to, cannot be ignored. Since the death of the Genteel Tradition the theme of the exiled individual in a meaningless universe—a universe in which precepts of religious orthodoxy seem increasingly less relevant—has challenged the imagination of American writers with an almost overwhelming urgency. Despite the persistence of institutional Christianity—as measured by church construction and attendance—modern man seems continually less able to find order and meaning in his life. While he seems increasingly reluctant to take the leap into faith, nihilism rarely produces card-carrying agnostics. Thus, what might be called the "religious quest" continues to exert a powerful influence on the minds of Western thinkers. Albert Camus suggested the reason for this determined questing when he said that "A world that can be explained even with bad reasons is a familiar world."[1] The world ceases to be familiar when even the worst reasons fail to be of any help in explaining or ordering it. All of the old ex-

[1] Albert Camus, *The Myth of Sisyphus*, trans. Justin O'Brien, p. 5.

planations—ethical and scientific—have failed where many modern
thinkers are concerned, bringing them face to face with an alien
universe in which orthodox "systems" can offer at best only a superficial reassurance.

Camus presented a thorough examination of man's hunger for
unity in the face of a disordered universe in *The Myth of Sisyphus.*
This persistent appetite for unity appears to be diametrically opposed
to the reality which contemporary man encounters, and the disproportion between man's "intention and the reality he will encounter"
Camus labels the "absurd." " 'It's absurd' means not only 'It's impossible,' but also 'It's contradictory'."[2] In regarding the absurd quest
for unity as essentially religious Camus is in accord with the prag-
matic anthropological definition of religion as anything which works
for a people insofar as it fulfills needs they define as "spiritual." In
no sense do Camus's writings attempt to establish a new religion, but
they recognize religion in the broad sense in striving to suggest an
outline of conduct with which modern Western man may face the
ethical problems of his age. Critic Charles Glicksberg spells out Camus's concern with those problems that have traditionally fallen
within the compass of theology:

the absence of God, the relationship of a God who is all-powerful and all-
knowing to the evil and the suffering that exist on earth, the contrast between the routine of life and the crisis of being lost and alone and doomed
that the Existentialist hero experiences, the disruption of familiar, human
reality by the knowledge of the inevitability and imminence of death, the
search for the authentic life on this journey to the end of night.[3]

What Camus eventually describes is a stance which man may take
in a universe in which the old codes of religious authoritarianism no
longer suffice to fulfill man's spiritual needs. The stance of Camus's
absurd man is anthropocentric, and its eventual opposition to both
suicide and murder is based on the assumption that all promise of

[2] *Ibid.,* p. 22.
[3] Charles A. Glicksberg, "Camus's Quest for God," *Southwest Review,* 44
(Summer, 1959), p. 250.

value rests in life itself. In reaffirming the potential meaningfulness of life, Camus established a new and distinctly modern basis for heroism, and he suggested both affirmation and heroism in choosing Sisyphus as the central figure of an essay designed to revaluate "the very warrant for continuing human existence and the possible resources of the human spirit in a universe that appears no longer to make sense."[4] It is a universe in which "right and wrong have lost their ancient names, as the ancient order that named them has crumbled; and the task, as he has seen it, is not to restore but to create anew."[5]

Camus's impression of the confrontation of intention and reality sets the stage for an interpretation of modern man's dilemma as little dependent on nihilism as it is on supernatural consolation, and Camus sees the novel as an ideal form for mirroring and confirming this confrontation. Not only does the novel itself represent a kind of revolt in favor of order, but "the growth of the novel corresponds, historically, to the beginnings of the modern metaphysical revolt . . ."[6] In his emphasis on art as a form of order Camus seems clearly opposed to the contemporary French "anti-novel." By selecting and rearranging elements from reality and composing them into an imaginative pattern the artist gives them a meaningfulness and a coherence which they would otherwise not have possessed. As an imaginative recreation of experience the novel can thus, in and of itself, become a revolt against a world which appears to have no logical pattern.

If the condition of the absurd is so widespread as Camus argues, and if the novel does indeed mirror the absurd as well as revolt against it, we might well expect to find contemporary novels of absurdity to which Camus's *Myth of Sisyphus* would serve as a key. Camus himself suggested that the concept of the absurd offered a critical aid in understanding the contemporary novel, and reviewers and critics have frequently noted that a knowledge of *The Myth of*

---

[4] R. W. B. Lewis, *The Picaresque Saint*, p. 60.
[5] *Ibid.*, p. 61.
[6] John Cruickshank, *Albert Camus and the Literature of Revolt*, p. 146.

Sisyphus is of great assistance in analyzing Camus's own fiction. While the philosophical essay and the novel are in many respects divergent forms, both are traditionally concerned with the ordering of experience, and Camus saw the novel as a form which harmonized certain of the metaphysical aspects of philosophy with the imaginative structuring of experience which is the traditional province of art. "It is true," as John Cruickshank argues in his study of Camus, "that each activity possesses its own particular climate, but this type of statement merely emphasizes the obvious fact that art is not philosophy and philosophy is not art. Clearly they do not coincide, but there can exist an interpenetration between them and both embody, at the present time, a common disquiet and similar anxieties."[7] It is this suggestive interpenetration between philosophy and art which makes Camus's philosophical writings especially pertinent to a study of contemporary fiction. The demonstration of Camusian elements of absurdity in the contemporary novel does not necessarily prove a borrowing or influence, and certainly does not suggest conscious artistic exercises on philosophical themes. What a demonstration of absurdity does indicate is a sympathetic response to the complex modern environment which Camus demandingly but compassionately explored, both in his fiction and in his philosophical essays. Many American novelists are considering the same disquiet, the same anxieties, and the same apparent lack of meaning and hope which Camus analyzed in *The Myth of Sisyphus,* and they share with Camus a common concern for religious and moral themes, especially in terms of the struggle to find value and fulfillment in a world without God.

The phenomenon of disproportion at the heart of the absurd has been the eternal problem of all great literature, and Camus frequently recognized that the concept of the absurd owed much to thinkers other than himself. Among those whom he cited in *The Myth of Sisyphus* were Husserl, Dostoevski, Nietzsche, and Sartre. What distin-

[7] *Ibid.*, p. 149.

guished Camus from the countless other thinkers who considered the conflict of intention and reality was his refusal of all conventional value systems as either explanation for this conflict or relief from it, and his desire not to describe a new metaphysics, but rather to suggest the basis on which such a metaphysics might eventually be established. Beginning with a *tabula rasa,* Camus proceeded to state what he considered the only pressing contemporary problem: suicide. Faced with a universe "suddenly divested of illusions and lights,"[8] man must decide either to live or to die. If suicide is eventually rejected as a solution to man's absurd situation he is left with the problem of how he should live. Camus admits that a recognition of the meaninglessness of the universe may lead man to defenestration, be it physical suicide or the intellectual suicide of the leap into faith, and his rejection of these reactions to the universe is largely emotional: he simply denies their validity as solutions. By eliminating one of the terms of the conflict between man's intention and the reality he encounters, suicide avoids the problem instead of solving it. Camus attempts to show that the only position of integrity is the one in which the paradox is preserved and in which the individual clings to the resulting tensions and conflicts as the only potential source of meaning. Camus repeatedly emphasizes that the absurd is not a feeling restricted to the province of the philosopher, but one which is as significant for the petty government clerk as it is for the conqueror or the creator. In fact, Camus's own first attempt at absurd fiction, *The Stranger,* centered around the colorless and insignificant clerk, Meursault.

The feeling of the absurd is born when suddenly the chain of mechanical daily gestures is broken, and in the void which results man has the opportunity to ask himself, "Why?" Out of this moment consciousness is born. In Camus's words:

It happens that the stage sets collapse. Rising, streetcar, four hours in the office or factory, meal, streetcar, four hours of work, meal, sleep, and

[8] Camus, *The Myth of Sisyphus,* p. 3.

Monday Tuesday Wednesday Thursday Friday and Saturday according to
the same rhythm—this path is easily followed most of the time. But one
day the "why" arises and everything begins in that weariness tinged with
amazement.[9]

A world which seemed to have order now has only a wearying rhythm. Some are lulled back to sleep by that rhythm, but those who
resist it and remain awake are the ones who must finally, with heightened consciousness, choose between suicide and life. There are many
manifestations of the absurd, of which the collapsing stage set is
only one. "Likewise the stranger who at certain seconds comes to
meet us in a mirror, the familiar and yet alarming brother we encounter in our own photograph is also the absurd."[10] But whatever
the physical circumstances of his absurd awakening, man becomes
detached from his environment. Like the Joycean epiphany, the
absurd moment—which may come in a telephone booth or in a factory or on a battlefield—shows forth to the observer the heart of
the world, and in Camus's vision that heart consists of the entire
meaningless picture of life, "the cruel mathematics that command our
condition." Many American writers—among them the early T. S.
Eliot, Ernest Hemingway, William Faulkner, and Wright Morris—
have noted similar manifestations of the absurd, but it is not with
manifestations so much as with consequences of the absurd vision
that Camus is concerned.

The viciously seductive rhythm of contemporary life is the source
of Camus's comparison of modern man to Sisyphus, for both are involved in exhausting, monotonous, and apparently unending tasks.
Camus's initial vision of the absurd seems nihilistic, but he continually
emphasizes that the apparently nihilistic "feeling of the absurd is not,
for all that, the notion of the absurd. It lays the foundations for it,
and that is all. It is not limited to that notion, except in the brief
moment when it passes judgment on the universe. Subsequently it

9 *Ibid.*, p. 10.
10 *Ibid.*, p. 11.

has a chance of going further"; the feeling of the absurd may be based entirely on the objective recognition of "the disproportion between [a man's] intention and the reality he will encounter."[11] Only that individual who takes the absurd as a truth of existence is able to realize the notion of the absurd, and, through heightened consciousness, bind himself so closely to absurdity that it becomes something to live for.

John Cruickshank has noted that while Valéry ironically commented on the well-developed muscles which Sisyphus achieved in the course of performing his absurd task, "Camus wants much more than this. He wants to discover whether some kind of spiritual muscularity can be obtained, and if so, to what positive use it may be put."[12] In the stages of observation leading to a notion of the absurd the world is seen to contain nothing worth living for and, consequently, nothing worth dying for. With the recognition of the absurd as a constant of experience, an observable (not an absolute) truth, man at last has something to live for and something which, under the appropriate arrangement of psychological circumstances, would be worth dying for. "The frustrated search for truth, which made him conscious of the absurd, is at least satisfied on one point in that it attains the truth of the absurd itself. Now this same desire for truth demands, he claims, that one should maintain and defend any truth that one discovers."[13] It is important to emphasize that the notion of the absurd is dependent on two ingredients: intention and reality. To deny either of those terms is to destroy the absurd, which exists only as a consequence of mind reflecting on the world. Thus, the notion of the absurd is one which leads us automatically to a consideration of the individual, and because the individual is essential to the absurd, our real concern is with the absurd man. If, as Camus says, the absurd demands defense as the only truth isolable in the

---

[11] *Ibid.*, p. 22.
[12] Cruickshank, *Albert Camus,* p. 57.
[13] *Ibid.*, p. 61.

modern environment, we are justified in projecting from the absurd man an absurd hero, one whose concern is with asserting a right to the particular disproportion which he exemplifies. A consideration of the concept of an absurd *hero* is in large part made necessary by the ubiquitousness with which Camus uses the word "absurd"—to refer to the meaningless universe, to the man who suffers in it, to the awareness of suffering, and to the work of art that describes such suffering. Clearly, however, Camus's final interest is not in the man who demonstrates just any kind of disproportion between intention and reality; it does not, for example, end with the individual who, armed only with a sword, singlehandedly attacks a machine-gun nest —although this is an absurd man. Camus's ultimate concern is with the man sufficiently strong to sustain a disproportion on the level of values, a man who persists in his demands for truth in a universe that says truths are impossible.

With the absurd hero, achievement ceases to be a question of victory or defeat but is rather success in sustaining an elemental disproportion. In terms of philosophy the idea that the struggle for truth becomes truth is hardly a new one. Emphasis is shifted from attainment to performance, and in the process of sustaining his performance, of defending his passion for the absurd, the absurd hero achieves fulfillment simply by defending a truth. Absurdity becomes a passion, and the test of the absurd hero is one designed to determine whether he can live with his passions, whether he can accept their law, "which is to burn the heart they simultaneously exalt."[14] Absurdity becomes a defiance of the universe, an extreme tension which will never permit the hero to rest, just as the tormented Sisyphus can never pause in his task. Maintenance of the absurd, moreover, is the only way in which man can rebel against the apparently meaningless universe, since rebellion that does not orient itself to truth is worthless. In the words of Germaine Brée, "The absurd for Camus requires no other universe than our daily world, our earth

[14] Camus, *The Myth of Sisyphus*, p. 17.

as we see it, our fellow men, ourselves. Thus integrated into our daily lives, it can be faced at every moment and, by our action, denied. Our revolt against the absurd begins when our consciousness of its existence is followed by the refusal to be obsessed and paralyzed by it. It is a state of mind. The emphasis which Malraux puts on death, Camus shifts to life. The emphasis which Sartre puts on the total liberty inherent in man's contingency, Camus puts on lucidity."[15]

Camus is able to draw three circumstances from the absurd: "My revolt, my freedom, and my passion." The absurd man becomes free the moment he recognizes his own absurdity, and thus "The myth of Sisyphus means for Camus that the most appalling truths can lose their power over us once we have absolutely recognized and accepted them."[16] A kind of glory descends on the man who is able to recognize and endure the absurd miseries of the world, and therefore Sisyphus, through such recognition, is not only free; at times he may even be happy. The tragedy of Sisyphus, Camus argues, comes solely from the fact that he is conscious, yet it is his very consciousness which causes the pain of his circumstances to vanish; Oedipus' conclusion that "all is well" is cited as "the recipe for the absurd victory."[17] At the moment of consciousness, tragedy begins, but so, too, does the stuff of happiness:

I leave Sisyphus at the foot of the mountain! One always finds one's burden again. But Sisyphus teaches the higher fidelity that negates the gods and raises rocks. He too concludes that all is well. The universe henceforth without a master seems to him neither sterile nor futile. Each atom of that stone, each mineral flake of that night-filled mountain, in itself forms a world. The struggle itself toward the heights is enough to fill a man's heart. One must imagine Sisyphus happy.[18]

Sisyphus becomes the incarnation of the absurd, and the strong appeal which this mythological figure has presented to man's imagina-

---

[15] Germaine Brée, *Camus*, p. 188.
[16] Cruickshank, *Albert Camus*, p. 38.
[17] Camus, *The Myth of Sisyphus*, p. 90.
[18] *Ibid.*, p. 91.

tion suggests something of the possibilities of the development of an absurd hero of great proportions. For Camus, both Don Juan and Don Quixote are companion figures to Sisyphus. Sisyphus is the hero of the absurd "as much through his passions as through his torment. His scorn of the gods, his hatred of death, and his passion for life won him that unspeakable penalty in which the whole being is exerted toward accomplishing nothing. This is the price that must be paid for the passions of the earth."[19] Obviously Camus's concept of the absurd goes beyond the classic figure of Sisyphus, for Sisyphus was forced back to Hades and his hands placed against the rock by his gods. No absolute or higher power commands the labors of the modern Sisyphus. Thus, Camus must reinterpret the Sisyphus myth to emphasize the fact that Sisyphus' labors are a defiance and negation of gods. "His fate belongs to him. His rock is his thing."[20] "Whatever facet of the problem we consider, the essay leads, nevertheless, to one conclusion: life is infinitely valuable to the individual; only by a clear consciousness of the given data of life can the individual reach happiness; happiness, at heart, can only be tragic. The absurd human being is by definition wedded to life; all evasion of life is a capitulation. Life is our rock."[21]

Camus's arguments on the absurd are impressionistic, and it would be unfair, therefore, to demand of them the logic and consistency of a finalized philosophical system. The author himself continually reminds us that they are neither definitive nor proscriptive. Faced with a world in which man's painful odyssey seems meaningless, Camus determines to find a source of meaning which will deny nihilism while avoiding recourse to traditional absolutes. In his *Lettres à un ami allemand*, Camus outlines this purpose, which was the motivation of his life's work:

I continue to believe that this earth has no superior meaning. But I know that something in it makes sense, and that is man, because he is the only

[19] *Ibid.*, p. 89.
[20] *Ibid.*, p. 30.
[21] Brée, *Camus*, p. 204.

being who insists upon it. The world has at least the truth of man, and our task is to give man his justification against fate itself.[22]

Both nihilism and orthodox faith negate the terms of man's conflict and justify fate by accepting it rather than giving man a justification *against* fate. Sartre, who was finally to become one of Camus's most extreme opponents, saw in Camus's very nature the injunction to justify man against fate by living the conflict between intention and reality: "For you bore within yourself all the conflicts of our time and went beyond them because of the ardor with which you lived them."[23] What Sartre saw in Camus was the primary injunction of the absurd: "Live the conflict, for only the conflict can make you free." The decision to live an unending essential conflict does not amount to the renunciation of hope, even though the absurd man does renounce hope in abstract "eternity" and in ever fully comprehending the universe which surrounds him. Life itself—life determined and walled in by absurdities—is now the source of hope.

The underlying, tacitly accepted premise of Camus's study of the absurd is that "man, without the help of the Eternal or of rationalistic thought, can create, all by himself, his own values."[24] The absurd becomes a new and extreme articulation of the necessity of man's appealing to himself as a source of values; its goal is to embrace life rather than to reject it, with the belief that through this embrace man can arrive at the joy of truth. Nevertheless, the absurd theory expounded in *The Myth of Sisyphus* tends more toward a quantitative than a qualitative ethics, as Camus himself suggested: "Belief in the absurd is tantamount to substituting the quantity of experiences for the quality."[25] Although granting the fact that in some cases quantity may constitute quality, Camus is unable—nor does he wish—to

[22] Quoted, *ibid.*, pp. 44–45.

[23] Jean-Paul Sartre, "Réponse à Albert Camus," *Les Temps Modernes* (August, 1952), p. 345. Translated by David D. Galloway.

[24] Albert Camus, *Actuelles, Chroniques* (1944–1948), p. 111. Translated by David D. Galloway.

[25] Camus, *The Myth of Sisyphus*, p. 45.

avoid the implication that the doctrine of the absurd allows for great latitude in human conduct. In the beginning of *Lettres à un ami allemand* Camus notes that both he and his imaginary German friend had begun from the same premise—that of the necessity of rebelling against the absurdity of the world. Their absurd stances were, in terms of the initial theory of *The Myth of Sisyphus,* equally valid, yet Camus had cast his lot with what he called "justice," while the German had cast his with brute terrorism. Because of his own political involvements, Camus thus found it necessary to redefine the absurd, to make it consider the question of murder as well as that of suicide. *The Myth of Sisyphus* had begun with questioning the latter, while *L'homme revolté* began by questioning the former.

A working definition of the absurd which can be applied to the contemporary American novel should generally avoid the theoretical qualifications Camus made in *The Rebel.* It is precisely because the concept of absurdity appears to have numerous contemporary applications that it suggests itself as a valuable critical thesis, and the unsystematic statements of *The Myth of Sisyphus* allow the individual artist the widest range of interpretation. The first step in the development of the absurd consists in the individual's shocking recognition of the apparent meaninglessness of the universe. The second step consists in the absurd man's living the now apparent conflict between his intention (his inner voice) and the reality which he will encounter; the third step consists in his assumption of heroic dimensions through living the conflict and making it his god. According to Leslie Fiedler, the most honest and promising vision of man which serious literature in our time can present is "not, as so often in the past, a view of man struggling to fulfill some revealed or inherited view of himself and his destiny; but of man learning that it is the struggle itself which is his definition."[26] The development from this struggle of a particular system of belief is not only possible but likely. The ethics of the absurd, however, are implicit rather than explicit.

[26] Leslie Fiedler, "No! In Thunder," *Esquire,* 54 (September, 1960), p. 79.

"L'homme absurde is a man without nostalgia. He has accepted his prison walls and the logical conclusion of Camus's argument. He is passionately wedded to life; he is an enemy of death. Therein lies the conscious affirmation of his humanity; he is against the natural order of the universe in which the words life and death are meaningless, against the gods—if there be any."[27] What gives this argument its ethical tone is that man is, through the absurd, affirming his own humanity. Thus far, however, we have at most an ethical direction, not an ethical code: but since man is in a position "to edify, without God, a humanism of high nobility,"[28] he is in a position to restore human dignity and thus to throw his weight on the side of ethical values.

The careful reader of *The Myth of Sisyphus* is well aware that Camus would cast his vote against murder even as he casts it against suicide. It is not the problem of murder which makes *L'homme revolté* inappropriate to the study of absurd fiction, but the fact that its central problem is the determination of the most efficacious channels which political activity should take in order to implement human dignity. What is significant in that work for the purposes of such an analysis is the light it sheds on the position and function of the artist. The novels, plays, and essays which followed *The Myth of Sisyphus* were not simple exercises on a theme, but all of them dealt in varying degrees with the problem of absurdity which that essay enunciates. Their conclusions differ, but the premise of an absurd universe and its absurd opponent remains the same, even when that universe is eventually given meaning by the joy of a Sisyphus-like struggle against it.

Since the words "absurd" and "alienated" have become such popular catchalls for the analysis of contemporary literature, it should perhaps be observed that literary critics no doubt often commit an unfortunate if understandable *lèse-majesté* in regarding the theme

[27] Brée, *Camus*, p. 199.
[28] Albert Maquet, *Albert Camus: The Invincible Summer,* trans. Herma Briffault, p. 108.

of alienation as the unique province of the contemporary artist, disregarding, as they do, the very fabric of tragedy and much that is best and most viable in romantic fiction; but their instincts are surely right, for with increasing frequency and persistence many contemporary writers would seem to suggest that alienation is not the result of the confrontation of a unique human spirit with a particular set of essentially external conditions, but that it is the fate of any and all men who think and feel with any intensity about their relationship to the world which surrounds them. Therefore man does not *become* alienated (the word itself ceases to have connotations of "process"): alienation is his birthright, the modern, psychologically colored equivalent of original sin. Thus, if contemporary alienation is not different in kind from that of previous ages, it is at least different in degree and, because it frequently presupposes the irrelevance of conventional value systems, significantly different in the results which it presupposes.

The four American novelists who are treated in this study—John Updike, William Styron, Saul Bellow, and J. D. Salinger—share a vision of the spiritual sterility and loneliness of the modern environment strikingly similar to the absurd universe which Camus described in *The Myth of Sisyphus*. These authors further share with Camus the belief that man must oppose this universe, even though his demands for order and meaning will make him absurd. Secular humanism is implied in the works of these authors as it is implied in *The Myth of Sisyphus* itself, thus forging an additional link with the early theories of Camus. Like Camus, these authors reject nihilism and orthodoxy, and like Camus too, they end by affirming the humanity of man. The absurd hero is by definition a rebel because he refuses to avoid either of the two components on which absurdity depends: intention, which is his desire for unity; and reality, which is constituted by the meaninglessness of life. The hope which absurd heroes offer to the secular societies of the West is that they may generate values to replace those which are lost as once sacred traditions disappear. Thus, revolt alone becomes revelatory of human values, giving the dimensions to human experience once provided by Christianity; the call to revolt is a call to humanize, to transform the inhumanity of the world. Like Camus, the absurd novelist does not attempt to establish a specific ethical system, but he does point toward a homocentric humanism which may well serve the function of prolegomena to a future ethic.

Just as the premise of the absurd defined in *The Myth of Sisyphus* permits a variety of conclusions—depending on the exact form of the two givens, intention and reality—so it permits, in fictive terms, a variety of forms. Sisyphus, as Camus reminds us, is first a portrait of tragedy and then a portrait of joy. The absurd hero in fiction may remain exclusively in the state of tragedy, or he may transcend that condition by his realization of the sheer joy of struggle; what concerns us here are the varieties of contemporary experience and the degrees of personal fulfillment accommodated by the absurd tension. To some degree, the potential joy following tragedy in the case of the absurd hero is not unlike the *anagnorisis* or discovery which follows the fall of the classical tragic hero: the "all is well" of Oedipus. In this respect, the development of the tragic hero follows Northrop Frye's "Theory of Myths," in which comedy and tragedy are viewed as related aspects of the quest-myth. When he first demonstrates a separation of intention and reality, the absurd man might well be the subject of burlesque, where the essential element of humor would rest in a contrast between the character's apparently exaggerated intention and the environment in which he is placed. At the next level, that of defense of the absurd, the character is involved, according to Camus's definition, in a tragic situation. When the joy that accompanies struggle fills the character, he is experiencing the comic sequel to tragedy.

If we are right [Frye argues] in our suggestion that romance, tragedy, irony and comedy are all episodes in a total quest-myth, we can see how it is that comedy can contain a potential tragedy within itself. In myth, the hero is a god, and hence he does not die, but dies and rises again. The ritual pattern behind the catharsis of comedy is the resurrection that follows death, the epiphany or manifestation of the risen hero . . . Christianity, too, sees tragedy as an episode in the divine comedy, the larger scheme of redemption and resurrection.[29]

At what stage the author picks up the absurd hero, and to what point he carries him along this spectrum is a question of individual "style," which Camus saw as an order "applied to the disorder of a particular time."[30] In its most exhaustive development, the absurd hero will be taken through all the stages from burlesque to comedy, and it is only after the joyous rebirth of the third and final stage that he may be prepared to derive a value system from his experience in the absurd. At any stage, however, the absurd is a symbol of hope. Like the characters in *The Plague* who give their lives meaning by fighting the epidemic even though there seems to be no hope of altering its course, the absurd hero holds out the message that though victory is questionable, defeat is not final. As a response to the futility which often seems to characterize the contemporary environment, that message is not without a kind of magnificence.

[29] Northrop Frye, *Anatomy of Criticism*, p. 215.
[30] Albert Camus, *The Rebel*, trans. Anthony Bower, p. 274.

THE ABSURD MAN AS *Saint*

John Updike's first novel, *The Poorhouse Fair,* was a novel of dismissal in which the author suggested the failure of various traditional systems to fulfill contemporary man's spiritual needs. The novel was an indictment of the life-denying impulses of an age, and while it offered no solution and raised no successful protagonist to this succession of denials, it had to be written to free Updike to create the absurd heroes who appear in *Rabbit, Run* and *The Centaur.* The bulk of Updike's attack in *The Poorhouse Fair* was against the presumably humanistic welfare state whose aim is to give security, coherence, and meaning to human life but which, Updike says, results only in a yet more precarious and obtrusive sterility.

Since the humanist's interests extend beyond the single individual to embrace the human race as a whole, he will eventually look toward the state as the only practicable organ for promoting the well-being and culture of man and for safeguarding the race. Thus, since the welfare state is the ultimate socio-political realization of humanism, almost all utopian literature runs either to criticism of the welfare state or proselytizing for it. *The Poorhouse Fair* is one of the two important books since the Second World War to have been added to this virtually timeless discussion. Its predecessor, B. F. Skinner's *Walden Two,* envisioned a paradise of experimentally conditioned people living together in perfect harmony and happiness. Art and individual expression proliferate at Walden II, and the author devotes considerable emphasis to their importance in the ideal society. Skinner was happily able to overlook the stress or neurosis theory of art—there being, of course, neither stresses nor neuroses at Walden II. The theory that man uses art to order his life is also a meaningless one in this environment, since every detail of life in Skinner's Utopia is synonymous with order. Indeed, there seems no motivation whatsoever for artistic expression—an oversight one would not have expected from an experimental psychologist. Skinner is wholly serious in his suggestion that conditioning is a panacea for the human race, and in advancing it he makes a supreme humanistic gesture to the suffering world. As a scientist he is certain that his plan will work, and as a man he sees no objection to the welfare state in which all needs and wants—the latter conditioned never to exceed the "reasonable" and attainable—are fulfilled.

Updike's examination of the welfare state of the late twentieth century is made through one of its agencies, the poorhouse, and through the humanist who administers to that agency, Mr. Conner. The poorhouse is actually a kind of old-folks home for those people financially unable to provide for themselves in their old age. Updike's criticism of the system comes through the presentation of three variously rebellious inmates, Lucas, Gregg, and Hook.

Conner is, in his own mind, a rebel and an idealist. His zeal for cleansing the world is unflagging. Standing in his office, he hears the gunshot fired by his assistant, Buddy; the fawning subordinate has followed Conner's orders by shooting a diseased cat that threatened to contaminate the grounds:

Buddy's rifle shot had sounded in here like a twig snapping. Conner had no regrets about ordering the animal killed. He wanted things *clean*; the

world needed renewal, and this was a time of history when there were no
cleansing wars or sweeping purges. when reform was slow, and decayed
things were allowed to stand and rot themselves away. It was a vegetable
world. Its theory was organic: perhaps old institutions in their dying could
make fertile the chemical world. So the gunshot ringing out, though a
discord, pleased the rebel in Conner, the idealist, anxious to make space
for the crystalline erections that in his heart he felt certain would arise,
once his old people were gone. For the individual cat itself he felt nothing
but sorrow. (*PFa*, 64)

There is no question about Conner's inclinations: while he feels sorrow for the individual, he is more than willing to sacrifice him for
the good of the "race," for achieving necessary fertilizer. Conner has,
unfortunately, been born too late for the kind of life he should have
preferred: "he envied the first rationalists their martyrdoms and the
first reformers their dragons of reaction and selfishness" (64). The
nature of Conner's administrative post would suggest impartial conduct; indeed, he himself felt that impartiality was "a crucial virtue"
(15). He frequently falls short in practice: he encourages an inform-
er in the midst of the old people, allowing the man benefits not available to the others, and he has a clear partiality for inmates who were
once wealthy or well educated. His impartiality with those whom
he feels to be ignorantly prejudiced is extreme. Despite Hook's education, Conner is angered by his defense of the concept of heaven,
and the administrator quickly yields to the desire "to pin his antagonist against the rocks that underlay his own philosophy" (109).

The reviewers of Updike's novels have repeatedly argued that he
refrains from committing himself to any of the philosophies which
he presents. Updike himself, in a fictionalized monologue on writing,
admits that he is "too tired" to attempt to draw philosophy from the
scenes which he creates, but he does hope that

once into my blindly spun web of words the thing itself will break; make
an entry and an account of itself. Not declare what it will do. This is no
mystery; we are old friends. I can observe. Not cast its vote with mine,

and make a decree: I have no hope of this. The session has lasted too long.
I wish it to yield only on the point of its identity. What is it? Its breadth,
its glitter, its greenness and sameness balk me. *What is it?* If I knew, I
could say.[1]

The mystery of the sea may perhaps eventually be revealed to the
writer through contemplation, just as the phenomenon that is modern
man may also reveal his secrets and flaws. In *The Poorhouse Fair*
Updike is primarily an observer, but he is neither completely dis-
sociated nor completely uncommitted. While he looks with ironic
compassion on the entire host of fools and meddlers which he exposes,
his final commitment is to the spirit of rebellion. Such commitments
are in some respects negative—we are scarcely in doubt of what he
disapproves. In standing on the side of rebellion, however, he sup-
ports no single character, but rather a germ which resides, with special intensity, in the three old men on whom the story centers.

Updike despises the simple, unthinking handmaid of church or
state as manifested through the well-intentioned meddlings of Hook
and Conner. Criticism of the welfare state and of Conner as its product is obvious from the opening page of *The Poorhouse Fair*. Two of
the old men approach their porch chairs to find them encumbered
with metal tabs bearing the names of their "owners." To Gregg this
obvious affront to individualism resembles the branding of cattle.
Hook's calmer reaction marks him as a well-trained and well-adjusted
cog of discipline in that he cautions in favor of tolerating such inane
examples of Conner's "tinkering." " 'Caution is the bet-ter part of
action'," he reasons. " 'No doubt it is an aspect of Conner's wish to
hold us to our place. An-y motion on our part to threaten his security
will make him that much more unyielding' " (11).

Through the novel runs a continuing undertow of criticism in the
form of a letter which Conner has received from one of the townspeople in nearby Andrews:

[1] John Updike, "The Sea's Green Sameness," *New World Writing*, 17 (1960),
p. 59.

Stephen Conner—

Who do you think you are a Big shot? Yr duty is to help not hinder these old people on there way to there final Reward. I myself have heard bitter complaint from these old people when they come into town where I live. They call you Pieface you and that moran Buddy. The nature of there complants I will disclose latter. And will write the U.S. gov.ment depending. Things have not gone so far these old people have no rights no pale peeny-notchin basterd can take away.

A "Town's person" (178)

The letter is a double-edged instrument, reflecting as much discredit upon the writer as it does on Conner, but its author has been chosen with intentional irony to highlight a central theme of the novel: Conner and his fellows are prolonging life and stifling living. The final judgment pronounced by the novel, however, is not directed so much against Conner as it is against the sterile world which has assigned the old people to a poorhouse which reduces life to its lowest denominator. Resignation characterizes their condition, but their resignation is not an acceptance of the prospect of death; it is, as the letter to Conner suggests, an acceptance of the tortuous necessity of continuing to live. Indeed, the old people revert to memories of the excitement of old wars and political campaigns and "dead" issues because of the necessity of putting some vitality, however ephemeral, into their lives. Thus, disappointed that rain has threatened to cancel their annual fair, the poorhouse inmates recall their former executive, Mendelssohn, and the warmth and vitality he had carried with him into their dining hall. In their total recollections Mendelssohn is far from perfect, but it is clear that the old man possessed a quality of life which won him their appreciation. Updike is later to describe this intense quality as "force."

Conner continually abuses the old people's memory of Mendelssohn, and by taking away much of their responsibility for the fair, considerably lessens its significance. The total boredom and passivity of these old people's lives remind one of Swift's description of the melancholy and immortal Struldbrugs. While Updike's comments reflect none of the brutality or bitterness found in Swift's description, they do contain a strikingly similar impression of futility.

Of the three "rebels" who emerge in *The Poorhouse Fair* Hook is the most intelligent: he is much too well disciplined to seek to reach Conner through violence. Gregg, on the other hand, incites the old people to stone their administrator, and Lucas attempts to defeat monotony with pain, jabbing at his ear with a match until the ear is badly inflamed. Lucas openly defies Conner's authority by buying a bottle of rye and slipping it into the main building to share with his rebellious cronies. It is, significantly, with these three men and their reactions to the dehumanizing humanism of the welfare state that Updike concludes his book:

THE MAN of flesh, the man of passion, the man of thought. Lucas slept. His body, stripped to underclothes and half-covered with a sheet, submitted in oblivion to a harmony of forms. Gregg hopped and chirrupped on the lawn, dazzling himself with the illumination and talking aloud in his self-delight, though tomorrow he would be as cross as ever. Hook sat up with a start. The pillow and his horizontal position had been smothering him, and the phlegm in his throat could not be rasped away. His heart doubled its speed of beating; and gradually slowed . . . His encounter with Conner had commenced to trouble him. The young man had been grievously stricken. The weakness on his face after his henchman had stolen his cigar was troubling to recall; and intimacy had been there [which] Hook must reward with help. A small word would perhaps set things right. As a teacher, Hook's flaw had been overconscientiousness; there was nowhere he would not meddle. He stood motionless, half in moonlight, groping after the fitful shadow of the advice he must impart to Conner, as a bond between them and a testament to endure his dying in the world. What was it? (184–185)

To be sure, Updike creates neither a *persona* nor a hero in any of these men. Hook is the most acceptable opponent of the poorhouse system, but Updike's sympathies lie with Hook's realization of his superior's weakness and his simultaneous desire to reach out and help—not with his Christian philosophizing. Hook remains too much a part of the system to be a true rebel. The *significaccio* of Updike's first novel does not rest in a proposed solution, but in the criticism of a system which provides "super" answers to man's physical needs while taking no notice of his spiritual desires and requirements. The lack of attention to the spiritual needs of the poorhouse inmates renders ludicrous the efficient medical treatment to which Lucas is subjected.

As we learn from the townspeople who attend the fair, the poorhouse is but one manifestation of the society which Updike has endeavored to expose. Their talk and their attitudes are shallow: "Heart had gone out of these people; health was the principal thing about the faces of the Americans that came crowding through the broken wall of the poorhouse fair. They were just people, members of the race of white animals that had cast its herds over the land of six continents" (158). They are harmless, but even more dispirited and empty than the old people at whom they gawk. In an attempt to allay the sterility of their lives, the younger Americans seek outlets in extremes of perversion or of respectable platitudinous behavior; and they attempt to regain something of America's once-vital heritage by collecting objects of early Americana and almost anything else which appears to be handmade.

The Poorhouse Fair is a projection into the year 1975, but like most exercises in the pastoral or utopian modes, it is an implied criticism of the contemporary environment. In *Rabbit, Run*, however, the author made a specific analysis of the spiritual shallowness of his own age. As Whitney Balliett commented after its publication, "*Rabbit, Run* bristles with enough dissatisfaction to let loose an affecting shout at human fumbling, which the first book never mustered up the indignation to do. There is no pity; nor, peculiarly, is there any humor, but there is a great deal of martinetlike understanding. *The Poorhouse Fair* was a brilliant but stiff setting-up exercise. *Rabbit, Run* goes many steps beyond."[2] Harry "Rabbit" Angstrom rebels against the wasteland into which he is born. In consistently opposing the

[2] Whitney Balliett, "Books," *The New Yorker*, 36 (November 5, 1960), 222.

reality which he encounters, Rabbit becomes an absurd hero, and because of the highly spiritual devotion of this gesture against the world, he becomes a saint, although a saint of a very special nature.

Like many absurd heroes, Harry Angstrom is a questing man and, because of the nature of his quest, he is set apart from the world in which he lives. Rabbit is rejected by both his own family and his wife and her family because of his dedication to " 'something that wants me to find it' " (*RR*, 127). The precise object of Harry's quest is never defined in more specific terms, although it is occasionally identified as "force." As a star basketball player, Harry was an idealist who never fouled and usually won. Unlike the idealism of Connor, Harry's is based upon devotion to an inner conviction; Conner's convictions are only the ideals of the state, unquestioningly absorbed. On its most obvious level, *Rabbit, Run* is a story of the *angst* of a young man who strives for the same perfection and skill in life that he had known on the basketball court. But Rabbit does not simply need to be a winner. The methods by which success can be achieved as a middle-class family man and car or kitchen-gadget salesman are not beyond his mastery; they simply do not interest him. Rabbit has broken away from the hypnotic mediocrity of his life long enough to realize its meaninglessness. Stepping apart from this routine, he is able to see himself, and the incredulous vision which greets him is the absurd. Camus argued that "the stranger who at certain seconds comes to meet us in a mirror, the familiar and yet alarming brother we encounter in our own photographs is also the absurd."[3] In a poem entitled "Reflection" Updike expressed a sensitivity almost identical to Camus's sensitivity to the mirror image. What at first glance appears to be an example of *New Yorker* preciousness is actually an extreme statement of the absurd:

> When you look   kool uoy nehW
> into a mirror   rorrim a otni

[3] Albert Camus, *The Myth of Sisyphus*, p. 11.

it is not	ton si ti
yourself you see	ees uoy flesruoy
but a kind	dnik a tub
of apish error	rorre hsipa fo
posed in fearful	lufraef ni desop
symmetry.	.yrtemmys[4]

Having glimpsed himself in the mirror, Rabbit flees from the apish error of his life, embarking on a quest for his real self.

The theme of the successful basketball star turned middle-class family man is one which Updike has explored in more than one fashion. In a story originally published in *The New Yorker*, Updike described "Ace" Anderson, a former basketball star disillusioned with small-town life and his job as a car salesman. In this story Ace is rejuvenated by the thought of producing a son whose grip and dexterity will match his own. Overcome with this idea, he seizes his angered wife in his arms and soothes her with dancing; as the music swells he imagines that "other kids were around them, in a ring, clapping" (*SD*, 26).

Updike's stories repeatedly urge the idea that few if any causes are worth man's sacrifice, that the world provides little room for heroism. Rafe, another of Updike's unfulfilled young moderns, is described in "Toward Evening" riding the bus up Broadway. Outside the windows numbers on the buildings begin to assume historical significance:

The clearly marked numbers on the east side of the street ran: 1832, 1836, 1846, 1850 (Wordsworth dies), 1880 (great Nihilistic trial in St. Petersburg), 1900 (Rafe's father born in Trenton), 1902 (Braque leaves Le Havre to study painting in Paris), 1914 (Joyce begins *Ulysses*; war begins in Europe), 1926 (Rafe's parents marry in Ithaca), 1936 (Rafe is four years old). Where the present should have stood, a block was torn down,

[4] John Updike, "Reflection," *The New Yorker*, 33 (November 30, 1957), p. 216.

and the numbering began again with 2000, a boring progressive edifice (SD, 63–64).

The present is a blank, the sky illuminated by a Spry sign, and the future holds forth only "a boring progressive edifice" like the poorhouse. The modern world as Updike sees it is a world of the superlative and the superfluous, but not a world of fulfillment:

> I drive my car to supermarket,
>   The way I take is superhigh,
> A superlot is where I park it,
>   And Super Suds are what I buy.
>
> Supersalesmen sell me tonic—
>   Super-Tone-O, for relief.
> The planes I ride are supersonic.
>   In trains I like the Super Chief.
>
> Supercilious men and women
>   Call me superficial—*me*.
> Who so superbly learned to swim in
>   Supercolossality.
>
> Superphosphate-fed foods feed me;
>   Superservice keeps me new.
> Who would dare to supersede me,
>   Super-super-superwho? (*CH*, 6)

In a world of such hyperbolic and self-defeating superlatives scant room exists for the hero except in the athletic events which seem increasingly to occupy contemporary America's minds. Another of Updike's former basketball stars, "Flick," finds nothing worthwhile on which he can lay his "fine and nervous" hands once he has retired from the basketball courts.

Updike's young basketball players—especially Harry Angstrom—recall Ring Lardner's innocence stories about the baseball diamond, and those stories offer a clue to Harry's quest. What attracted Lardner to the game of baseball was that there one could find rules, that there right conduct was rewarded and wrong-doing punished, and the prize awarded to the person who dedicated himself to the game. Real heroism and integrity could be expressed through baseball, and the baseball diamond became a surrogate spiritual environment whose values transcended the individual player. The famous World Series "fix" virtually broke Lardner's heart. Harry Angstrom is, of course, a perfectionist and an idealist, but he is not simply a former basketball hero determined to be in all things star and winner. Harry's former coach, Tothero, emphasizes that what he has inspired in his boys is " 'the will to achieve'." He adds, " 'I've always liked that better than the will to win, for there can be achievement even in defeat. Make them feel the, yes, I think the word is good, the *sacredness* of achievement, in the form of giving our best' " (RR, 61). It is part of Updike's essential irony that this message comes from a pathetic neurotic. One is nevertheless reminded of Camus's suggestion of the great joy which Sisyphus realizes in his apparent defeat.

Harry's quest is for that environment in which he can give his best. He cannot do it in the television-and-booze-tinted world of his wife Janice, nor in any of the other "worlds" which he samples in Brewer, Pennsylvania. Harry's intention is to find that world in which he can again experience the sacredness of achievement. Janice unwittingly touches the core of her husband's experience when she asks after hearing that he has given up cigarettes, " 'What are you doing, becoming a saint?' " (9). Whenever he is disillusioned by the world in which he finds himself Rabbit begins to run. The gesture is impulsive, but it is fundamental to his spiritual nature. As he runs Rabbit becomes a social outcast, rejecting his family and the responsibilities which life seems to place on him. These rejections are part of his saintliness. Rabbit has sampled conventional ethics and found them wanting. He longs for total absorption in the present moment, for an opportunity to express his compassion for the human race. This expression of compassion—the desire to embrace the very soul of man—is a concomitant of sainthood. Rabbit hopes that he can give in this fashion to Ruth Leonard, a prostitute with whom he lives after leaving his wife, and that he can give his best in this new experience:

He turns her roughly, and, in a reflex of his own, falls into a deep wish to give comfort . . . As they deepen together he feels impatience that through all their twists they remain separate flesh; he cannot dare enough now that she is so much his friend in this search . . . She feels transparent; he sees her heart. (78, 83, 84)

While Ruth cannot completely fulfill Harry's desire to give, she is nonetheless able to recognize the intensity of his quest more fully than any of the other characters in the novel. She likes Harry, and when he presses her for a reason, she answers, " 'Cause you haven't given up. Cause in your stupid way you're still fighting' " (91). Standing with Ruth at the top of Mt. Judge, Harry has a compassionate, Pisgah-like vision of death and suffering. He opens "the lips of his soul to receive the taste of the truth about it, as if truth were a secret in such low solution that only immensity can give us a sensible taste" (112).

Ruth is not wholly alone in recognizing this struggle in Rabbit. Eccles, the sympathetic Episcopal minister, also recognizes it, but the struggle is foreign to his orthodoxy, and "duty" demands that he reject it. Countering Rabbit's saintly declarations, Eccles says that Jesus taught " 'that saints shouldn't marry' " (127). There is, of course, nothing about the high level of a saint's emotional experience which dictates the requirement of celibacy. Eccles has chosen to deny Rabbit's quest because it is foreign to the neat theological patterns into which the minister has organized his life. Rabbit's peculiar saintliness demands, in fact, that he not be celibate, for it is largely through sex that he is able to express his desire to comfort and heal; it is through sex that he is able to see Ruth's "heart." Updike reiterates this idea of salvation through sex in "Lifeguard," a monologue in which a young, devoted divinity student considers the advantages of his summer job as a lifeguard. He lusts after many of the women who parade before him, but he emphasizes that "To desire a woman is to desire to save her. Anyone who has endured intercourse that was neither predatory nor hurried knows how through it we descend, with a partner, into the grotesque and delicate shadows that until then have remained locked in the most guarded recess of our soul: into this harbor we bring her" (*PFe*, 216–217).

When Eccles chides Rabbit about his lack of celibacy he is being decidedly ironic, but as his knowledge of this dissenter increases, the seriousness and force with which Eccles attacks Rabbit also increase:

"Harry," he asks, sweetly yet boldly, "why have you left her? You're obviously deeply involved with her."

"I *told* ja. There was this thing that wasn't there."

"What thing? Have you ever seen it? Are you sure it exists?"

Harry's two-foot putt dribbles short and he picks up the ball with trembling fingers. "Well if you're not sure it exists don't ask me. It's right up your alley. If you don't know nobody does."

"No," Eccles cried in the same strained voice in which he told his wife to keep her heart open for Grace. "Christianity isn't looking for a rainbow. If it were what you think it is we'd pass out opium at services. We're trying to *serve* God, not *be* God."

They pick up their bags and walk the way a wooden arrow tells them.

Eccles goes on, explanatorily, "This was all settled centuries ago, in the heresies of the Church."

"I tell you, I know what it is."

"What is it? What *is* it? Is it hard or soft, Harry? Is it blue? Is it red? Does it have polka dots?"

It hits Rabbit depressingly to know that he really wants to be told. Underneath all this I-know-more-about-it-than-you heresies-of-the-early-Church business he really wants to be told about it, wants to be told that it is here, that he's not lying to all those people every Sunday. As if it's not enough to be trying to get some sense out of this frigging game, you have to carry around this madman to swallow your soul. The hot strap of the bag gnaws his shoulder.

"The truth is," Eccles tells him with womanish excitement, in a voice agonized by embarrassment, "you're monstrously selfish. You're a coward. You don't care about right or wrong; you worship nothing except your own worst instincts" (*RR*, 132–133).

Rabbit is, of course, selfish after the manner of any man in search of truth, and his life is a struggle for self-knowledge that is comically heralded by a television Mousketeer: " 'Know Thyself, a wise old Greek once said' " (9).

In light of Rabbit's renunciation of traditional Christianity Updike's choice of one of Pascal's fragments from the *Pensées* as an introduction to the novel may seem somewhat enigmatic. It need not seem so if we think of the *Pensées* as a testimony to the spiritual struggle of man and not as a testimony to the struggle of Christian man. "The motions of Grace, the hardness of the heart; external circumstances." In citing Pascal, Updike emphasizes the spiritual nature of Rabbit's quest. It is, perhaps, only through the action of something akin to the Christian concept of grace that a voice calls to Harry that does not call to other men; his pursuit of that voice demands a hardness of the heart and a definite obliviousness to external circumstances. All of Pascal's religious writings rest on the foundation of a personal religious experience of a peculiarly intense nature. The *Pensées* themselves, as one of their best critics has noted, "reconstruct in logical terms—the speech of common mortals—a spiritual pilgrimage and a mystical experience."[5] Eccles, to some degree, may be thought of as representing that Reason which, for Pascal, would never alone be capable of achieving truth. Rabbit himself suggests Pascal's description of the man who is seeking for Jesus but who has not found him:

Mais *ceux qui cherchent Dieu de tout leur coeur*, qui n'ont de déplaisir que d'être privés de sa vue, qui n'ont de désir que pour posséder, et d'ennemis que ceux qui les en détournent, qui s'affligent de se voir environnés et dominés de tels ennemis, *qu'ils se consolent*, je leur annonce une heureuse

[5] F. T. H. Fletcher, *Pascal and the Mystical Tradition* (Oxford: Basil Blackwell, 1954), p. 47.

nouvelle: il y a un Libérateur pour eux, je le ferai voir, je leur montrerai qu'il y a un Dieu pour eux: je ne le ferai pas voir aux autres.[6]

This kind of seeker is *malheureux et raisonnable,* but in his very struggle to find essential truth (in Pascal's terminology, Jesus), he *has* found it.

Rabbit is not a Christian saint precisely because Christianity is one of the unsuccessful environments which fail him and which he must reject. He has no taste for what Updike later calls "the dark, tangled, visceral aspect of Christianity, the *going through* quality of it, the passage into death and suffering that redeems and inverts these things, like an umbrella blowing inside out" (*RR,* 237). It is true that he is attracted to the church, but only so long as it promises to fulfill his needs. When it fails him, the stained-glass church window which had once "consoled him by seeming to make a hole where he looked through into underlying brightness" becomes "a dark circle in a stone facade" (306). There can be no doubt that Updike intends us to look upon Rabbit as a saint and to see his experiences as spiritual. Nonetheless, Rabbit is a saint who exists outside the Christian tradition. This exclusion is based, first of all, upon his own inability to conceive of a God in the traditional Christian sense, and secondly on the fact that Rabbit's "saintly" quest is a wholly solipsistic one. In discussing the novels of Ignazio Silone, R. W. B. Lewis finds it necessary to speak of a new kind of saint who is both rebel and outlaw, what he finally terms "the picaresque saint":

If we accept Silone's hints and speak of Spina as a kind of contemporary saint, we must add that he is a saint just *because* he is a martyr; he is a saint just *because* he is a man. His sanctity is manifested not in a private communion with God, but in an urgent communion with his fellow men: in his dedication of himself to assuaging a little the human sufferings of his time. That dedication requires of him that he be forever a wanderer, for-

---

[6] Blaise Pascal, *Pensées,* p. 692.

ever pursued and pursuing. It requires of him that, in the view of that much of the world that oppresses and hurts, he appears as a rogue.[7]

The world as Rabbit knows it is filled with nothing but oppressions and hurts, and this is the condition which dictates his peculiar kind of isolation; to everyone but Tothero and Mrs. Smith he is a perfect rogue. His absolute devotion to a quest for meaning dictates his absolute aloneness in a society which knows nothing of meaning. To these people he is not only an enigma, but he is destructive, even unto death, which he comes to represent for Ruth. Like Heller's *Catch*-22, *Rabbit, Run* emphasizes that man is victimized by life itself, and it remains for him to seek salvation alone—even when that means a rejection of human solidarity. Yossarian decides that self-preservation is more important than the insane commands and rituals of military life, but like Rabbit, he deserts only after he has tried all that can be expected of him as an individual.

Mrs. Smith, whose garden Rabbit has cared for and restored to beauty, says, " 'That's what you have, Harry: life. It's a strange gift and I don't know how we're supposed to use it but I know it's the only gift we get and I know it's a good one' " (*RR*, 223). Harry has noted this quality in others and defined it as "force." Because Tothero represents a kind of spiritual force, Rabbit for a while thinks of him as the Dalai Lama, the object of his quest, but while Tothero has helped to inspire Rabbit with the sense of spiritual achievement, his realization of that impulse must come on a larger ground than that which is defined by a single individual.

Updike consistently avoids every opportunity to affirm the ethical values of Christian humanism. His most dramatic opportunity comes during the grave-side reunion of Harry with his family and with Eccles. The people are united at the funeral of Harry's infant daughter, who was drowned through the inattentiveness of her intoxicated

---

[7] R. W. B. Lewis, *The Picaresque Saint* (Philadelphia: J. B. Lippincott, 1959), pp. 159–160.

mother. One would anticipate that this tragedy might finally give the family the common bond they have lacked, but for Harry reconciliation must be formed in truth, not in grief—a conviction his fellow mourners are unable to understand.

When faced with the loneliness and lack of values of the modern world, man can do one of three things. He can seek an escape through sensualism; he can attempt to find reconciliation with his fellows through some form of humanism; or he can break from all conventional ethics and systems and actively pursue new ones. It is the last category to which the absurd hero must be limited; and since his search is a search for values, his struggle is primarily religious. Any consideration of a religious system without God (or with only an irrelevant God) involves paradoxical inversions of values. Charles Glicksberg has pointed out that writers like Camus, in their stern negation of God, are more obsessively involved with God than writers who take Him for granted. God is present, then, even in the negation, for "even when a man denies God, he may in fact be affirming the existence of God."[8] If such a paradoxical inversion is involved in the writings of Camus or Updike, the God affirmed is not representative of traditional Christianity, which these writers see stripped of all power and significance. Nonetheless, Rabbit Angstrom does demand confirmation of a voice which calls to man and asks him to make life meaningful. Heroes like Rabbit reject formal Christianity because it is not religious enough. What they seek is not the consoling reinforcement of dogma or ritual but some transcendent inner vision of truth that will make life meaningful. Despite its secular origins there is something holy in such austere dedication to truth. Rabbit remains true to a standard of good by which he attempts to live, and the intensity of his loyalty to this standard can only be described as "religious." Everything in his world is in flux, but his intention is, in the presumed absence of God, to impose order and value on that flux.

Updike's characters occasionally claim the existence of a Divine

[8] Charles Glicksberg, "Camus's Quest for God," *Southwest Review*, 44 (1959), 244.

Being, but their faith is intermittent, subjective, and often capricious, and the object of their belief is, in any event, rarely equatable with traditional Western concepts of divinity. As a group, Christians in Updike's stories emerge as "a minority flock furtively gathered within the hostile enormity of a dying, sobbing empire" (*PFe*, 250). David Kern, the hero of several Updike narratives, has a resurgence of faith when, after vindictively shooting pigeons who are covering the floor of his father's barn with their droppings, he is seized by the beauty of the dead birds:

As he fitted the last two, still pliant, on the top, and stood up, crusty coverings were lifted from him, and with a feminine, slipping sensation along his nerves that seemed to give the air hands, he was robed in this certainty: that the God who had lavished such craft upon these worthless birds would not destroy His whole Creation by refusing to let David live forever. (149–150)

A later David Kern story, however, chronicles his profound disillusionment and his fear of the enormities and absurdities of life; he concludes that "the God who permitted me this fear was unworthy of existence. Each instant my horror was extended amplified God's non-existence" (261). Earth packed by human feet becomes more meaningful to Kern than God, because this packing and the paths that it produces represent a spontaneous ritual of human beings giving shape to their lives. Like the packing of dirt, churchgoing (important even when faith is being drained away), acts of human kindness, and even driving an automobile are rituals which sustain man in a godless universe. Speaking to a sailor hitchhiker, Kern tries to explain his purpose as a writer: "We in America need ceremonies, is I suppose, sailor, the point of what I have written" (279).

In the descriptive outline for a story about Fanning Island, Updike pictures an island occupied solely by shipwrecked men. Doomed to extinction because there is no woman with them, the men make wives of one another and struggle to maintain remembered rituals. Updike took the theme for his Fanning Island outline from Pascal:

Qu'on s'imagine un nombre d'hommes dans les chaînes, et tous condamnés à la mort, dont les uns étant chaque jour égorgés à la vue des autres, ceux qui restent voient leur propre condition dans celle de leurs semblables, et, se regardent les uns et les autres avec doleur et sans espérance, attendent à leur tour. C'est l'image de la condition des hommes. (243)

Salvation from this enslaved condition does not rest in the hands of an overseeing God, but in the hands of the man determined to live his life meaningfully. There is no question that Updike intends Fanning Island to stand as a microcosm of contemporary society, but the story of its inhabitants is to be one of joy:

This is the outline; but it would be the days, the evocation of the days . . . the green days. The tasks, the grass, the weather, the shades of sea and air. Just as a piece of turf torn from a meadow becomes a *gloria* when drawn by Durer. Details. Details are the giant's fingers. He seizes the stick and strips the bark and shows, burning beneath, the moist white wood of joy. For I thought that this story, fully told, would become without my willing it a happy story, a story full of joy; had my powers been greater, we would know. As it is, you, like me, must take it on faith. (245)

Like Pascal's man in chains, Rabbit is a man without hope, cast up on a deserted island of death, but his dedication brings the novel to a conclusion which is almost paradoxically joyful. In part, we are asked to take Rabbit's sainthood on faith even as we are asked to take the joy of the Fanning Island story on faith.

What alienates Harry from the world around him is his intention, and the disproportion of that intention to the reality which he encounters is responsible for his absurd stance. "And meanwhile his heart completes its turn and turns again, a wider turning in a thinning medium to which the outer world bears decreasing relevance" (*RR*, 129). Since the saint's goal is to love absolutely and entirely, he cannot give preference to any particular individual or system. In order to be true to the quest he has assumed, Harry must free himself from both the rationalism of the Springers and the spiritual subjectivism of Eccles (in itself a kind of rationalism). He is alone and an outcast, but he is still running, and now that all ties have been broken there is hope of a sustained achievement for him. Harry doubts that he can succeed, but Tothero has emphasized for us the fact that achievement can come even in defeat. For the saint, it is the struggle, not the success of the struggle, which is significant. At the thought of being unable to capture his goal, Rabbit panics, but the panic is "sweet," and the final words of the novel, "he runs. Ah: runs. Runs" (307), are exultant.

Responding to those inner voices which warn him that escape from the pretensions and inconsistencies of the world is the only course by which he can maintain his integrity, Rabbit, like Huck Finn, lights out for the wilderness: escape becomes fulfillment and irresponsibility becomes responsibility. The child hero (or the childlike hero) is thus reiterated as one of the major devices in American literature, and again it is the socially disreputable hero in whom ultimate values reside. Updike portrays Rabbit as a contemporary saint who cannot resist the search for truth, even when the search ironically converts him into an ominous figure of death. The reader is constantly reminded that Rabbit has a gift to give to man—and not just a sexual one; at one point in the novel he himself jokingly defines his gift as faith. Strangled beneath the net of traditional Christian Humanism, Eccles, Janice, Ruth, and Rabbit's parents cannot recognize this gift. In fact, the love and integrity which Rabbit offers is so antithetical to their world that it appears poisonous.

In his third novel Updike illustrates the far-reaching significance of the modern saint's apparently solipsistic experience. *The Centaur* was originally conceived as a companion piece to *Rabbit, Run.* Its hero, George Caldwell, is in some respects merely an older and slightly more conventional Harry Angstrom; both men had once excelled as athletes, and both are enmeshed in a narrowly circumscribed world which repeatedly diverges from the principles they value. Updike has again chosen to represent this stultifying middle-class world by a small, mid-state Pennsylvania town. While Rabbit defends his values by running, George Caldwell maintains his intentions in the face of a hostile reality by retreating into a mythological kingdom in which Olinger, Pennsylvania, becomes Olympus. George's experiences are almost wholly psychological, but like Rabbit's they constitute a significant rebellion against the meaninglessness of life.

In his dreamlike, mythological world, George Caldwell becomes Chiron, the wise Centaur renowned among the Greeks as prophet, healer, and teacher of such famous heroes as Jason, Achilles, and Aeneas. Updike is by no means the only contemporary writer to have followed Joyce's lead in adapting ancient legend for purposes of exploring the modern milieu. Frederich Buechner depended heavily on the Philomela myth in *A Long Day's Dying*, Bernard Malamud wove the legend of Sir Percival into *The Natural*, and J. F. Powers drew obscure but interesting allusions to Arthurian legend in *Morte D'Urban*. Myth and legend would seem to serve two functions in modern literature: to suggest, after the manner of Jung, universal, archetypal experiences; or to demonstrate, by comparison, modern man's decreased stature and relevance. Updike's use of the Chiron myth serves both functions.

The mythological Chiron, wisest and noblest of all the Centaurs, was accidentally wounded by a poisoned arrow while attending a wedding feast among the Lapithae of Thessaly. The famed healer was unable to heal himself and, tormented by his wound, begged to be permitted to give up his immortality. His death was finally accepted as atonement for the sins of Prometheus. A loving, in many respects wise, public-school science teacher, George Caldwell is not entirely lacking in those qualities which distinguished Chiron, but unlike Chiron he is tormented by self-doubts, by feelings of persecution, and by the agonizing realization that his life is being expended in trivia. Physically he drives himself to the breaking point, giving his life up for his son, Peter, the "Prometheus" of the novel.

When *The Centaur* opens, Caldwell is standing before a characteristically unruly class attempting to impress upon them the immensity of the probable age of the universe. As he turns, an arrow strikes him in the ankle. "The class burst into laughter. The pain scaled the tender core of his shin, whirled in the complexities of his knee, and swollen broader, more thunderous, mounted into his bowels" (C, 3). Struggling to retain consciousness, Caldwell moves painfully down the hall with the arrow scraping the floor behind him. "Each time the feathers brushed the floor, the shaft worked in his wound. He tried to keep that leg from touching the floor, but the jagged clatter of the three remaining hooves sounded so loud he was afraid one of the doors would snap open and another teacher emerge to bar his way" (4–5). It is a tribute to Updike's enormous skill as a literary craftsman that he can make the transition from Caldwell, the fifty-year-old science teacher, to Chiron the Centaur with such apparent ease. The result of these fluid transitions is that *The Centaur* is not merely a retelling of the myth of Chiron but a suggestion of the mythical dimensions of even the most ordinary contemporary experience.

George Caldwell fears that the arrow which has pierced his ankle has spread poison through his body—a poison representing the hatred he imagines his students feel for him. In fact, while they delight in baiting him and in parodying his mannerisms, Caldwell's students both love and respect him. Updike has included in the novel an "obituary" on Caldwell; written in maudlin journalese by a graduate of Olinger High School, it nonetheless indicates that the students' true feelings for their teacher are far from hatred. In his fears and his insecurity, Caldwell is a personification of modern man—worried about cancer, grocery bills, decaying teeth, and the power of authority as represented by Zimmerman, the high-school principal who plays Zeus to Caldwell's Chiron. Caldwell dresses in worn, ill-fitting clothes and seems a source of endless awkwardness and mediocrity.

The one redeeming quality which Caldwell has to offer is love. His gestures of affection, like Rabbit's, are often misunderstood in an age which sings "a material hymn to material creation" (10). While it finds its ripest expression in his relationship with his son, Caldwell's love spreads so widely that it even includes a degenerate hitchhiker whom he picks up against Peter's protests. " 'You cook!' " he marvels. " 'That's a wonderful accomplishment, and I know you're not lying to me' " (82).

The goal of Caldwell's life has been "to bring men out of the darkness" (94); the tragedy of his life is that he does not realize that it is as a man who loves and not as a teacher that he is best equipped to fulfill this challenge. He does, however, remind his Olympian students that " 'Love set the universe in motion. All things that exist are her children' " (99). The scope of Caldwell's imagination and of his desire to give to his fellow man can be comprehended only in mythological terms, but he drily notes about the time in which he lives that " 'It's no Golden Age, that's for sure' " (17). There is, in fact, virtually no difference between Olinger, Pennsylvania, and Rabbit Angstrom's home town of Brewer, Pennsylvania (and from the windows of the Olinger High School Caldwell can look out at the lane leading to the county poorhouse). In a world apparently devoid of meaning—even when he imagines himself dying of cancer, his money runs out, his car breaks down, and he and Peter become snowbound—he never ceases to believe that there is meaning. As Peter himself muses,

"And yet, love, do not think that our life together, for all its mutual frustration, was not good. It was good. We moved, somehow, on a firm stage, resonant with metaphor. When my grandmother lay dying in Olinger, and I was a child, I heard her ask in a feeble voice, 'Will I be a little debil?' Then she took a sip of wine and in the morning she was dead. Yes. We lived in God's sight." (50)

The metaphor through which the Caldwells move is the metaphor of love created by "Chiron" Caldwell, who maintains not only the ability to keep going, but also to keep on loving, in a world where no pleasant rewards encourage his struggles. Although he is finally mesmerized by the thought of death, he continues to radiate a quality of life and energy which affects even those who scorn him as an incompetent nuisance. The old enemies of rationalism and orthodoxy again emerge as the hero's major opponents. Rationalism is represented by Zimmerman, an authoritarian not unlike Conner, the poorhouse administrator; in a report to the school board Zimmerman suggests that Caldwell slights "humanistic values" in his presentation of the sciences. When he returns to his classroom after having the arrow removed from his ankle, Caldwell finds Zimmerman supervising his class:

Zimmerman's lopsided face hung like a gigantic emblem of authority, stretching from rim to rim of Caldwell's appalled vision. With a malevolent pulse, it seemed to widen still further. An implacable bolt, springing from the center of the forehead above the two disparately magnifying lenses of the principal's spectacles, leaped space and transfixed the paralyzed victim. The silence as the two men stared at one another was louder than thunder. (31)

Spiritual subjectivism is suggested by the Reverend March, a handsome, arrogant minister who attends an Olinger basketball game and spends his time ogling the local Aphrodite, Vera Hummel, a sensual, middle-aged gym teacher. When Caldwell tries to question him about "god's mercy," March rebuffs him with meaningless aphorisms. Updike notes that despite the fact that March has been "tested" as a combat soldier, and "Though his faith is intact and as infrangible as metal, it is also like metal dead. Though he can go and pick it up and test its weight whenever he wishes, it has no arms with which to reach and restrain him. He mocks it" (237). Both Zimmerman and March instinctively recognize that Caldwell presents a threat to their systems of values.

Like Harry Angstrom, Caldwell represents both life and death, but the paradox is more successfully realized in Caldwell's case by an almost Whitmanesque vision of the significance of death. He outlines for his class the various stages in the formation of the earth and emphasizes the role of the microscopic volvox which theoretically introduced the phenomenon of death. There is nothing in the plasmic substance which forms the basis of life that should necessarily come to an end: "Amoebas never die." The volvox, however, pioneered in the idea of cooperation.

". . . while each cell is potentially immortal, by volunteering for a specialized function within an organized society of cells, it enters a compromised environment. The strain eventually wears itself out and kills it. It dies sacrificially, for the good of the whole. These first cells who got tired of sitting around forever in a blue-green scum and said, 'Let's get together and make a volvox,' were the first altruists. The first do-gooders. If I had a hat on, I'd take it off to 'em." (42)

Just as the cooperative cell dies sacrificially, so did ancient Chiron, by surrendering his immortality that Prometheus might be pardoned, die sacrificially for fire-stealing man. Like Chiron and the volvox, Hook, Rabbit Angstrom, and Caldwell all suggest Christ-figures, although in the intensity of his love Caldwell comes closer than any of Updike's other characters to something like a traditional concept of Christ. The mythological metaphor of the novel, however, continually reminds us that the principles Caldwell represents are far more ancient (and in many respects more universal) than those represented by Christ.

George Caldwell is the first of Updike's major protagonists to have joined hands with community; if Rabbit is a kind of Huck Finn, Caldwell is Updike's Tom Sawyer, but Caldwell's saintliness, moreover, is stripped of the romantic sentimentality for which Twain began to dislike Tom, more traditional than Rabbit's since it seeks social rather than asocial forms of expression. While George Caldwell's dedication to a ceaseless, exhausting struggle for value in a world from which value seems to have abnegated is "absurd," he lacks the awareness of absurdity which Camus asserts to be a crucial ingredient of the absurd experience. Dramatically, however, such awareness is provided by Peter Caldwell, who is often painfully aware of the disparity between his father's intentions and the reality which he encounters. While George Caldwell is clearly the narrative and philosophical focal point of *The Centaur,* the novel is also, and significantly, the story of Peter's education. When the boy has at last grasped the gravity of the threat of his father's death, "even at its immense stellar remove of impossibility" (93), he has begun to understand the significance of his father's life.

Both the modern Chiron and his son Prometheus are chained to the rock of mediocrity; the "curse" laid on Prometheus takes the form of adolescent awkwardness and psoriasis. The entire mythological structure is devaluated in its application to the modern environment. Chiron's conversation with "Aphrodite" Hummel in the girls' locker room of the school emphasizes this devaluation. Chiron attempts to defend the majesty of the gods, but Aphrodite answers that Zeus is " 'A lecherous muddler'," Poseidon " 'A senile old deckhand' " whose beard stinks of dead fish, Appollo an " 'unctuous prig'," and her husband Hephaestus simply a ditherer (25–26). Ours is not, we are continually reminded, a Golden Age. The mythological story of Chiron's pain and sacrifice defines the significance of Caldwell's experience, and the value of his struggle and of his ritualistic death is undimmed by this devaluation. What the devaluation accomplishes is to serve as a reminder that the experiences described in *The Centaur* are human experiences, even though their significance may have mythological dimensions. Updike prefaced his novel with a quotation from Karl Barth: " 'Heaven is the creation inconceivable to man, earth the creation conceivable to him. He himself is the boundary between heaven and earth'." As his mind shifts between Olinger and Olympus, Caldwell continually reminds us of this boundary; he is lower than the gods, but he transcends the physical through the intensity of his struggle and transmogrifies the commonplace through the power of love.

Mythological references in *The Centaur* therefore both illustrate the narrowness and mediocrity of the modern environment and suggest the overriding, universal significance of the human struggle. It is, however, on the level of Caldwell the man rather than that of Caldwell the centaur that the novel has its greatest significance. The mythological level is provocative, but Updike quite possibly took his mythological construct too seriously. The index appended to the novel serves to make the reader too aware of a narrative device which, in the hands of a less skillful writer, would be little more than a gimmick. Any referential system of this kind must be organic to the work of art which it serves; the description of "Hephaestus" Hummel's garage and repair shop is possibly the best example of Updike's success in achieving this unity. Caldwell goes there to have the arrow removed from his ankle, and as he moves tremblingly into the garage he descends into a kind of underworld:

> A deep warm blackness was lit by sparks. The floor of the grotto was waxed black by oil drippings. At the far side of the long workbench, two shapeless men in goggles caressed a great downward-drooping fan of flame broken into dry spots. Another man, staring upward out of round eyesockets white in a black face, rolled by on his back and disappeared beneath the body of a car. His eyes adjusting to the gloom, Caldwell saw heaped about him overturned fragments of automobiles, fragile and phantasmal, fenders like corpses of turtles, bristling engines like disembodied hearts. Hisses and angry thumps lived in the mottled air.
> . . . This tumble, full of tools, was raked by intense flashes of light from the two workmen down the bench. They were fashioning what looked like an ornamented bronze girdle for a woman with a tiny waist and flaring hips.
>
> .   .   .   .
>
> He walked to the door but Hummel limped along with him. The three Cyclopes gabbled so loud the men turned. (7–8, 10, 17)

Even in his earliest poems and stories Updike was fascinated with that hallmark of twentieth-century American culture, the service station. He possibly sees in the trade of the mechanic the same chance of fulfillment, the vital contact between worker and product, which Paul Goodman sees there. Like the athletic field, the service station is an arena in which skill is rewarded and in which the individual can establish a vital contact with his world. Caldwell even envies George Hummel his craftsmanship, but this world too, as we are reminded, is being squeezed out by mass production and large national organizations.

Three days in the life of George Caldwell and his son are described in objective chapters told by Caldwell himself and retrospective chapters narrated by Peter. As Caldwell blunders his way through the Augean stables of Olinger High School searching for relief from the pain that has begun to gnaw at his entrails, we realize that the episodes of these three days are intended not merely to suggest the tediousness and frustration of his life, but also to foreshadow his death. The novel ends as it begins, with the figure of Caldwell merging with that of Chiron: "Chiron accepts death." According to one version of the Chiron myth, the centaur had begged for death not because of his pain, which was tolerable, but because (like the inmates of Updike's poorhouse) he was weary with life. It is weariness which leads Caldwell to the abyss and makes him yearn for death, but for all his longing, he never considers suicide as a solution. So long as he has strength, he continues the struggle; there is no more compelling requirement for any of Updike's characters than that of existing—no matter how essentially absurd the struggle for life may be.

Clearly one of the most skillful stylists of our age, Updike has nonetheless been challenged by numerous critics for becoming so involved with stylistic technique that he fails to create either intensity or scope. The critic, to be sure, is traditionally suspicious of technical adroitness, especially (and probably unreasonably) when that adroitness is associated with a *New Yorker* apprenticeship. Updike has chosen to give us insights into the modern world through the commonplace; he reveals to us the drama of the common man, a representative twentieth-century type who is often either dead-beat or slob, but whose significance, Updike urges, must not be slighted. His major creative problem is to stimulate us to see this significance without resorting to the sentimental, the sensational, or the sordid. It is here that his technical adroitness serves him in good stead. The refinements and subtleties of language ask us to pause over characters who would otherwise seem undeserving of our attention, to see drama in conventional middle-class situations which would otherwise seem singularly undramatic. Updike's hero invariably suffers from the weariness which Camus described as "Rising, streetcar, four hours in the office or factory, meal, streetcar, four hours of work, meal, sleep . . ." To his characteristic technical adroitness Updike adds a mythological superstructure in *The Centaur* to reinforce the significance of the drama he depicts. Here, too, Updike's stylistic virtuosity assists him in achieving graceful, economical transitions between Olinger and Olympia. The index at the conclusion is, however, an unfortunate addition insofar as it makes the reader overly conscious of the mythological ingredients of the novel, rendering them less organic to the work as a whole.

It is the most dramatic example of an aesthetic self-consciousness which jeopardizes even the best of Updike's fiction; thus, for all the virtuosity of technique, *The Poorhouse Fair* seems as lifeless a novel as the characters it portrays, and no doubt what Updike has to say in that book could have been as effectively conveyed in a philosophical essay. Rabbit Angstrom's disillusionment and his uncompromising dedication to an inner voice permit the triumph of imagination over mere form, but form obtrudes so rudely in *The Centaur* that the novel succeeds at all only by placing the most strenuous burden on Updike's increasingly lyrical technique.

Thus, while Updike's saintlike heroes are finely calibrated and philosophically persuasive, they lack the force and vitality of Edward Lewis Wallant's Norman Moonbloom or Sammy; they lack, as well, the comic richness of Wallant's creations. Intellectually, Updike's Rabbit and Harry Angstrom are no doubt more viable and more significant for the modern reader than Kerouac's child saints, Gerard and Tristessa, both of whom depend for credibility on an old-line sentimentality which, if moving, is unconvincing. What such writers share is the belief that the individual is the sole hope in the dislocated modern environment. The demonstration of Rabbit's and Caldwell's pursuit of their particular saintly visions is an optimistic assertion of man's ability to overcome his environment and to project his compassion and concern to the degree of absurdity at the heart of the religious experience. Jeopardized as it is by Updike's involvement with purely verbal and otherwise formal elements of prose, that vision carries its own magnificence, and it is the force which, in the best of Updike's work, humanizes the technician and establishes his significant place in any serious study of the contemporary novel in America.

THE ABSURD MAN AS $Tragic\ Hero$

During a *Paris Review* interview held in 1954, William Styron was asked whether he thought the current generation of American writers worked under greater disadvantages than their literary predecessors. He answered that

Writers ever since writing began have had problems, and the main problem narrows down to just one word—life. Certainly this might be an age of so-called faithlessness and despair we live in, but the new writers haven't cornered any market on faithlessness and despair, any more than Dostoevski or Marlowe or Sophocles did. Every age has its terrible aches and pains, its peculiar new horrors, and every writer since the beginning of time, just like other people, has been afflicted by what that same friend of mine calls "the fleas of life"—you know, colds, hangovers, bills, sprained ankles, and little nuisances of one sort or another. *They* are the constants of life, at the core of life, along with nice little delights that come along now and then. Dostoevski had them and Marlowe had them and we all have them, and they're a hell of a lot more invariable than nuclear fission or the Revocation of the Edict of Nantes. So is Love invariable, and Unrequited Love, and Death and Insult and Hilarity. Mark Twain was as baffled and appalled by Darwin's theories as anyone else, and those theories

seemed as monstrous to the Victorians as atomic energy, but he still wrote
about riverboats and old Hannibal, Missouri. No, I don't think the writer
today is any worse off than at any other time.[1]

There are, Styron emphasizes, constants in life, day-to-day pleasures and perils which man can fasten to for their continuity, but even
so, each age does have "its terrible aches and pains, its peculiar new
horrors." Life in mid-twentieth-century Newport News, Virginia,
where Styron was born, is not essentially different from Twain's life
in Hannibal, Missouri. Love, Unrequited Love, Death, Insult, Hilarity are still the constants about which peculiar horrors or joys gather.
In Twain's Hannibal as in Styron's Newport News there were the
years of horror and anxiety in the face of mounting threats that the
"world" would be blown apart. It matters little so far as the constants
are concerned that it was a civil war which threatened Twain's world
and, as the most obvious manifestation, submarines in Chesapeake
Bay which threatened Styron's. For Henry Adams the threat of disintegration was posed ironically in the dynamo, an apparent symbol
of power and progress which nonetheless threatened to make men
"mere creatures of force around central powerhouses." The particular
horrors of a new age do become significant, however, when we realize
that they will dictate the terms of an artist's answers to the constant
problems of life. In the same interview quoted above Styron goes on
to point out that the "morbidity and gloom" of so many young writers
today is the product of greatly increased knowledge about "the human self—Freud—that is, abnormal psychology, and all the new
psychiatric wisdom. My God, think of how morbid and depressing
Dostoevski would have been if he could have gotten hold of some of
the juicy work of Dr. Wilhelm Stekel, say *Sadism and Masochism*."[2]
This knowledge is part of the *status quo*, but a *status quo* which, Styron concedes by analogy, makes the problem of the contemporary

[1] Peter Matthiessen and George Plimpton, "William Styron," *Writers at Work*,
p. 280. This interview was originally published in *The Paris Review*, 5 (Spring,
1954), 42–57.
[2] *Ibid.*, p. 281.

artist at least more deviously complex than that of, say, Dostoevski. While it is unquestionably true that young writers have cornered no market on despair, it is certainly equally true that they are frequently faced with unique difficulties in meeting the peculiar new horrors of their age.

In an article appearing in *Nation* in 1953, Maxwell Geismar attempted to look ahead to what might honestly be expected from such promising young talents as William Styron, outlining at the same time the peculiar amalgam of circumstances which seemed to surround the contemporary artist:

Pity the poor artist! The retreat either to the modes of personal sensibility, or those of religious and social authoritarianism may be a refuge for him. But it is hardly a source of great art anymore. The real drama and content of this period lie directly at the center of the chaos that surrounds him. It is there he must turn to come close to the spirit of the age, if he can only catch it. And surely no literary subject matter could offer him so many opportunities along with so many dangers. For our part we can only keep the boundaries of the middle way as wide as possible for him, preserve him from false orthodoxy, let him speak his mind without benefit of Congress—or even of captious critics.[3]

Lie Down in Darkness was indeed such a plunge into chaos, and like Updike's *Poorhouse Fair* it is a dismissal of more pervasive traditional "answers" to that chaos and an enumeration of contemporary absurdities. In the structure of this book is something of the baroque glory that abounds in Sir Thomas Browne's "Urn Burial," from which Styron took his title. Styron has admitted that the greatest problem which faced him in writing this first novel was the problem of "the progression of time,"[4] but the many complex episodes of the novel are so smoothly handled that the reader may tend to slight the enormous skill and concentration which were necessary to bring them

[3] Maxwell Geismar, "The Postwar Generation in American Arts and Letters," *Saturday Review*, 36 (March 14, 1953), 60.

[4] Matthiessen and Plimpton, "William Styron," *Writers at Work*, p. 275.

off. A rereading of the book is clearly essential if the reader is to be conscious of Styron's exceptional technical virtuosity.

What we might call the centralizing action of *Lie Down in Darkness* occurs in the space of a few hours, beginning as Milton Loftis awaits the arrival of the train that bears the disfigured body of his daughter, and concluding shortly after her burial on the same day. With apparent casualness, the book manages to embrace all the events of more than a quarter century which bring Loftis, his estranged wife, and his mistress together for this tragic funeral. Styron's debt to the interior monologues of Joyce (especially in Peyton's final, frenzied, Molly Bloom-like soliloquy) and to Faulkner's experiments with time—most notably those in *The Sound and the Fury*—is obvious and tremendous. "I'm all for the complexity of Faulkner, but not for the confusion,"[5] Styron once commented, later extending those comments to include Joyce. That Styron is able to succeed so well and so personally with techniques that are associated with Faulkner and Joyce is in part, of course, a tribute to his enormous skill as a writer, but in part, too, the result of historical accident; for Styron is not essentially an experimenter, and therefore does not run the dangers which Joyce and Faulkner often ran of becoming overwhelmed by technique itself. Character and story are of immense importance to Styron, and his intense, fully drawn characters give the novel concentration and unity, just as such characters give substance to Faulkner's best work.

It is significant that Styron's greatest problem in writing this first novel should have been focused on "the progression of time," for even by arranging events on a merely temporal basis, man can begin to see in them some order or purpose. What Styron was forced to make orderly in this book was precisely what Geismar saw as the main challenge for the young writer: "the chaos that surrounds him." Emotionally, socially, and spiritually, *Lie Down in Darkness* is a painful chronicle of chaos, lightened only by the fact that the worst of

[5] *Ibid.*, p. 275.

the chaos is now relegated to the past, where it can be regarded with, if not calmness, at least objectivity.

The chief concern of this novel is with the efforts of Milton and Helen Loftis and their daughter Peyton to arrive at some sort of personal identification. At moments the book seems to verge on what might be classified as a Jungian integration of personality, except that psychoanalysis fails Peyton and would, we know, fail the other characters, too. For all his psychoanalytic inclinations, Styron tends to see his characters as figures from a Greek drama, as bared, tormented, and destined souls, in essence far removed from the aid of the analyst. That Peyton has an Electra complex and that much of the tension of the novel derives from repressed Oedipal desires is obvious, but it is equally obvious that all of the characters are somehow doomed to play out their fates without external interference. They do not, and Styron seems to say *cannot*, achieve any personality integration, can never reach full or complete identification because their incompleteness, like the writer's knowledge of "the human self," is part of the *status quo* of this first novel. Psychoanalysis can help to describe existing conditions, but it seems to offer no hope of resolving them. The fruitlessness of the quest for identification is most resounding in the case of Peyton, for she represents the promise of youth and sensibility; but rejected, unable to find the constant, Love, she continues a nymphomaniacal quest for peace and wholeness which is brought to an end only when she leaps, naked, briefly free, from the loft of a garment factory in Harlem. Unidentified for several days, her body is interred in a Potter's Field on Hart's Island, and even this temporary burial among unnamed dead suggests the horror of Peyton's frustrated quest for identity.

The first step toward the absurd is, according to Camus, the awakening that occurs when "the stage sets collapse" and man is forced to ask "Why?" It is then that he becomes conscious of the weary, enigmatic circles in which his life has run, and then that he has the chance to return gradually into the "chain" or to achieve a real awakening. It is at a somewhat dissipated but still youthful fifty years

that Milton Loftis first comes to this absurd awakening: "At the age
of fifty he was beginning to discover, with a sense of panic, that his
whole life had been in the nature of a hangover, with faintly unpleas-
ant pleasures being atoned for by the dull, unalleviated pain of
guilt" (*LDD*, 152). Suddenly Loftis knows himself to be a failure as
a father, as a husband, and as a lawyer. He exists now in what Camus
called "that weariness tinged with amazement."[6] "The stranger who
at certain seconds comes to meet us in the mirror"[7] becomes for Loftis
"a wasted, aging satyr" (*LDD*, 250), a mocking symbol of his hollow
vanity. Loftis vacillates between a definitive awakening and being
lulled back into the rhythmic chain of meaningless gestures from
which he has only recently been aroused. His marriage is, perhaps,
the most extreme example of the absurdity of his life, for he is in
love with and married to a woman who is incapable not only of loving but even of being loved except in the make-believe, idealistic
world of childhood which is kept alive for her in a demented daughter.

Beginning with consciousness of his failure as a husband, Loftis
has made a primary absurd discovery, but it is the consequences of
the absurd discovery which are of primary importance. For a year
after the death of his retarded daughter, Loftis is reunited with his
wife in something like a conventional marital relationship. He has
totally rejected his mistress, and he even hopes that Helen may forget herself long enough to draw Peyton back into the family, for
only Helen herself has the ultimate power to keep Peyton in the family circle or to drive her out. Loftis's intentions in this year of reconciliation are clearly opposed to reality. Helen and Peyton despise each
other, partly because of their rivalry over Milton, partly because they
are such wholly different creatures—Helen frigid and precise, Peyton sexual and flamboyant. Helen had had Maudie, the perpetual
child, as the recipient of her own brand of sexless love, and Milton
has had Peyton, has been stimulated by her sexuality, and has sought

[6] Albert Camus, *The Myth of Sisyphus*, p. 10.
[7] *Ibid.*, p. 11.

relief from sexual frustrations with his mistress, Dolly. It is inconceivable that the family, after so many years of harsh and agonizing separation, could suddenly draw together. By flaunting his intention against this reality, by refusing to be lulled to sleep again by alcohol and by the vulgar attentions of Dolly, Milton promises to emerge with something of the acuteness of the absurd hero; this promise is based not merely on the fact that Milton is involved in an absurd situation, but on the additional circumstance that he is aware of the absurdity. But when reality crashes down about him on the day Peyton returns home to be married, when he stands and watches the blood flow from the gouges which Peyton has made on Helen's cheeks, he reverts to alcohol and to Dolly, gladly sinking into a blurred mechanical chain and refusing to recognize any conflict in his life. After two years of this drugged existence, the stage sets collapse once more with the news of Peyton's suicide; Milton again rejects Dolly and pleads with Helen to take him back. They are standing with Carey Carr in the vestibule of the cemetery chapel waiting out a sudden rain storm. Loftis takes advantage of their refuge to draw Helen aside, and his pleading voice reaches Carey as "high, hysterical, tormented." Helen breaks away from Loftis and urges him not to make a scene. " 'Scene! Scene!' Loftis shouted. 'Why, God damn you, don't you see what you're doing! With nothing left! Nothing! Nothing! Nothing!' " With a horror that causes him to moan to himself, " 'Oh, my Lord, You shall never reveal Yourself'." Carey Carr sees Loftis seize Helen and begin to choke her. " 'God damn you!' Loftis yelled. 'If I can't have . . . then you . . . nothing!' " (387–388). The moment of violence ends as abruptly as it began, and Loftis runs from the chapel in despair. Helen's final words echo Milton's and express the meaninglessness and emptiness of their lives: " 'Nothing! Nothing! Nothing! Nothing!' " (399).

"The absurd is born," Camus says, of the "confrontation between the human need [for happiness and for reason] and the unreasonable silence of the world. This must be clung to because the whole consequence of a life can depend on it. The irrational, the human nostalgia, and the absurd that is born of their encounter—these are the three characters in the drama that must necessarily end with all the logic of which an existence is capable."[8] Milton Loftis feels this longing and witnesses the dramatic confrontation of his own needs with the unreasonable silence of the world, but he lacks the strength to remain "awake" in the face of these contradictions. His occasional isolated gestures against a life of chaos never involve a thorough or sustained commitment.

Peyton, however, does achieve an awakening, and she is then faced with the choice of suicide or recovery. She is too weakened to struggle conclusively with the irrationality of the universe, and since she cannot find a smooth, clean world like the inside of the clock which she comes to worship, she has no choice but suicide. Peyton has never really known the hypnotic rhythms of life which lull Milton back to sleep, although she seeks them in the image of the clock, knowing that she lacks the strength to come to grips with the real world:

I went back to the windowsill and got the clock. I cupped my hands around it, looking at the dots and hands, which shone with a clear green light in the darkness: we have not been brought up right, I thought, peering down into the alarm hole: there in the sunny grotto we could coast among the bolts and springs and ordered, ticking wheels, riveted to peace forever. Harry would like to know: rubies he'd love and cherish, in that light they'd glow like the red hats of Breughel dancers. I could hear the serene and steady whir, held it closer to my ear for the ticking—an unfitful, accomplished harmony—perfect, ordered, whole. (344–345)

Peyton is too sophisticated, knows too much of the inner self to be able to escape through alcohol or sex, and when no other alternatives appear, she commits suicide.

Throughout *Lie Down in Darkness* there is a continuous stress on the return to childhood itself, as there is in much of the work of J. D.

---

[8] Camus, *The Myth of Sisyphus*, p. 21.

Salinger; this yearning for the experience of innocence may also be
the attempt, neurotic or sentimental, to avoid coming to terms with
the insuperable evils of the present. For Helen, Peyton, and even
Loftis himself, recurrent urges toward the apparently uncomplicated
world of childhood are efforts to avoid both the devastating complexities of adult life and—more importantly—the very absurdity of a
loveless existence. The image of perfect innocence and uncomplicated love is given special vividness in the book by Maudie, whose
"Mamadear" and "Pappadaddy" not only vividly recall the innocence
of childhood, but also parody this innocence to a monstrous degree.
Sitting in a Charlottesville hospital and waiting for Maudie's im-
pending death, Helen tells Peyton and Loftis that Maudie "knows":
" 'I said, even if they don't know, well, Maudie knows, and that's
enough. She knows! Want me to tell you about her my dears?' " (219).
Maudie had known how to love, and had actually been in love with
a small, thin, half-Negro, half-Indian man who performed tricks for
her. Although she had seen him only a few times, and then separated
by a high fence, she could recognize love as a potential force. Helen
revels in the idea of Maudie's knowledge, partly because of her intense desire that Maudie know some kind of happiness, but largely
because the girl's love experience conformed to Helen's own roman-
ticized, sexless view. Helen erred fatally in seeing Maudie's love as
ideal and in failing to realize that an adult is incapable of living completely if such childhood perspectives are artificially retained.

What Styron has given the reader in this book is not a picture of
an absurd man but rather a group of absurd situations: absurd marriage, absurd love, absurd death, brought into conjunction only
through the passage of time. Helen, seeking order through the church,
is frustrated by Carey Carr's primness and is aware that beneath
his immaculate Virginia-Episcopal surface lies his own grief at the
failure of personal revelation. Carey comments to his wife on the way
to Peyton's wedding that a wedding ceremony " 'is the symbolic
affirmation of a moral order in the world' " (248), but the wedding
itself, like all the Loftis reunions which begin with such high hopes,

ends in a cataclysm of despair and violence. Loftis anticipates the wedding as a great victory, one which will somehow compensate for the uneventfulness of his life:

A man so unaccomplished, he reflected, might achieve as much as great men, give him patience and a speck of luck; though his road slopes off to a bitter sort of doom—and the wind, blustering down the night through chill acres of stars, suddenly made Loftis feel cold, and his life a chancey thing indeed—he has had his moment, a clock-tick of glory before the last descent. You know this man's fall: do you know his wrassling? *Bring home the bride again, bring home the triumph of our victory.* (260)

Like Sisyphus, Loftis is poised near the top of the hill, his shoulder bitten painfully by the enormous rock which he is attempting to lift, but unlike Sisyphus, he has reached such a point of decay that he is unable to "wrassle" it up even once.

The only figure in this novel who offers any real promise of completeness is Harry Miller, Peyton's Jewish husband. Harry is a painter, and the fierceness of his aesthetic intentions is suggested by the fact that he is able to create his most successful painting in the midst of Peyton's unfaithfulnesses and with the radio blaring the news of the atomic destruction of Nagasaki.

He was painting an old man. In grays, deep blues, an ancient monk or rabbi lined and weathered, lifting proud, tragic eyes toward heaven; behind him were the ruins of a city, shattered, devastated, crumbled piles of concrete and stone that glowed from some half-hidden, rusty light, like the earth's last waning dusk. It was a landscape dead and forlorn yet retentive of some flowing, vagrant majesty, and against it the old man's eyes looked proudly upward, toward God perhaps, or perhaps just the dying sun. (374)

As she watches him paint, Peyton pleads for another chance, but Harry cannot understand the birds of guilt that torment Peyton and are driving her to her death. The picture we receive of Harry is never

complete, but his speech to Peyton, recalled in her lengthy monologue, represents a major thematic climax:

There are a lot of things I'd like to talk about. Do you realize what the
world's come to? Do you realize that the great American commonwealth
just snuffed out one hundred thousand innocent lives this week? There
was a time, you know, when I thought for some reason—maybe just to
preserve your incomparable beauty—that I could spend my life catering
to your needs, endure your suspicions and your mistrusts and all the rest,
plus having to see you get laid in a fit of pique. I have other things to do.
Remember that line you used to quote from the Bible, "How long, Lord?
or something—" "Remember how short my time is," I said. "Yes," he said.
"Well, that's the way I feel. With your help I used to think I could go a
long way, but you didn't help me. Now I'm on it alone. I don't know what
good it'll do anyone but me, but I want to paint and paint and paint because I think that some agony is upon us. Call me a disillusioned innocent,
a renegade Red, or whatever, I want to crush in my hands all that agony
and make beauty come out, because that's all that's left, and I don't have
much time—" (377).

Despite the heroic assertiveness of this statement, Harry Miller appears too infrequently to be the hero of the novel, although Styron
clearly regards him as a symbol of hope. Since the figure of Harry is
incomplete, the hope he offers cannot triumph over the despairing
cries of "Nothing!" which Milton and Helen have uttered. There is
no room in *Lie Down in Darkness* for the kind of positive, creative
force which Harry represents. In sketching the heroic outlines of
Harry's vision, Styron seems to be suggesting the direction which a
later novel might take; it is, significantly, another painter who rises
to tragic insight as the absurd hero of Styron's third book, *Set This
House on Fire.*

Styron's second book, *The Long March,* was originally published in
discovery magazine. There is undoubtedly more than a passing note
of subjective protest in this novella, for its indictment of the authoritarianism of military life followed shortly after Styron was himself

recalled to the Marines. Stylistically, *The Long March* is in almost total contrast to *Lie Down in Darkness*. The book is a vivid and often savage trajectory covering approximately twenty-four hours in the life of a "peace-time" Marine company. Its central figure is Captain Mannix, a hulking Jew from Brooklyn, who finds first that he is too old to be a Marine but finally comes to wonder whether he could ever be anything else. A concentrated treatment of action and character provides emphasis for the day's two major events: the explosion of short rounds which causes the death of eight young recruits and the maiming of fifteen more, and the brutal, thirty-six–mile forced march which H&S Company undertakes.

Mannix's company was composed largely of men who had been in civilian life for six years and were recalled during the Korean War. Untrained, soft, they were in no condition for a forced march of any length. Colonel Templeton, however, demanded the march as proof of his battalion's readiness, and especially as a reminder to Mannix and his company that they were, above all else, Marines. The painful march through a hot Carolina night and morning, like the senseless death and crippling which occur when old ammunition is fired, is simply an extreme dramatic illustration of the "never-endingness of war"(*LM*, 420). Mannix and Culver, the latter being a kind of persona for Styron, have both known what they thought to be an enduring peace, but both have now learned that war is, after all, the human condition. Culver felt that "all of his life he had yearned for something that was as fleeting and incommunicable, in its beauty, as that one bar of music he remembered, or those lovely girls with their ever joyful, ever sprightly dance on some far fantastic lawn" (419). Stripped of their illusions, Mannix and Culver nonetheless cling to something more fundamental, a vision of themselves. It is not as members of H&S Company or as Marines that they struggle to complete the long march, but as men who refuse to be intimidated by what they regard as a senseless authority. War has become, for the time at least, the reality of their lives, and with the last ounce of strength they cling to that intention which opposes the notion that war should be never-ending.

The Long March offers a bleak panorama, and at each turn Styron reminds his reader that this world whose aim is to keep alive the sufferings of war is, in fact, a world of absurdity. Unlike such professional Marines as Major Lawrence, Mannix refuses to be lulled to sleep by this world but determines instead to fight, regardless of the personal consequences. Mannix knows, as the true absurd hero always knows, that he has virtually no chance for victory, but he must be true to his intentions: "Born into a generation of conformists, even Mannix (so Culver sensed) was aware that his gestures were not symbolic, but individual, therefore hopeless, maybe even absurd, and that he was trapped like all of them in a predicament which one personal insurrection could, if anything, only make worse" (388). Challenging the absurd universe with such intensity and determination, Mannix becomes a true rebel, and as Camus emphasizes, "In every act of rebellion, the rebel simultaneously experiences a feeling of revulsion at the infringement of his rights and a complete and spontaneous loyalty to certain aspects of himself."[9] Mannix, like Camus's rebel, is prepared to support this rebellion precisely because he has been driven to the point where his most important loyalty—his loyalty to himself—has been challenged:

No, perhaps Mannix wasn't a hero, any more than the rest of them, caught up by wars in which, decade by half-decade, the combatant served peonage to the telephone and the radar and the thunderjet—a horde of cunningly designed, and therefore often treacherous, machines. But Mannix had suffered once, that "once" being, in his own words, "once too goddam many, Jack." And his own particular suffering had made him angry, had given him an acute, if cynical, perception about their renewed bondage, and a keen nose for the winds that threatened to blow up out of the oppressive weather of their surroundings and sweep them all into violence. And he made Culver uneasy. His discontent was not merely peevish; it

9 Albert Camus, *The Rebel*, pp. 13–14.

was rocklike and rebellious, and thus this discontent seemed to Culver to be at once brave and somehow full of peril. (*LM*, 383)

The absurdity of the mock war maneuvers in which these Marines are engaged—"this new world of frigid nights and blazing noons, of disorder and movement and fanciful pursuit" (378)—reaches a dramatic climax in the march itself, one longer and more strenuous than most severe marches in actual wartime. Mannix's determination to complete the march and to drive his men to complete it as well is simply his way of scorning, through a kind of rebellion in reverse, the world which the Colonel represents. As the Colonel pushes out at the head of the vicious march, there comes from the rear the voice of the Captain, which reaches Culver as a huge force "dominating the night" (403).

Maxwell Geismar has called *The Long March* "a tour de force on the side of the angels, so to speak, and against the demons of industrial, scientific, and militaristic twentieth-century American life."[10] Certainly the movement from Milton Loftis's tentative, febrile gropings after rebellion (and his return to Helen is also a kind of "rebellion in reverse") to Captain Mannix's limited but successful rebellion is a very great step. In *The Long March* Styron demonstrated his ability to do more than simply enumerate the absurdities of the world; he suggested the possibility of a character who is capable of rising up against them. In *Set This House on Fire* Styron was to extend his view of the rebel and to place him in a background of stylistic and thematic richness comparable to that of *Lie Down in Darkness*.

In an article written for *Nation* in 1953 William Styron noted his peculiar inability to enjoy "practically any visually artistic representation":

I think this blindness of mine, though, has had its worthy effects, for if it has helped to keep me from understanding the more beautiful things about

[10] Maxwell Geismar, *American Moderns: From Rebellion to Conformity*, p. 250.

Europe it has also conspired with a sort of innate and provincial aloofness in my nature to make me more conscious of my *modern* environment, and self-consciously aware of my emotions as an American within that environment.[11]

That Styron has italicized the word modern becomes particularly significant in light of the dramatically affirmative conclusion of *Set This House on Fire*. Again Styron has attempted to highlight the grotesqueries and frustrations of the contemporary environment, but in this novel he finds a unity and order infinitely more significant than the mere order of time which emerged from *Lie Down in Darkness*.

The very title of Styron's third book—and especially the source of the title—suggests the change which had come in his philosophical point of view. Both Peyton and Loftis had chosen to lie down in darkness, while Cass Kinsolving, his body shaken by fires and fevers, learns that such fires are preferable to exile from whatever power rules the moral universe. Thus, the fire of purgation cancels that of destruction and self-destruction, for as in T. S. Eliot's *Four Quartets* there is only one "discharge" from hatred and self-pity: "The only hope, or else despair/Lies in the choice of pyre or pyre—/To be redeemed from fire by fire." Styron took the title for his first novel from Browne's "Urn Burial"; for *Set This House on Fire* he went to Donne's sermon "To the Earle of Carlile, and his Company, at Sion," and specifically to a passage suggesting the horror of separation from God. Both metaphysicals, Browne and Donne had in common the interest in exploring experience by way of the intellectual excitements and preoccupations of their day. Despite their many resemblances, perhaps most striking in any comparison of Donne and Browne is the contrast in their prose styles and in the attitudes which those styles suggest. In Browne's prose the balance of the words and clauses, the leisurely spacing and punctuation, induce a slow, relaxed rhythm. The effect is to make the reader curious as to what might follow—but not excited, and the rhythms create neither pressure nor urgency. In

[11] William Styron, "Prevalence of Wonders," *Nation*, 176 (May 2, 1953), 370.

contrast it is often difficult to cut across the constant jet of thought in Donne's prose; clause springs from clause and sentence from sentence with a complex criss-cross and overlay of ideas which demands a continual reference back and catching up with the sense. There is a similar contrast between the prose styles of *Lie Down in Darkness* and *Set This House on Fire*. In the former book Styron was largely concerned with a somewhat static enumeration and articulation of the various absurdities of modern life, while in the latter his involvement is direct and energetic. The two novels reflect stylistically the different impulses from which they were written. In *Lie Down in Darkness* Styron avoided any passionate moral commitment, but in *Set This House on Fire* his commitment was specifically and passionately an affirmation, through the attempted creation of a tragic hero, of the order of the universe.

In *Set This House on Fire*, as in his first two books, Styron has given considerable time to establishing the absurdity of the environment in which his characters are placed. Like his earlier work, this novel suggests an environment dominated by a profound desuetude of order and value, and again the action centers around the events of a single day. Unlike the day described in *Lie Down in Darkness*, that in *Set This House on Fire* does not simply *centralize* what would otherwise be the chaotic action of the book, but contains the *central* action of the novel. *Set This House on Fire* opens, several years after the tragic events which occurred in Sambuco, Italy, with the reminiscences of Peter Leverett, the fairly detached observer of the results of the two acts of horror which occurred on that day. Leverett serves much the same function in the novel that Nick Carraway served in *The Great Gatsby*, that of synthesizer and commentator. He does not, as did Nick, tell the story solely through his own reminiscences (the story is so much bigger and more complex that a single-narrator retelling would be virtually impossible), but he does provide the catalyst which induces Cass Kinsolving to fill in the gaps in his own knowledge of that day in Sambuco and offer a passive but critical commentary on the other characters. Peter Leverett further resembles Carraway in that he represents to some degree the older values of rural America and remains the only uncorrupted male character in the book.

Remembering, even with only the most vague knowledge, the events that had turned his day in Sambuco into one of almost unrelieved horror, Peter Leverett is tortured by dreams:

One of them especially I remember; like most fierce nightmares it had the habit of coming back again and again. In this one I was in a house somewhere, trying to sleep; it was dead of night, wintry and storming. Suddenly I heard a noise at the window, a sinister sound, distinct from the tumult of the rain and the wind. I looked outside and saw a shadow—the figure of someone who moved, an indefinite shape, a prowler whose dark form slunk toward me menacingly. Panicky, I reached for the telephone, to call the friend who lived nearby (my best, my last, dearest friend; nightmares deal in superlatives and magnitudes); *he*, somehow, I knew, was the only one dear enough, close enough, to help me. But there was no answer to all my frantic ringing. Then, putting the phone down, I heard a *tap-tap-tap*ping at the window and turned to see—bared with the malignity of a fiend behind the streaming glass—the baleful, murderous face of that self-same friend. (*STHF*, 5–6)

This first note of horror which the book strikes comes like a fearful prelude to the story, gothicly foreshadowing the violence which follows. Leverett knows that he will be haunted by such dreams until and unless he is able to find some order within the chaos of his day in Sambuco, and especially in the almost surrealistic episodes which occurred on the day of his arrival. He is fully confident that such an order exists if only he can find its key. Motivated by the desire to determine this order and to locate the moral responsibility for two inadequately related acts of violence, Peter Leverett journeys south, stopping briefly in Virginia, the source of those "older values" which he represents. His intention at this time is to visit Cass Kinsolving, the only person alive who might help him piece out a complete story; his stop is significant as an almost ritualistic preparation for the ordeal of discovery he is soon to undergo with Cass Kinsolving. As he prepares to leave Virginia, Peter thinks:

In times of stress and threat, I've heard it said, in times of terror and alarms, of silence and clinging, people tend to hold on to the past, even to imitate it: taking on old fashions and humming old songs, seeking out historic scenes and reliving old ancestral wars, in an effort to forget both the lack-luster present and a future too weird and horrible to ponder. Perhaps one of the reasons we Americans are so exceptionally nervous and driven is that our past is effaced almost before it is made present; in our search for old avatars to contemplate we find only ghosts, whispers, shadows: almost nothing remains for us to feel or seem or to absorb our longing. That evening I was touched to the heart: by my father's sweetness and decency and rage, but also by whatever it was within me—within life itself, it seemed so intense—that I knew to be irretrievably lost. Estranged from myself and from my time, dwelling neither in the destroyed past nor in the fantastic and incomprehensible present, I knew that I must find the answer to at least several things before taking hold of myself and getting on with the job. (18–19)

These thoughts, provoked by the idea of people who "tend to hold on to the past," recall John Updike's descriptions of the poorhouse inmates who struggle to maintain something of value in their lives by clinging to mementos of the American past.

From Leverett's point of view the disintegration of all apparent order began on the day he left Rome for a visit with his wealthy, oversexed, arrogant, but somehow gracious friend, Mason Flagg, whose name is perhaps suggestive of his flamboyant manner. Leverett dates the events which occur in Sambuco from the moment he left Rome. Setting out at night, he is forced to sleep in his car, fighting intense heat and swarms of mosquitoes. Later, almost driven off the road by a speeding Alfa Romeo, Leverett himself begins to speed, and he is doing over sixty miles an hour when he smashes into a motorscooter bearing a one-eyed, accident-prone Italian peasant. After being upbraided by the peasant's mother for wartime raping, stealing, bombing, and looting, Leverett, suffering from extreme nervous exhaustion, proceeds toward Sambuco in his wrecked car. The speedy building up of absurd incidents creates a tone of high comedy which finally becomes hysteria and ends only after sounding a note of total horror.

When Leverett reaches Sambuco, after a dreamlike encounter with Cass and his wife, it is only to blunder into the apparently serene village square to find himself in the middle of a movie set, intimidated by arc lights and cameras and outraged directors. Styron has achieved here a masterful comic tone, and with it has established the absurdity of this environment by introducing into the beautiful ancient village a movie crew engaged in the filming, in modern dress and with numerous unsuccessful scripts, of a costume novel about Beatrice Cenci. Assembled to work on the film is perhaps the greatest single collection of neurotics since Nathaniel West's *Day of the Locust*. The Hollywood phantasmagoria offered Styron, as it offered West, a kind of microcosm of the world's distortions and illusions; and the description of the half-American, half-Italian cast brought together for the movie creates the nightmarish humor of the surrealist jokesmith without necessitating the manipulation of environment which surrealistic imagery usually presupposes.

It is Cass Kinsolving who forms the dramatic center of this novel, and Cass's only involvement with the movie crew is in the fact that Mason Flagg forces him to perform disgusting pantomimes for their amusement. Like John Updike's "Rabbit," Cass is continually running. Slotkin, a "kindly old Navy brain doctor," once told him, " 'You will be running all your life' " (314). What Cass is running after is something "which had indeed flowed right on out of me, and which to save my very life I knew I had to recapture" (278). On the day he gratefully surrendered his chastity to a teen-age religious fanatic and nymphomaniac, she had referred to his orgasm as the loss of the "divine spirit"; Cass later accepts her description as one of particular significance. Commitment to an absurd marriage with a blissfully irresponsible, totally disorganized, and wholly devout Catholic (Cass comes from a staunch Episcopal family) hardly seems to have aided his search, and further agonized by his failures as a painter, Cass has become an alcoholic and acquired the added tortures of an ulcer. Cass had caught Mason Flagg in what was perhaps the only painful faux pas of his career, and the wealthy American embarked with such severity on a program of degrading and dehumanizing the young painter that he threatened to destroy him completely.

Largely as a result of Flagg's tortures, Cass has lost almost all touch with reality, a loss which would have been complete were it not for his intense love for an Italian peasant, Francesca, and his friendship with a semi-Fascist policeman, Luigi. It is chiefly Luigi who reminds Cass of his responsibilities—not necessarily to his family—but to himself as a man and, consequently, to life itself. Luigi's role in the novel and his emphasis on "force" are closely parallel to those of To-thero in *Rabbit, Run*. Trying to halt Cass's course of alcoholic annihi-lation, Luigi argues:

"I'm not a religious man . . ., and this you well know. However, I studied among the humanist philosophers—the Frenchman Montaigne, Croce, the Greek Plato, not to speak, of course, of Gabriele D'Annunzio—and if there's one thing of the highest value I've discovered, it is simply this: that the primary moral sin is self-destruction—the wish for death which you so painfully and obviously manifest. I exclude madness, of course. The single good is respect for the force of life. Have you not pictured to yourself the whole horrible vista of eternity? I've told you all this before, Cass. The absolute blankness, *il niente, la nullità*, stretching out for ever and ever, the pit of darkness which you are hurling yourself into, the nothingness, the void, the oblivion? Yet are you unable to see that although this in itself is awful, it is nothing to the moral sin you commit by willing yourself *out* of that life force . . ." (195–196)

Luigi's statement that "the primary moral sin is self-destruction" might almost have been taken from the pages of Camus's *Myth of Sisyphus*, for Camus's entire argument in that essay is eventually con-cerned with the problem of suicide and the subsequent affirmation of life itself. Sisyphus, it should be remembered, was sentenced to his unending task precisely because of his persistent commitment to life. Since Cass has lost virtually everything of value and since life appears to him to be hopeless, meaningless, and absurd, he has no desire to live; but through his very fall he is to realize the meaning of life, and through Luigi's intervention he will be given the chance to live it.

It is in Sambuco that Cass first begins to have the "visions" which will eventually assist him in rising to the heights of an absurd hero. The first of these visions is recorded in a diary kept fitfully during his early days in Sambuco:

"What saves me in the last analysis I have no way of telling. Sometimes the sensation I have that I am 2 persons & by that I mean the man of my dreams and the man who walks in daylight is so strong and frightening that at times I am actually scared to look into a mirror for fear of seeing some face that I have never seen before." (361)

This "stranger who at certain seconds comes to meet us in the mirror"[12] later reappears to Cass: "Then—wonder of wonders—he had withdrawn from himself. Standing aside, clammy and wet with horror, he saw his other self, naked now, step into the shower and, with the numb transfixed look of one already dead, turn on all the faucets full blast" (*STHF*, 368). The "other self" has actually turned on jets of gas. This dream, like the vision of horror in the mirror, comes to Cass immediately before he meets Mason Flagg, and as Flagg begins to dominate him there is doubt that the visions will ever be productive of true rebellion; in fact, it is only the most severe circumstances which shake Cass out of the chain into which he has sunk. Without Luigi, he would long before have been crushed by the weight of his desire for " 'a long long spell of darkness' ":

He recovered himself momentarily, focusing upon me his hot crowned eyes. "Yes, I'll tell you how you can help old Cass," he said somberly. "Now I'll tell you, my bleeding dark angel. Fetch him the machine, fetch him the wherewithal—a dagger, see, a dirk, well honed around the edges—and bring it here, and place it on his breastbone, and then with all your muscle drive it to the core." He paused, swaying slightly from side to side, never

12 Camus, *The Myth of Sisyphus*, p. 11.

removing his gaze from my face. "No bullshit, Pete. I've got a lust to be gone from this place. Make me up a nice potion, see? Make it up out of all these bitter-tasting, deadly things and pour it down my gullet. Ole Cass has had a hard day. He's gone the full stretch and his head aches and his legs are weary, and there's no more weeping in him." He held out his arms. "These limbs are plumb wore out. Look at them, boy. Look how they shake and tremble! What was they made for, I ast you. To wrap lovely ladies about? To make monuments? To enfold within them all the beauty of the world? Nossir! They was made to destroy and now they are plumb wore out, and my head aches, and I yearn for a long long spell of darkness." (238)

Camus stated that his aim in examining the absurd was

. . . to shed light upon the step taken by the mind when, starting from a philosophy of the world's lack of meaning, it ends up by finding a meaning and depth in it. The most touching of those steps is religious in essence; it becomes obvious in the theme of the irrational. But the most paradoxical and most significant is certainly the one that attributes rational reasons to a world it originally imagined as devoid of any guiding principle.[13]

Cass Kinsolving's world was devoid of any guiding principle from the moment Mason Flagg came to Sambuco and tossed him the first bottle of whiskey—a bottle that was to enslave him; but even as he is losing all perspective, Cass is laying a firm basis for its re-establishment through his love for the peasant girl Francesca. He has walked with her back into the primitive, timeless valley where she was born, and has tried to save the life of her tubercular father. Helping Michele has given Cass something to live for, and while his mind is still too tormented to be able to realize fully the significance of this experience, the seeds of self-regeneration are planted:

On some wet black shore, foul with the blackness of death's gulf, he was searching for an answer and a key. In words whose meaning he did not know he called out through the gloom, and the echoed sound came back to him as if spoken in an outlandish tongue. Somewhere, he knew, there

[13] Camus, *The Myth of Sisyphus,* pp. 31–32.

was light but like a shifting phantom it eluded him; voiceless, he strove to give voice to the cry which now, too late, awakening, he knew: "Rise up, Michele, rise up and walk!" he roared. And for the briefest space of time, between dark and light, he thought he saw the man, healed now, cured, staunch and upright, striding toward him. *O rise up Michele, my brother, rise!* (*STHF*, 425)

Cass knows that he has tried to give Michele something he does not really possess himself, that in rejecting life he has lessened his own ability to give life to others, and he thinks with sudden horror, "Michele will die because I have not given. Which now explains a lot . . . hell is not giving" (453).

Cass's nostalgia, his desire to give, and his blind rage for justice will, however, finally combine to cause him to break out of the weary chains in which Mason has bound him. "Every act of rebellion expresses a nostalgia for innocence and an appeal to the essence of being. But one day nostalgia takes up arms and assumes the responsibility of total guilt; in other words, adopts murder and violence."[14] Circumstances conspire to make all of Cass's "stage sets" collapse, and finally, jarred from his alcoholic chrysalis, he is able to perform a conscious, overt act in the name of order and value. Ironically, this act—the murder of Mason Flagg—is a profound moral wrong—not just because Cass has misjudged circumstances, but because he has a sudden realization of Flagg's humanness, and through that an insight into the meaning of life.

While the absurd hero may take many forms, underlying them all is the fundamental struggle with environment—the refusal to surrender personal ethics to environmental pressures. The tragic hero is perhaps the most intense example of the absurd, for his opposition is directed against the moral order of the universe itself. His "disproportion," while a strong affirmation of individual will, is nonetheless of such a nature that, at some point, it will be broken. This breaking

[14] Camus, *The Rebel*, p. 105.

or "fall" of the tragic hero is in itself an affirmation of the *logos* of the universe, of the fact that the world is governed by "rational reasons." Life may appear to be cruel to the tragic hero, but this apparent cruelty is necessary to affirm the existence of moral cause and effect in the world. In the fate of the tragic hero a pattern is given to experience, and that pattern is visible not alone to the hero himself, but to the observer of his fall. The optimism inherent in tragedy is the result of this affirmation of a moral order and the assertion that man has not only sufficient power to challenge that order but sufficient nobility to achieve wisdom through his fall. It is absurd to come into collision with the universal law of righteousness (or, like Ahab, with the universal law of unrighteousness), but it is also the height of heroism. Perhaps the most significant reason for the failure of modern authors to create tragedy in its classical fullness is simply that tragedy demands for its full implementation a belief in a moral order superior to the individual. Without such a belief the ultimate tragic creation, the tragic hero, is inconceivable. In *Set This House on Fire* Styron has perhaps come closer than any other modern author to actualizing this creation.

One of the earliest facts which we learn about Cass is that he is a psychotic, dismissed uncured from a Navy hospital. He is frequently violent in public, he abuses his family, and he goes through the ritual of degrading songs and gestures whenever Mason Flagg demands this "payment." We also learn near the beginning of the novel that upon his discharge from the hospital Cass was presented with "a two-volume edition of Greek drama" (129). Cass refers at length to *Oedipus*, and in the course of the evening preceding his murder of Mason he quotes at length from the tragedy. Such passages alone suggest that Cass is meant to be compared to a classical tragic hero, and on the brink of his "fall" he seems to grasp the drama which he is now destined to play out:

"Hold on! Let me tell you what we'll do. Together you and me we'll pull a Prometheus on 'em. We'll bring back tragedy to the land of the Pepsi-

Cola and the peanut brittle and the Modess Because. That's what we'll do, by God! And we'll make the ignorant little buggers like it. No more pop-corn, no more dreamboats, no more Donald Ducks, no more wet dreams in the mezzanine. *Tragedy,* by God, that's what we'll give 'em! Something to stiffen their spines and firm up their joints and clean out their tiny little souls. What'll you have? *Ajax? Alcestis? Electra? Iphigenia? Hoo-*boy!" Once more his hand plunged into the neck of his T-shirt. " 'I would not be the murderer of my mother, and of thee too. Sufficient is her blood. No, I will share my fortune, live with thee, or with thee die: to Argos I will lead thee . . .' " (118–119)

What Cass does not know at this time, but what he will learn as a participant in the tragedy of the following day, is a fundamental les-son of all tragedy: ". . . the harder you kite upward like that the harder you hit the ground when you fall" (267).

Cass, like Updike's Rabbit, had not only the opportunity but also the ability to become "a good family man, striving for the sunny ideal of *mens sana,*" but he rejected this alternative in deference to "that necessary part of the self which saw the world with passion and reck-lessness, and which had to be flayed and exacerbated and even mad-dened to retain its vision" (296–297). It is because of this passion and recklessness that Cass finds himself in a situation in which he must sin, albeit unwittingly. W. H. Auden has argued that the tragic "situation" in which a character appears to have no choice but to sin is actually "a sign that he is guilty of another sin of hybris, an over-weening self-confidence which makes him believe that he, with all his *arete,* is a god who cannot be made to suffer." Perhaps the most common instance of hybris is man's failure to recognize human limita-tions, in trying to operate with presumably complete knowledge and control when, of course, the effects of his actions can never be known in their entirety. Oedipus presumes to act as though he could totally control the results of his actions, and his final symbolic blinding is a recognition of his limitations, of what the Greeks would have rec-ognized as *ate.*

Presuming to be godlike, the tragic hero often takes upon himself the responsibility of becoming a judge. Such was Oedipus' impetuous attack on his own father. Cass, too, demonstrates a lack of control, and we have, in his participation as a boy in the destruction of the Negro cabin, an example of the kind of hybris which we see when Oedipus strikes his father. Cass does not appear to know what made him participate in the willful destruction of all which this family owned or revered, but he suggests it in his observation that "all the clichés and shibboleths I'd been brought up with came rolling back— a nigger wasn't much more than an animal anyway" (378). It is the overweening, blind pride of a white Southerner which makes him strike the face of the humanistic moral universe. The tragic hero presumes to act like a god, sitting in judgment as Cass had done in his treatment of the Negro. Cass must bear the guilt and shame of this episode, must be half-smothered for his blind violation, and he later notes to Peter Leverett that "this figured in what happened to me there in Sambuco" (379). The essential, final ingredient of the tragic hero is that he must realize his own blindness, his own limitations, and accept the obligations of his guilt. At the point of Cass's recognition Styron becomes particularly specific:

Cass fell silent again. Then he said: "But to kill a man, even in hatred, even in revenge, is like an amputation. Though this man may have done you the foulest injustice in the world, when you have killed him you have removed a part of yourself forever. For here was so-and-so. Here was some swine, some blackguard, some devil. But what made him tick? What made him do the things he did? What was his history? What went on in his mind? What, if you had let him live, would he have become? Would he have stayed a swine, unregenerate to the end? Or would he have become a better man? Maybe he could have imparted to you some secrets. You do not know. You have acted the role of God, you have judged him and condemned him. And by condemning him, by killing him, all the answers to those questions pass with him into oblivion. Only *you* remain—shorn of all that knowledge, and with as much pain as if somehow you had been dismembered. It is a pain that will stay with you as long as you live . . ." (446)

It is through Peter Leverett that the scene in Sambuco is first set

for tragedy. The macabre experiences of his trip lend the feeling of
a surrealistic dreamscape to his arrival. The deserted square almost
assumes the character of a stage awaiting its actors, and the personalities of the "movie folk clustered beneath the lights" (57), as they un-
fold in the following chapters, help to reaffirm the feeling that we are
watching something performed in the theatre. From the moment of
Leverett's arrival at Mason's palace, when he observes that "a confusing amber light played over the scene" (99) until his horrified
viewing of the "act" that Cass performs for Mason, this theatrical feeling becomes increasingly frenzied and helps to prepare the reader for
the scenes which follow.

Mason Flagg has raped Francesca, the graceful peasant girl who
represents for Cass all the beauty and value which have gone out
of his life. Cass knows of the rape and has determined to be revenged
on Flagg, but before he can formulate a plan he learns that Francesca
has been raped a second time, and that this time she has also been
hideously, fatally mutilated. Never questioning Mason's guilt, Cass
tracks and brutally murders the young American dilettante. This
"justice" is executed against a classical setting: before a ruined villa
with a "sagging façade and blasted columns" (463), a kind of temple
bearing the inscription *DUM SPIRO SPERO*, the adopted motto of
Cass's home state, South Carolina. As if to illustrate and support the
argument of tragedy, Styron repeatedly suggests classical episodes
and settings. Earlier in the novel, when Cass considered ways of
breaking free of Mason, he had looked out to sea and observed "above
Salerno, aloft, unbelievably high in space . . . a mist, a churning rack
of cloud, terrible and only faintly discerned, as of the smoke from re-
mote cities sacked and aflame: he gave a stir, touched on the shoulder
by an unseen, unknowable hand" (406).

The tragedy that takes place in Sambuco first comes to Leverett
through a series of wailing cries similar to those which might be made
by the chorus in a Greek play. The first words of explanation which
he hears are " 'Quelle horreur! . . . Quelle tragedie' " (219). Pressed
for more details, the money-conscious hotel owner, Windgasser, can

only mutter, " 'Overpowering twagedy, my God. It's like the *Gweeks*, I tell you, but far worse!' " (220). Describing the crowded square into which he runs, Leverett notes that "A squad of carabinieri entered in a riot truck, stage right . . ." (221), and when the horrifying events of the day are over, Cass comments to Leverett, *"Exeunt omnes.* Exit the whole lousy bunch" (239). Thus, as seen through Leverett's eyes, the tragedy which occurs in Sambuco observes the unities of time, place, and action; it constitutes, in fact, a kind of play within the novel.

As a modern version of the tragic hero Cass has not challenged the authority of a god or a group of gods, but he has challenged the purposive ordering of the universe in which right action is somehow rewarded and wrong action punished, if only within the confines of the individual conscience. Like Camus himself, Styron avoids commitment on words like "god," but also like Camus he is finally able to maintain that the world, which appears to lack all vestiges of order, is in fact governed by "rational reasons." Camus stated that the absurd does not lead to God because "the absurd is sin without God."[15] What Camus undoubtedly intended to assert was that the sense of sin must come from within, not from some set of traditional rules handed down from an abstract higher power. Perhaps it is sufficient to say that what Cass violates is Rabbit Angstrom's "something out there that wants me to find it." Important to the creation of the modern tragic hero as it is to the modern saint, is the emphasis that there is, after all, *something* out there, some convergence of individual consciousness in the formation of transcendent values, even though none of the traditional definitions of that "something" are acceptable. In terms of Cass's own particular vision we might describe it as the humanistic order of the universe; even so, Cass must discover and shoulder his own sin, for there is no authority dictating punishment —least of all is there a threat of punishment after death. Even at the moment of killing Flagg, Cass is aware of his violation of this hu-

[15] Camus, *The Myth of Sisyphus,* p. 30.

manistic order as he had not been aware at the time of the destruction of the Negro cabin:

Perhaps it was then that he drew back, understanding where he was,
and what he had done. He does not recall. Perhaps it was only the "Doll-
baby," echoing belatedly in his mind, that caused him to halt and look
down and see that the pale dead face, which was so soft and boyish, and in
death as in life so tormented, might be the face of almost anything, but
was not the face of a killer.

Children! he thought, standing erect over the twitching body. *Children!*
My Christ! All of us!

Then in his last grief and rage he wrestled Mason's body to the parapet,
and wearily heaved it up in his arms and kept it for a moment close to his
breast. And then he hurled it into the void. (464–465)

What Cass learns after the murder is that Mason Flagg had not
attacked and mutilated Francesca on the path outside the village, but
that this atrocity was committed by Saverio, the village idiot who had
earlier been apprehended in an almost identical crime. The authori-
ties, however, are convinced that Flagg committed suicide after attacking Francesca; only Cass and his soul mate Luigi know the
truth. In desperation Cass, who has had no use for religion, turns to
a priest with the words, "Help me." The priest cannot help him any
more than Slotkin, the psychiatrist to whom Cass once literally
prayed, can help him to resolve this moral dilemma. Only the funda-
mentally humanistic Luigi can assist Cass by convincing him that he
must, in order to achieve knowledge, not wallow in his guilt, but expiate it and eventually defeat it by living. Cass "had come to the
end of the road and had found there nothing at all. There was nothing. There was a nullity in the universe so great as to encompass and
drown the universe itself. The value of a man's life was nothing, and
his destiny nothingness' " (489). Despite this bitter pronouncement,
Cass still feels "that old vast gnawing hunger," a hunger for order
and meaning in the face of a meaningless universe. Luigi admonishes
Cass to expiate his guilt, refusing him the right to sin in his guilt by

cultivating it. He urges that Cass must, like Oedipus, become a penitent in life. Cass's choice now is the choice between suicide and life
which Camus poses in *The Myth of Sisyphus,* and Cass chooses life.
Again there is the vagueness in terms and the refusal to accept traditional formulas characteristic of all the novelists considered in this
study, but there is no doubt that the author sees Cass possessed of a
kind of vision for which he had only groped tentatively before his
"fall":

> "Now I suppose I should tell you that through some sort of suffering I
> had reached grace, and how at that moment I knew it, but this would not
> be true, because at that moment I didn't really know what I had reached
> or found. I wish I could tell you that I had found some belief, some rock,
> and that here on this rock anything might prevail—that here madness
> might become reason, and grief joy, and no yes. And even death itself
> death no longer, but a resurrection.
>
> "But to be truthful, you see, I can only tell you this: that as for being
> and nothingness, the one thing I did know was that to choose between
> them was simply to choose being, not for the sake of being, or even the
> love of being, much less the desire to be forever—but in the hope of being
> what I could be for a time. This would be an ecstasy." (500–501)

Styron sees Cass as a modern Oedipus, and Camus saw Oedipus as
an example of the absurd man:

> Happiness and the absurd are two sons of the same earth. They are in-
> separable. It would be a mistake to say that happiness springs from the
> absurd discovery. It happens as well that the feeling of the absurd springs
> from happiness. "I conclude that all is well," says Oedipus, and that re-
> mark is sacred. It echoes in the wild and limited universe of man. It teaches
> that all is not, has not been exhausted. It drives out of this world a god who
> had come into it with dissatisfaction and a preference for futile sufferings.
> It makes of fate a human matter, which must be settled among men.[16]

"Oedipus gives," Camus says, "the recipe for the absurd victory,"
and suggesting the link between the classical Oedipus and Oedipus

---

[16] Camus, *The Myth of Sisyphus,* pp. 90–91.

as the absurd hero, he adds, "Ancient wisdom confirms modern heroism."[17]

If the above speech, in which Cass announces his choice of being, makes no affirmation of the idea of knowledge, it does suggest hope that he will eventually achieve something like knowledge. Indeed he seems to demonstrate such an acquisition in one of the two letters appended to the novel, in which he writes, "Who was it in Lear who said ripeness is all. I forget, but he was right" (*STHF*, 506). As an artist he has turned social critic out of a desire for reform, and he thus demonstrates the increasing tendency of the existential hero to return to society. In triumphing over himself, in defeating his sense of guilt, in establishing a love for humanity, Cass has achieved a singular victory, and it is necessary to think of him as Camus intended that we think of Sisyphus, as "happy."

[17] *Ibid.*, p. 90.

THE ABSURD MAN AS *Picaro*

In his first two short novels Saul Bellow presented heroes who served as acutely impressionable centers of consciousness reflecting the dislocations of metropolitan life. In both *Dangling Man* and *The Victim* distortions of contemporary values and victimization by environment are greatly simplified, but the simplifications are fruitful in delineating the milieu in which later Bellow characters are to function.

Paul Levine has noted that "In its style, philosophical content, and hypothetical nature, *Dangling Man* stands in a unique place in our contemporary literature, more closely resembling a novel by Albert Camus than one by any American novelist writing today."[1] Certainly the Camus novel to which *Dangling Man* is a counterpart is *The Stranger,* and the similarity goes far beyond the incidental fact that Camus avowedly adopted for that book certain stylistic techniques from the American novel. Both *Dangling Man* and *The Stranger* describe the absurd experience rather than suggest a specific absurd metaphysics, and Meursault and Joseph ultimately arrive at absurd

---

[1] Paul Levine, "Saul Bellow: The Affirmation of the Philosophical Fool," *Perspective,* 10 (Winter, 1959), 165.

stances as a result of the same ironic, although apparently indiscriminate, clustering of circumstances. These experiences seem to fit no
logical pattern: they are simply there, and their presence announces
itself with the same apparent lack of reason to both reader and participant. An effect of immediate involvement is achieved in both novels
through the use of narrators who observe without attempting to analyze; Bellow accomplishes this sense of involvement through the device of Joseph's journal, and Camus through having Meursault tell
his own story directly to the reader. Both writers have taken a form
usually intended to reach profound depths of introspection and have
used it in a way that is predominantly objective.

Like Meursault, Joseph is a petty clerk who suddenly finds himself
a metaphysical outsider, dangling between commitments and value
systems. Also like Meursault, Joseph is initially caught up in the stifling ritual of daily activity and is highly susceptible to external stim-
uli; living empirically in a prolapsed world, he grows from philosophical innocence to a state of aggravated consciousness in which he
questions the very nature of human existence. Neither Joseph's nor
Meursault's reaction to his environment is wholly negative. Sitting in
his room writing his journal, Joseph is given a chance to derive a personal value system to oppose (without denying) the "real" world,
just as Meursault, shut away in prison, at last drafts a personal code
which both scorns the ministrations of the church and rejects the
consolation of death as an escape from human misery.

The shock which destroys the monotonous routine of Joseph's daily
life comes in the form of a draft notice. His life interrupted, he can
finally look upon it for what it is really worth, and he finds it devoid
of all significant meaning. In the face of this meaninglessness Joseph
develops the intention to spin a life out of his own spirit, having the
opportunity to do this as he "dangles" between a regular job and in-
duction into the army. His temporary dislocation at first suggests that
a hostile universe deprives contemporary man of all significant inner
life. Looking out the window before he begins his journal, Joseph sur-
veys the run-down buildings, dingy warehouses, and smoking chim-

neys which make up his physical as well as his spiritual horizon, and
concludes:

It was my painful obligation to look and to submit to myself the invariable
question: Where was there a particle of what, elsewhere, or in the past, had
spoken in man's favor? There could be no doubt that these billboards,
streets, tracks, houses, ugly and blind, were related to interior life. And yet,
I told myself, there had to be a doubt. There were human lives organized
around these ways and houses, and that they, the houses, say, were the
analogue, that what men created they also were, through some transcendent means, I could not bring myself to concede. There must be a difference,
a quality that eluded me, somehow, a difference between things and persons and even between acts and persons. Otherwise the people who lived
here were actually a reflection of the things they lived among. (*DM*, 24–
25)

Pressing his forehead against the glass, Joseph looks out on the
reality of his life, and confronts a barren insignificance to which he
refuses to concede his belief in some transcendent meaning. It is Joseph's intention to affirm the basic humanity of man in a universe
which speaks to him largely through "taverns, movies, assaults,
divorces, murders." So far as metaphysical progression is concerned,
Dangling Man moves in an inverse direction to that of *The Stranger*;
Joseph begins with a stance remarkably similar to that which Meursault is able to strike only in the last moments of his life. The final
test of the absurd hero, however, rests in his ability to live the conflict between intention and reality; Meursault is not asked to submit
to this test, and Joseph is unsuccessful in maintaining his intention;
thus neither character wholly qualifies as an absurd *hero*, although at
the most intense point of his rebellion Joseph is as close to Camus's
concept of the absurd man as is any other character in American
fiction.

Joseph adopts none of the minor badges of social defiance which
often denote the rebel, for the small arenas of nonconformity do not
interest him; he conserves his strength and his energies so that he can
give "all his attention to defending his inner differences, the ones that

really matter" (28). Just as he refuses the socially obvious representation of his differences, so too he refuses obvious philosophical posi-
tions; life is neither good nor bad, but an experience, and his anxiety
stems from the desire to see that experience as a reflection of forces
which are ultimately compassionate and creative. The vision which he
requires is frequently thwarted, however, by what he calls "treasons:
There were so many treasons, they were a medium, like air, like water;
they passed in and out of you, they made themselves your accom-
plices; nothing was impenetrable to them" (56). Everywhere he turns
Joseph finds these treasons and betrayals, which constantly hammer
at the life he is struggling to define. At a cocktail party they reveal
themselves in an intensely personified form as Joseph watches a
friend torture a hypnotized woman whose body is incapable of regis-
tering the indignities to which she is subjected. The state of hypnosis
itself is perhaps the most successful single representation of that
spiritual drowsiness and emotional lethargy which Camus described
in *The Myth of Sisyphus* as the almost universal condition of modern
man. The figure of the hypnotizer becomes for Joseph a representation of all the cruelties and injustices which the world imposes:

This was only the beginning. In the months that followed I began to discover one weakness after another in all I had built up around me. I saw
what Jack Brill had seen, but, knowing better, saw it more keenly and
severely. It would be difficult for anyone else to know how this affected
me, since no one could understand as well as I the nature of my plan, its
rigidity, the extent to which I depended on it. Foolish or not, it answered
my need. The plan could be despised; my need could not. (57)

Joseph finds the same frustration of this need in his pompous, money-
oriented brother, in the spoiled niece who accuses him of attacking
her, and eventually in his own wife, and his own stance is continually
refined as life presents him with one disappointment after another.
His consciousness of a divorce from the world becomes more intense
as the novel progresses, and while he had once envisioned the possibility of deriving some strength through recourse to friends and rela-

tives, he becomes increasingly aware that his struggle is to be a lonely one. Like Camus's Meursault, he finds no meaning in the social life, and he rejects the order of men when he suddenly realizes that his friends band together for mutual protection, behaving the way the group expects them to behave, asserting group values, and ridiculing anything that threatens their mutual definition. Joseph's disillusionment with people is the prelude to a total deracination characterized by a "feeling of strangeness, of not quite belonging to the world at large" (30). An indifferent world precludes belief in a beneficent personal God, and Joseph asserts that "there are no values outside of life. There is nothing outside of life" (165).

"What, in fact, is the absurd man?" Camus asks. "He who, without negating it, does nothing for the eternal. Not that nostalgia is foreign to him. But he prefers his courage and his reasoning. The first teaches him to live without *appeal,* to get along with what he has; the second informs him of his limits."[2] It is when Joseph has the revelation of the necessity of living without appeal and within narrowly circumscribed limits that his original intention becomes sufficiently refined to suggest his possibilities as an absurd hero; he is, in this moment of revelation, at least an absurd *man.* Joseph's revelation comes while he is listening to a Haydn *divertimento* for the cello. The sober opening movement of Piatigorsky's performance convinces him that he is yet an apprentice in suffering and humiliation, and that he is foolish to imagine avoiding further indignities; it was not among human privileges to be exempt from them:

What I should do with them, how to meet them, was answered in the second declaration: with grace, without meanness. And though I could not as yet apply that answer to myself, I recognized its rightness and was vehemently moved by it. Not until I was a whole man could it be my answer, too. And was I to become this whole man alone, without aid? I was too weak for it, I did not command the will. Then in what quarter should

2 Albert Camus, *The Myth of Sisyphus,* p. 49.

I look for help, where was the power? Grace by what law, under what order, by whom required? Personal, human, or universal, was it? The music named only one source, the universal one, God. But what a miserable surrender that would be, born out of disheartenment and chaos; and out of fear, bodily and imperious, that like a disease asked for a remedy and did not care how it was supplied. The record came to an end; I began it again. No, not God, not any divinity. That was anterior, not of my own deriving. I was not so full of pride that I could not accept the existence of something greater than myself, something, perhaps, of which I was an idea, or merely a fraction of an idea. That was not it. But I did not want to catch at any contrivance in panic. In my eyes, that was a great crime. Granted that the answer I was hearing, that went so easily to the least penetrable part of me, the seldom-disturbed thickets around the heart, was made by a religious man. But was there no way to attain that answer except to sacrifice the mind that sought to be satisfied? From the antidote itself another disease would spring. It was not a new matter, it was one I had frequently considered. But not with such a desperate emotion or such a critical need for an answer. Or such a feeling of loneliness. Out of my own strength it was necessary for me to return the verdict for reason, in its partial inadequacy, and against the advantages of its surrender. (*DM*, 67–68)

Joseph's emphasis on courage, reasoning, and lack of appeal might have been drawn directly from Camus's own answer to the question, "What, in fact, is the absurd man?"

In the first part of the novel, Joseph, like Meursault, has an acute awareness of the passage of time, but also like Camus's hero, he eventually begins to lose all sense of time's regular passage. Metaphysically, this distorted time sense emphasizes an attitude of indifference to the physical and "withdrawal from temporal existence in the world of sense into more speculative and timeless self-awareness."[3] Joseph and his wife spend a lonely New Year's Day in their drab apartment, and feel "set aside" by the absence of any celebration or diversion.

What such a life as this incurs [Joseph comments] is the derangement of

[3] John Cruickshank, *Albert Camus and the Literature of Revolt,* p. 159.

days, the leveling of occasions. I can't answer for Iva, but for me it is certainly true that days have lost their distinctiveness. (*DM*, 81)

Joseph's absurd intention takes him increasingly farther out of life, and his contacts with the world become little more than open hostilities. He comes to envy an artist friend, John Pearl, who is able to carve for himself a life of the imagination in which he sustains a "real world" of "art and thought."

Realizing that he lacks the resources of imagination which sustain John Pearl, Joseph is cast into a yet deeper state of despair, and as the novel progresses he is eventually faced with the idea of suicide as a solution to his acute loneliness; even while he doubts his own ability to live a life of curtailed expectations, he is yet unable to accept the obliteration of expectation which death entails. "The sense in which Goethe was right: Continued life means expectation" (148).

With the possible exception of Asa Leventhal in *The Victim*, all of Saul Bellow's heroes are consciously questing figures, and Joseph introduces this gallery of contemporary knights when he says:

The quest, I am beginning to think, whether it be for money, for notoriety, reputation, increase of pride, whether it leads us to thievery, slaughter, sacrifice, the quest is one and the same. All the striving is for one end. I do not entirely understand this impulse. But it seems to me that its final end is the desire for pure freedom. We are all drawn toward the same craters of the spirit—to know what we are and what we are for, to know our purpose, to seek grace. And, if the quest is the same, the differences in our personal histories, which hitherto meant so much to us, become of minor importance. (154)

Joseph's quest is not wholly successful, and he must confess that he has not done well "alone" in the world. Thus, in the final pages of the novel he gives himself up to the regulation of army life with shouts of joy for regular hours, "supervision of the spirit," and regimentation. His idiopathic freedom has isolated him so painfully that he at last seeks social accommodation within the ranks of the army. While our final view of Joseph is not essentially heroic, it is of a sympathetic character who possesses all the sensitivity of spirit prerequisite to the creation of an absurd hero, and his return to the world ironically foreshadows the more successful reconciliations of Henderson and Moses Herzog. Joseph has purposely committed himself to the mechanistic universe which was once so repulsive to him, but he leaves us with the hope that "the war could teach me, by violence, what I had been unable to learn during those months in the room. Perhaps I could sound creation through other means. Perhaps. But things were now out of my hands. The next move was the world's" (191).

At the heart of Bellow's work rests the conviction that man's problems derive from a profound dislocation of his social and political universe. While *Dangling Man* opens with the vision of a character intensely determined to put such dislocations to rights, *The Victim* opens with the inverse picture of a middle-class magazine editor who appears unaware of any fundamental disharmony in his universe; Asa Leventhal's greatest concerns seem to be an illness in the family, a vacationing wife, and a dirty apartment. Despite his apparently contented surface, we soon learn that Asa has come perilously near falling spiritual prey to the same grey environment which Joseph was regarding when *Dangling Man* opened:

He occasionally said to Mary, revealing his deepest feelings, "I was lucky. I got away with it." He meant that his bad start, his mistakes, the things that might have wrecked him, had somehow combined to establish him. He had almost fallen in with that part of humanity of which he was frequently mindful (he never forgot the hotel on lower Broadway), the part that did not get away with it—the lost, the outcast, the overcome, the effaced, the ruined. (V, 20)

Because he has enjoyed some measure of success, Asa feels that he has been able to overcome the tragic destiny which usually awaits modern man, and in the complacency that results from this judgment, he falls into a lethargy as deadening as that which surrounds "the overcome, the effaced, the ruined."

It is through Kirby Allbee that Asa will achieve an awakening that will allow him "to know what he is, to know what he is for, to know his purpose, to seek grace" (*DM*, 154). Several years before the novel opens, Kirby Allbee had secured Asa Leventhal an interview with his employer. Whether at Allbee's instigation or from natural maliciousness, Mr. Rudiger mercilessly attacked the young man, and Asa, in turn, flew back at him with all the stored-up vehemence of weary, fruitless months of job seeking. Shortly after this encounter, Kirby Allbee was fired. Years later, having exhausted his dead wife's insurance money, Allbee returns as a kind of *alter ego* antagonist to remind Asa of his "guilt." At first Allbee seems only a hopelessly degenerate anti-Semite, but he becomes a significant catalyst, forcing Asa to break out of his complacent mold and to admit, if only on the Conradian level of potentiality, the fact of his guilt.

Asa, who has always prided himself on the position he has won in the literary jungle, is repulsed by Allbee's suggestion that the individual has no responsibility in the world. " 'The day of succeeding by your own efforts is past'," Allbee argues. " 'Now it's all blind movement, vast movement, and the individual is shuttled back and forth. He only thinks he's the works. But that isn't the way it is. Groups, organizations succeed or fail, but not individuals any longer' " (*V*, 70–71). Often when he paints such pictures of human insignificance Allbee reasons speciously, and indeed, his accusations against Asa are a clear indication of the fact that he believes in individual responsibility. But as he manipulates for an advantage with Asa, Allbee is revealing to the incredulous Jew the very face of the absurd universe, which is clearer, as delineated in this novel, to Allbee's vision than it is to Asa's.

Kirby Allbee had been at best a questionable employee who was always subject to alcoholic evasions. In the face of this reality, his intention of touching Asa for a new start in life appears absurd, and Asa turns to his friends for confirmation of "the absurdity, the madness of the accusations" (86). But when Asa has reconciled himself to the tentative but significant validity of Allbee's social absurdity, he himself will be better equipped to understand metaphysical absurdities. "There was something in people against sleep and dullness, together with the caution that led to sleep and dullness. Both were there, Leventhal thought" (99). His first defense is to assume a guise of sleep and dullness, until Allbee begins to antagonize a sense of values which refuses sleep, and Asa's recognition of those values also entails an admission of his guilt.

Gradually, as his conflicts with Allbee increase in number and intensity, Asa begins to see himself in a new light. After an especially painful encounter with Allbee, Asa takes his young nephew to the zoo, where he is maddened by the fear that Allbee is hiding somewhere in the crowd: "He tried to put him out of his thoughts and give all his attenion to Philip, forcing himself to behave naturally. But now and then, moving from cage to cage, gazing at the animals, Leventhal, in speaking to Philip, or smoking, or smiling, was conscious of Allbee, so certain he was being scrutinized that he was able to see himself as if through a strange pair of eyes: the side of his face, the palpitation in his throat, the seams of his skin, the shape of his body and of his feet in their white shoes. Changed in this way into his own observer, he was able to see Allbee, too" (107). Later in the novel Leventhal has "an unclear dream in which he held himself off like an unwilling spectator; yet it was he that did everything" (168). This shifting of perspective in which Asa becomes both pursuer and pursued alarms him, and he strives against "countering absurdity with absurdity" (108).

Asa Leventhal is not totally unaware of the suffering and evil which dominate the modern world; he knows something of what it is to be a "victim." He merely chooses not to concern himself with this aspect of life, and the isolation into which he recedes is not unlike that glacial, betraying hardness of the heart which characterized many of Nathaniel Hawthorne's characters. Allbee accuses him of keeping his spirit "under lock and key," where it is unnecessary to have to make the kind of reconciliations which Joseph tried to make in *Dangling Man*. " 'It is necessary for you to believe'," Allbee argues, " 'that I deserve what I get'."

"It doesn't enter your mind, does it—that a man might not be able to help
being hammered down? What do you say? Maybe he can't help himself?
No, if a man is down, a man like me, it's his fault. If he suffers, he's being
punished. There's no evil in life itself. And do you know what? It's a Jewish
point of view. You'll find it all over the Bible. God doesn't make mistakes.
He's the department of weights and measures. If you're okay, he's okay,
too. That's what Job's friends come and say to him. But I'll tell you something. We do get it in the neck for nothing and suffer for nothing, and
there's no denying that evil is as real as sunshine. Take it from me, I know
what I'm talking about. To you the whole thing is that I must deserve what
I get. That leaves your hands clean and it's unnecessary for you to bother
yourself. Not that I'm asking you to feel sorry for me, but you sure can't
understand what makes a man drink." (146)

Against his will, Leventhal is at last convinced that it is no longer
possible to think in the old dichotomous terms, and later, at the funeral of one of his nephews, he rejects the consolation which the chapel
and its crucifix seem to offer. "Prompted by an indistinct feeling, he
thought to himself, 'Never mind, thanks, we'll manage by ourselves . . .'" (180). Leventhal is learning to live without appeal either
to the neat patterns with which he had once regulated his life or to
any kind of supernatural consolation. His former evasions had been
perpetrated with a kind of innocence, but as he gradually moves toward consciousness, he realizes that innocence itself can often be ma-
liciously destructive. " 'Wake up!' " a friend urges him. " 'What's life?
Metabolism? That's what it is for the bugs. Jesus Christ, no! What's
life? Consciousness, that's what it is. That's what you're short on. For
God's sake, give yourself a push and a shake. It's dangerous stuff, Asa,
this stuff' " (264).

Leventhal moves closer to consciousness as Allbee comes to occupy
an increasingly intimate role in his life. The climax to both consciousness and intimacy occurs when Leventhal returns home from a night
at a friend's house to find Allbee making love to a prostitute in Leventhal's bed. After driving the couple from his apartment, he reflects on

the look of terror in the woman's eyes, and "Both of them, Allbee and the woman, moved or swam toward him out of a depth of life in which he himself would be lost, choked, ended. There lay horror, evil, all that he had kept himself from" (277).

Kirby Allbee helps Asa to learn that "Each man is responsible for his actions because he is accountable for their consequences" (166), and at the same time Asa's eyes are opened to suffering and evil which he had never felt strong enough to reckon with. But he does not become a perpetually suffering martyr as does Nathanael West's Miss Lonelyhearts, whose vision of suffering and responsibility are in many ways similar to Asa's. He now knows the meaning of responsibility, but he also knows its limitations. When Allbee tries to involve Asa in a dual suicide without first getting his permission, Asa is at last able to break the bonds that have joined them, and in the moment when he struggles with Allbee in the gas-filled apartment, he casts his vote with life, despite all the horror and evil which have just been revealed to him. Allbee is to some degree the victim of Asa's narrowness, but both are victims of a world which at every turn warns that man may be "lost, choked, ended."

Asa Leventhal had feared extending his consciousness to include humanity as a whole because he doubted his own ability to live with the vision that would await him. At the conclusion of the novel he is, after a symbolic reunion with his wife, not only able to live with this vision but able to live happily. Life apparently holds out empty promises to most men, turning them away when they present themselves to make their claims, but Asa doubts that this is the final picture. "For why should tickets, mere tickets, be promised if promises were being made—tickets to desirable and undesirable places? There were more important things to be promised. Possibly there was a promise, since so many felt it. He himself was almost ready to affirm that there was. But it was misunderstood" (V, 286). While Asa's vision is only fragmentary, this undefined "promise" which he derives from it brings

The Victim to a conclusion more significantly, if as vaguely, affirmative as that of *Dangling Man.*

Both *Dangling Man* and *The Victim* are brief, arresting trajectories written in a terse prose which, after two novels, readers came to expect from Saul Bellow. *The Adventures of Augie March*, therefore, appeared to many to be more of a departure than it really was. Its flowing, demotic language, its bumptious hero, and its mammoth episodic structure make it a modern picaresque, and it has in fact been compared to all the great picaresque novels of the past. As the story of a young boy cast adrift in life and gradually proceeding toward a defined system of values, it is perhaps closer to *The Adventures of Huckleberry Finn* than to any other picaresque novel. As an analysis of rebellion and of man's lonely attempt to spin a life of his own, the book grew logically from the themes of Bellow's first novels. While in his earlier works Bellow saw this spinning concentrated in a single dramatic episode, he now sees it in its full organic process. From his earliest recollections as a fatherless child in the Chicago slums, Augie has had, like Huck Finn, to improvise, to live by his wits and his instincts, and often to travel incognito. Both Huck and Augie have a profound and premature knowledge of human depravity, and yet both approach the world with a remarkable tenderness; their resilient good humor is perhaps their best defense against nihilism and self-pity.

Through the episodic structure of this novel Bellow has done far more than reveal a single state of mind; he has re-created an era and peopled it with an enormous and varied fictional population. One of the most significant early influences in Augie's life is Grandma Lausch, an eccentric old Russian Jew with a vaguely romantic past who is taken in by the March family as a boarder and comes to rule over them as a semibenevolent tyrant. It is Grandma Lausch who teaches Augie the values of expedient lying, as when she sends him with a trumped-up story to the Public Health Department in order to get glasses for his half-blind mother. Given a mission and given credit for understanding the "set up" behind it, Augie is easily persuaded to play an appropriate role. He warns, however, that he is not trying to create the impression that, because of his willingness to rise to such challenges, he might have been a Cato or "a young Lincoln who tramped four miles in a frontier zero gale to refund three cents to a customer. I don't want to pass for having such legendary presidential stuff. Only those four miles wouldn't have been a hindrance if the right feelings were kindled. It depended on which way I was drawn" (*AAM*, 23).

Augie is drawn many ways in the course of this novel—to deceit, sacrifice, love, theft, and pain. At moments he seems to have some of the qualities and a measure of the fate of Nathanael West's parodic Lemuel Pitkin—another picaresque "voyager"—but something always brings Augie back to a middle ground, and he says no—though often at the last minute—before he is drawn over the brink. He flirts with every kind of radicalism which a big city offers, but such digressions never stir "the right feelings," and Augie drifts away from them. As a young boy he spends one summer with a group of enterprising relatives who are able to give him odd jobs, and Cousin Anna undertakes a comically macaronic program of religious instruction based on the Hebrew calendar and her own vague knowledge of the Old Testament. "I have to hand it to her," Augie comments, "that she knew her listener. There wasn't going to be any fooling about it. She was directing me out of her deep chest to the great eternal things" (27). The entire episode is written in a high comic style, but somehow Augie's life does become vaguely directed "to the great eternal things."

Even while he is learning from such people as Cousin Anna and Grandma Lausch, Augie is continually saying "no," refusing to be limited by loyalties which threaten his independence. It is Einhorn, his shadily but monolithically powerful employer, who first notices this quality in Augie when he confronts him about his role in a petty neighborhood theft:

". . . were you looking for a thrill? Is this a time to be looking for a thrill, when everybody else is covering up? You could take it out on the roller coasters, the bobs, the chute-the-chutes. Go to Riverview Park. But wait. All of a sudden I catch on to something about you. You've got *opposition* in you. You don't slide through everything. You just make it look so."

This was the first time [Augie notes] that anyone had told me anything like the truth about myself. I felt it powerfully. That, as he said, I did have opposition in me, and great desire to offer resistance and to say "No!" which was as clear as could be, as definite a feeling as a pang of hunger. (116–117)

Like so many *picaros*, Augie is singularly "adoptable." Almost everyone he meets wants either to adopt him or at least to plan his life. The first people to demonstrate this inclination are Grandma Lausch and Cousin Anna. When Augie begins to work for the Einhorns they continually emphasize the fact that he will not be remembered in their will, but that their entire commercial empire will go to their son—almost as a defense against Augie's adoptability. Mrs. Renling, a wealthy carriage-trade shopkeeper, takes control of Augie's life, teaches him how to dress, how to handle himself socially, and finally tries to begin formal adoption proceedings. Augie is perhaps the most adoptable character in American literature since Huckleberry Finn, but it is essential that the opposition in him arise in time to leave him absolute control over his own spirit. His persistent refusal to become involved or to conform to the will of others is positive criticism of things as they are. Even when he falls in love with women who try to "adopt" him, he refuses to be wholly recruited to their views of reality. What Augie fears when such overtures are made is the destruction of the self, and to him the contemporary world seems awesomely resourceful in the techniques of destruction.

Augie's brother Simon cultivates the very kind of emulation which Augie resists. Having lost everything his family owns as the result of his infatuation for a bosomy neighborhood blonde, Simon determines to marry a wealthy commercial heiress. In a short while he has so thoroughly indoctrinated himself to the tastes and mannerisms of Charlotte Magnus's family that he becomes virtually their most representative member. On his way to becoming a commercial tycoon, Simon plans a similar course for Augie, setting him up as an ideal husband for Lucy Magnus, Charlotte's cousin. Since his love for his brother is so great, Augie plays Simon's game with thoroughness if not with enthusiasm, but he eliminates himself as a matrimonial candidate when he becomes involved with the efforts of a neighbor, Mimi Villars, to get an abortion. The child is not Augie's, but circumstances are against him, and Simon gives up all hope of being able to reform Augie's life, rejecting him as a *schlemiel*. Mimi, meanwhile, as one of the few people who do not want to adopt Augie, becomes a significant influence on his life. Her view of the world is statically fatalistic, and life for her is only a malicious joke through which man must suffer. In his rebellion against her morbid vision, Augie first begins to formulate his own impressions of life:

Me, I couldn't think all was so poured in concrete that there weren't occasions for happiness that weren't illusions of people still permitted to be forgetful of permanent disappointment, more or less permanent pain, death of children, lovers, friends, ends of causes, old age, loathsome breath, fallen faces, white hair, retreated breasts, dropped teeth; and maybe most intolerable the hardening of detestable character, like bone, similar to a second skeleton and creaking loudest before the end. (255)

It is this intense determination to see life as eventually meaningful which makes Augie realize "the shame of purposelessness" demonstrated by the WPA crew to which he belongs for a short while. He is suddenly aware that he is no longer a child, and that it is no longer sufficient for him merely to believe; he must implement his beliefs. There is never hope that Augie will be able to escape from reality into a world of childish innocence, even though his own innocence is perhaps his most outstanding characteristic. As in *Lie Down in Darkness*, the uncomplicated world of childhood is given an overtone of horror

in being represented by a demented child—in this case Augie's brother Georgie, whose simple-minded song foreshadows Augie's efforts
to find love:

> Georgie Mahchy, Augie, Simey
> Winnie Mahchy, evwy, evwy love Mama. (3)

From the moment of his realization of the shame of purposelessness,
we see Augie's picaresque humor in a new light, as he himself reminds
us that "Even the man who wants to believe, you sometimes note kidding his way to Jesus" (302). If Augie is to succeed in his quest for a
metaphorical Jesus he must maintain the defenses which have protected him from invasion by an adoption-minded world. The greatest single crisis of his life comes when he falls in love with the eccentric socialite, Thea Fenchel, whose romantic, adventurous view of life
threatens to strip Augie completely of the liberty which has always
protected him. In Simon as well as in his own mother, Augie has an
example of a family tendency toward surrender of freedom, and he
has, in fact, become involved in so many "schemes" that he imagines
himself as the family's least stable member. As he prepares to leave
for Mexico with Thea, Augie visits his mother, who instinctively fears
that this new involvement will make her son unhappy. "And what lay
behind this, I believe, was that if Simon hadn't helped me to choose,
if I had picked for myself, my mother thought me to be sufficiently
like her to get myself in a bad fix. I said nothing of the hunting to her,
but it did occur to me how it was inevitable for the son of a Hagar to
go chase wild animals at one time or another" (322). Having committed himself to Thea's almost monomaniacal plan to hunt giant
iguanas with an eagle, Augie begins to assume a more than casual
parallel to Melville's Ishmael, that other son of Hagar.

There is no Queequeg to guide this modern Ishmael as he sets out
on his mysterious voyage to Mexico (although there is such a figure in
Bellow's *Henderson the Rain King*). It seems Augie's special fate to
face the world alone, just as Joseph and Asa Leventhal faced it alone.

If there is promise of a kind of rebirth in this pilgrimage to Mexico and in Caligula, the savage eagle which Thea and Augie carry with them to hunt the prehistoric lizards, the promise is quickly dispelled. The cul de sac which Augie encounters in Mexico is foreshadowed in the novel by the experience of Eleanor Klein, who goes to Mexico for the ostensible purpose of marrying a well-to-do cousin but finds herself exploited as part of a sweatshop labor system. Rather than fulfillment and promise, Augie finds sordidness and infidelity in Mexico, and even Caligula—whom he fears, abhors, accepts, and finally in some respects admires—proves to be a failure; he is afraid of reptiles. As the bizarre life they have created begins to disintegrate around them, Thea and Augie gradually resume their individualistic poses. Augie strives vainly to reconstruct their romance, but gradually turns to alcohol and gambling in the hope of making his anxious days pass more quickly. Somehow Augie has managed to maintain his innocence, a quality which makes him a natural success at poker, for the people with whom he plays can never tell whether he is bluffing. " 'Nobody can really be as innocent as all that'," an opponent scoffs, and Augie admits, "This was true, though I would have said I actually did intend to be as good as possible" (369). Even when he learns of Thea's affair with another man (and, ironically, when he makes love to Stella, a young movie starlet), he still maintains his intention to be as good as possible, although reality has taught him that it is those people who try to be good (his mother, his brother Georgie, Sophie Geratis) who somehow always end by being cheated. Augie's point of view—the maintenance of an intention which is opposed at almost every turn by reality—begins gradually to define him as an absurd man, even an absurd man with a specifically practical idea of his own intention:

Everyone tries to create a world he can live in, and what he can't use he often can't see. But the real world is already created, and if your fabrication doesn't correspond, then even if you feel noble and insist on there being something better than what people call reality, that better something needn't try to exceed what, in its actuality, since we know it so little, may be very surprising. If a happy state of things, surprising; if miserable or tragic, no worse than we invent. (378)

In refusing to succumb to the grimness of reality Augie becomes a rebel, and he invents for himself "a man who can stand before the terrible appearances" (402) of external life. This instinct, Augie notes, is characteristic of inventors and artists and leaders of men, and is almost always used to recruit followers and therefore sustain the individual in his make-believe. Just as Augie refuses to be recruited to others' defenses against external life, so he initially declines to proselytize for his own creation, an image which "wanted simplicity and denied complexity" (402). Since Augie is a lone pilgrim by necessity rather than by choice, it becomes evident that he does not play the role of recruiting officer himself, for the simple reason that the object of his quest lacks sufficient definition; Augie's experiences are not intended to be programmatic, precisely because such a straightforward conception of experience—the presumption life can be arranged on a taut line—is foreign to Bellow's feeling for the vagaries of life. Augie's goal is similar to that of Rabbit Angstrom, since, although it is vague and elusive, its value comes from the fact that it repeatedly denies external reality as a final or total expression of human potential.

In his pilgrimage after what his friend Clem Tambow refers to as " 'a worth-while fate'," all that Augie seems to have achieved is a fractured skull, lost teeth, and a broken heart. Because he continues to pursue his vague goal with such determination, Clem accuses him of having " 'A nobility syndrome. You can't adjust to the reality situation. I can see it all over you. You want there should be Man, with capital M, with great stature'." " 'Tell me, pal, am I getting warm or not?' " Clem asks. " 'You are, yes you are' " (434–435), Augie answers. Clem argues that Augie must reconcile his vague goals with reality, and Augie refuses. " 'I'll put it to you as I see it. It can never be right to offer to die, and if that's what the data of experience tell you, then you must get along without them' " (436). In refusing to rec-

oncile himself to an adverse reality and in rejecting the idea of death
as a solution to his dilemma, Augie increasingly asserts his position as
an absurd man. Gradually, too, his conception of the general nature of
his goal begins to come clear. He aims, he says, for the "axial lines of
life, with respect to which you must be straight or else your existence
is mere clownery, hiding tragedy" (454). In the painful struggle
against reality man will suddenly come into harmony with these lines,
and his life will be filled with joy, just as Sisyphus himself will suddenly be flooded with happiness as he shoulders the impossible
weight of his stone. " 'I have felt these thrilling lines again'," Augie explains. " 'When striving stops, there they are as a gift . . . Truth, love,
peace, bounty, usefulness, harmony!' "

"At any time life can come together again and man be regenerated, and
doesn't have to be a god or public servant like Osiris who gets torn apart
annually for the sake of the common prosperity, but the man himself, finite
and taped as he is, can still come where the axial lines are. He will be
brought into focus. He will live with true joy. Even his pains will be joy
if they are true, even his helplessness will not take away his power, even
the wandering will not take him away from himself, even the big social
jokes and hoaxes need not make him ridiculous, even disappointment after
disappointment need not take away his love. Death will not be terrible to
him if life is not." (454–455)

What Augie has described is a life lived without appeal, a life in
which, other truths being denied, pain and disappointment not only
become something to live for; they may even be a source of joy. Augie
has paraphrased, in this vision of "axial lines," the absurd formula em-
bodied in the figure of Sisyphus. Augie's greatest desire is to be no
more and no less than human, retaining a moral vision in terms of the
axial lines he has discovered. In rejecting the temptations of wealth
and success to which Simon yields, he becomes a rebel, but deflec-
tion from society is, as Camus argues, "profoundly positive in that it
reveals the part of man which must always be defended." It was his
failure to realize the positive aspects of Augie's revolt which led Rob-

ert Penn Warren to refer to him as "a man with no commitments."[4]
While it is true that Augie resists limiting commitments to society, he
does so in order to protect his commitment to himself.

Although this positive aspect of his quest—his belief in the presence of axial lines—is slow in achieving definition, through it Augie
envisions founding a home where he can board and teach orphaned
children. The height of his fervor for this project becomes almost
comic, and the reader sees him as a kind of overgrown "catcher in the
rye." Augie's adoption scheme—an ironic and to some degree philosophically inconsistent reversal of his own earlier independent position—fades as he becomes carried away with the idea of the Second
World War: "Overnight I had no personal notions at all" (*AAM*, 457).
Through the war and his hasty marriage to Stella, Augie becomes
again the peripatetic hero. Torpedoed at sea, he climbs into a life boat
with the only other survivor of the shipwreck—a monomaniacal bi-
ologist who claims to have discovered a process for creating life. Bateshaw, who does all he can to recruit Augie to his schemes, becomes a
tragic and bitter parallel to Augie's own struggles against reality:

"The shoving multitude bears down, and you're nothing, a meaningless
name, and not just obscure in eternity but right now. The fate of the
meanest your fate. Death! But no, there must be some distinction. The soul
cries out against this namelessness. And then it exaggerates. It tells you,
'You were meant to astonish the world. You, Hymie Bateshaw, *Stupor
mundi*! My boy, brace up. You have been called, and you will be chosen.
So start looking the part. The generations of man will venerate you as long
as calendars exist!' This is neurotic, I know—excuse the jargon—but to be
not neurotic is to adjust to what they call the reality situation. But the
reality situation is what I have described. A billion souls boiling with anger
at a doom of insignificance." (503)

Bateshaw speaks with more insight into the boredom of the human

----

[4] See Robert Penn Warren, "Man with no Commitments," *New Republic*, 129
(November 2, 1953), 22–23.

spirit and the need to resist the "reality situation" than anyone Augie has ever known before, and it is an essential irony of the novel that this man who seems to speak so wisely of "unused capacities" is a hopeless neurotic.

As the novel closes we have a view of Augie playing what, on the surface at least, is the most conventional role of his life. He is involved in selling (often in blackmarketing) surplus goods in Europe, and his wife Stella is working in Paris as a movie actress. War has tempered Augie, and a relatively successful marriage has helped to smooth down some of his rough edges. The experience with Bateshaw has affected his ideas of opposition to reality, but he still maintains the belief that "Death is going to take the boundaries away from us, that we should be no more persons. That's what death is about. When that is what life also wants to be about, how can you feel except rebellious?" (519). He is still affirmative, even though hope, as represented by the idea of a home for children where he can unite his mother and demented brother, is now transferred to his unborn children.

It seems essential to the picaresque structure of *The Adventures of Augie March* that we leave the hero as we found him—a wanderer. Saul Bellow has at least shown us a moment of absurd vision which, however transitory, offers a promise not enjoyed by Leventhal or Joseph and only exceeded in *Henderson the Rain King* and *Herzog*. In the laughter which concludes the novel, however, we are inevitably reminded of the man "you sometimes note kidding his way to Jesus." Augie has gone out of his way to drive Stella's maid, Jacqueline, to Normandy, where she will visit her family. When his car breaks down, Augie hikes with her across the frozen winter fields, singing to keep warm. As they near her home, he learns that the dream of her life is to go to Mexico, and remembering how the same dream had once seemed to be the hope of his own life, he begins to laugh. But he realizes that after all, it is no more laughable that Jacqueline should hope to find fulfillment in Mexico than that Augie now sought the same fulfillment in her native France. Later,

I was still chilled from the hike across the fields, but thinking of Jacqueline
and Mexico, I got to grinning again. That's the *animal ridens* in me, the
laughing creature, forever rising up. What's so laughable, that a Jacqueline,
for instance, as hard used as that by rough forces, will still refuse to lead
a disappointed life? Or is the laugh at nature—including eternity—that it
thinks it can win over us and the power of hope? Nah, nah! I think. It
never will. But that probably is the joke, on one or the other, and laughing
is an enigma that includes both. Look at me, going everywhere! Why, I
am a sort of Columbus of those near-at-hand and believe you can come to
them in this immediate *terra incognita* that spreads out in every gaze. I
may as well flop in this line of endeavor. Columbus too thought he was a
flop, probably, when they sent him back in chains. Which didn't prove
there was no America. (536)

And Augie, trying to beat the dark to Bruges to close an illicit deal for
purchasing nylon, with his movie starlet wife awaiting his return in a
moldy Paris apartment, nevertheless does not disprove the existence
of "axial lines."

In *Seize the Day*—a collection consisting of a novella, three short
stories, and a one-act play—Saul Bellow returned to the terse prose
and muted action which characterized *Dangling Man* and *The Victim*. In the novella which gives this book its title, we are presented
with a painful picture of a morbid gerontocracy obviously intended to
represent the same oppression and dehumanization which Bellow
constantly endeavors to expose in his work. Tommy Wilhelm, the
pathetic failure who is the hero of "Seize the Day," seems to have
wandered up almost every dead end which the world has to offer. His
early career as a screen star was a hopeless joke; his marriage has
ended in a torturous separation; a once rejuvenating love affair has
simply faded away; and he has resigned, out of pride, a lucrative and
well-established sales position with a large Eastern manufacturing
company. Like Bellow's Joseph, Tommy Wilhelm is a dangling man,
suspended between jobs and between loves; and like Leventhal he
is a strange kind of victim-victimizer.

The action of this novella is concentrated in a single day in the life of Tommy Wilhelm, an impulsive, in many respects childlike, man. During that day Wilhelm is compelled to review the course of his life in an effort to comprehend his needs as well as his weaknesses. In the figure of his father, Wilhelm has a constant reminder of the demands which the external world makes on a man, and Dr. Adler has measured up to those demands with great vigor. He is distinguished, moneyed, respected, neat, "sensible," and his son (who has maintained the "stage" name he was given years before) is a perpetual source of disappointment. Wilhelm's pursuit of mercy and tenderness is unrelenting, but these are not qualities to be found in Dr. Adler, or in the aging residence hotel to which the father has retired, or in the indifferent, fast-paced city about which Wilhelm blunders.

If Dr. Adler is intended to suggest the superficialities of the urban system, Dr. Tamkin, a shady psychiatrist, represents its corrupting influences. Tamkin is the only person to whom Wilhelm can talk, and while he seems at first to represent a kind of salvation, he turns into the same deceitful but distinctly comic maniac as Bateshaw in *The Adventures of Augie March*. Winning Tommy's confidence with free psychiatric "advice" and a willing ear, he enlists him in a stock-market scheme which seems Tommy's last hope for recouping his dwindling resources. Tamkin tries to teach Wilhelm that the real universe is " 'the present moment. The past is no good to us. The future is full of anxiety. Only the present is real—the here-and-now. Seize the day' " (*SD*, 66). He emphasizes to the younger man the necessity of distinguishing his "real" soul from his "pretender" soul. Much of what Tamkin argues seems true to Wilhelm—especially the psychiatrist's description of the human soul as something "howling from the window like a wolf when night comes" (67), and Wilhelm momentarily accepts his line of reasoning and agrees to cooperate in his schemes. The charlatan-psychiatrist draws a picture of the world as " 'a kind of purgatory' " populated by " 'poor human beasts' " (71), a description which seems tailored to Wilhelm's experience, but it presupposes a nihilism which he cannot accept. Even while he is cringing beneath the blows which life is delivering him, Wilhelm maintains his intention to find tenderness and kindness. His quest amounts simply to an effort to reaffirm man's humanity, to restore an idea of dignity to the human race, and his intention is both reflected and parodied in one of Tamkin's poems:

Mechanism vs Functionalism
Ism vs Hism

If thee thyself couldst only see
Thy greatness that is and yet to be
Thou would feel joy-beauty-what ecstasy.
They are at thy feet, earth-moon-sea, the trinity.

Why-forth then dost thou tarry
And partake thee only of the crust
And skim the earth's surface narry
When all creations art thy just?

Seek ye then that which art not there
In thine own glory let thyself rest.
Witness. Thy power is not bare.
Thou art King. Thou art at thy best.

Look then right before thee.
Open thine eyes and see.
At the foot of Mt. Serenity
Is thy cradle to eternity. (75)

The quest which this poem ambiguously describes has been encouraged by something like an absurd vision which had occurred to Wilhelm several days before the novella opens. As he passed through an underground corridor he suddenly imagined himself embracing and blessing all mankind, and the memory of that vision returns to him as he sits in the stock exchange waiting for Tamkin:

A queer look came over Wilhelm's face with its eyes turned up and his silent mouth with its high upper lip. He went several degrees further—when you are like this, dreaming that everybody is outcast, you realize that this must be one of the small matters. There is a larger body, and from this you cannot be separated. The glass of water fades out. You do not go from simple *a* and simple *b* to the great *x* and *y*, nor does it matter whether you agree about the glass, but, far beneath such details, what Tamkin would call the real soul says plain and understandable things to everyone. There sons and fathers are themselves, and a glass of water is only an ornament; it makes a hoop of brightness on the cloth; it is an angel's mouth. There truth for everybody may be found, and confusion is only—only temporary, thought Wilhelm. (84)

As these thoughts pass through Wilhelm's mind Tamkin is in the process of losing the rest of their money on the stock exchange, and in the crowded room in which Tommy Wilhelm sits men are frantically worshipping the golden calf of speculation. In this environment his deepening convictions seem increasingly absurd.

Tamkin vanishes, and Wilhelm is left alone to contemplate his complete financial ruin. Turning to his father in a final, desperate plea for grace, Wilhelm is rejected more bitterly than ever before. His vision of truth and of brightness seems to have faded completely, but in the final moments of the story crowds force him into a funeral procession, and before he knows what is happening he is standing over a coffin looking down into the face of a total stranger. Suddenly he begins to cry for this man, "another human creature," who comes to represent everyone he had ever loved, everyone from whom he had wanted kindness. Like the true Christian knight, Wilhelm has cast off the burden of pride, "bending his stubborn head, bowing his shoulders, twisting his face" (117–118), and achieving at last the feeling of oneness with humanity which has been the object of his quest. As the funeral music comes to his ears he sinks "deeper than sorrow, through torn sobs and cries toward the consummation of his heart's ultimate need" (118). As one of Bellow's critics has commented, "This is a vision . . . that transcends defeat, transcends, in fact, both love and death because it fastens on the means of their reconciliation."[5] The

[5] Ihab Hassan, "Saul Bellow: Five Faces of a Hero," *Critique*, 3 (September, 1960), 30.

Bellow hero can run no longer; beaten and exhausted, Wilhelm is forced in his extremity to find a meaning to life or to die. In his final, desperate adventure he finds himself moving "toward a consummation of his heart's ultimate need," a need for existence itself. The movement from isolation to affirmation of existence in the world is reiterated in *Henderson the Rain King* as "Grun-to-molani." Henderson himself is able to carry the principle farther because his energies and ambitions demand to know the form and the goal which existence should adopt. All Bellow heroes begin by trying to throw off responsibility and the chaotic weight of the world, but love for mankind finally brings them back to the business of living in the real world, even when the real seems chaotic and destructive.

Throughout Bellow's work there is an increasingly modulated emphasis on the almost Jamesian notion that the lack of money will enslave the individual to the artificialities of contemporary life; in a world which typically measures success by the material, it becomes increasingly difficult for the individual to escape the dehumanizing marketplace. Only in the wealthy (three million dollars after taxes) Henderson do we have a successful Bellow "knight" completely free of financial pressures. In the three short stories which accompany "Seize the Day," as well as in the one-act play "The Wrecker," Bellow continues to crystallize his comments on reality around society's compulsion for material success. Rogin, the central character of "A Father-to-Be," realizes that "Money surrounds you in life as the earth does in death" (*SD*, 123). He has a sudden feeling of hope, however, in the idea that all men are similarly enslaved, and while we know that Rogin's elated feeling can be only temporary, Bellow's last view of him is of a man overwhelmed by "his own secret loving spirit" (133), as his anger at his spendthrift mistress gradually fades away.

Like Henderson, Clarence Feiler in "The Gonzaga Manuscripts" has sufficient financial independence to pursue an economically undisturbed quest, but his very financial independence eventually leads him to bitter disappointment. Feiler travels to Spain in search of the

mysterious manuscripts which give this story its title. That he is related to all of Bellow's other heroes is clear from the fact that he
chooses to devote himself to the obscure Spanish poet Gonzaga rather
than to modern English history, which to him " 'doesn't express much
wish to live'." He is in touch, he feels, with " 'a poet who could show
me how to go on, and what attitude to take toward life' " (163). Gonzaga becomes an *in absentia* Sancho Panza or Queequeg, and by locating the lost manuscripts Feiler hopes to make a gift to the world
as well as to give shape to his own life. "He was becoming an eccentric; it was all he could do with his good impulses. As yet he did not
realize that these impulses were religious" (163–164). Bringing to
light the testimony of a great man is to be his gesture both against a
superficial world and in behalf of it. Clarence Feiler is led through a
minor peccadillo of mistaken identities and tweaked noses, almost always looked at askance as the boorish, insensitive caricature of the
American tourist. At last, however, he seems to have found the object
of his quest. Standing beneath "a harshly crowned Christ" (189) in a
Segovian church, Clarence reaches out to his contact man for the
long-sought manuscripts. The moment has all the solemnity and ecstatic expectation of a communion service, a mood which is broken
only when the American looks down to discover that he is holding
mining stocks. The great symbol of life which he sought has been re-
placed by stock in a pitchblende mine—*"Para la bomba atomica"*
(190), as his guide explains.

"Looking for Mr. Green" chronicles the lonely search of a Chicago
relief worker for an elusive Mr. Green. It is George Grebe's duty to
see that the man receives his relief check, and as he wanders through
the Negro district he begins to learn something of the distrust which
poorer people feel for the person who claims to have something to
"give" them. He comes "as an emissary from hostile appearances"
(160), but finding Mr. Green becomes more than just the opportunity
to perform well in his new job. For George Grebe the search becomes
a symbolic opportunity for expressing his desire to reach out and help
his fellow man. Even though the circumstances under which he de-

livers the check are humiliating, he is nevertheless elated by the knowledge that Mr. Green " '*could* be found!' " (160).

In the one-act play "The Wrecker" a man is determined to destroy the dingy apartment that represents his enslavement to the city, and to emphasize the relationship between contemporary slavery and the drive for material success. Bellow has his "wrecker" turn down a $1,000 bonus in order to remain in his apartment after other tenants have vacated the building and have the pleasure of destroying it himself. He is able to defeat his wife's appeal to the joys of love-making which the bedroom represents for her, and in the end she joins him in the destruction of their home. While the play is nonsensical and often frivolous, it is not an inappropriate conclusion to a volume which emphasizes the idea of money as the image of an oppressive public world. The wrecker's gesture of defiance is dramatically satisfying, and the contrast between his destructive intention and the reality of the massive stone walls he has vowed to destroy is a clear example of the absurd.

All of the variety of Bellow's earlier work and all of his concern with the individual who is able to maintain his intention in the face of an opposing reality come together to form an intense and unified testament to the absurd hero in *Henderson the Rain King*. Joseph dangles and drops; Levanthal is only partially awakened; Augie's vision wavers with the buffetings of fate; and Tommy Wilhelm's consummation comes as the result of a push from the crowd. Only the prodigious Henderson is a consistently and devotedly conscious seeker, and the consummation of his quest creates a feeling of magnificence unknown in Bellow's other novels—even in the more complex resolution of *Herzog*. But Henderson is closely related to Joseph, Leventhal, Wilhelm, Augie March, and Moses E. Herzog in that they are all faced by the crossroads where "one path leads to the society, the other away from the community." Henderson is able to rejoin society on satisfactory terms, reinforcing Richard Lehan's observation of the tendency for the new existential hero to take the path toward society, as in the case of Camus's Rieux, Tarrou, and D'Arrest, and Bellow's Leventhal and Wilhelm.[6] Like Camus's later heroes and like Tommy Wilhelm and Asa Leventhal, Bellow's Henderson is an example of the contemporary absurd hero's possession of a new and strangely ennobling compassion.

Much of *Henderson the Rain King*—especially the opening description of Henderson's bizarre life as the pig-raising, law-breaking, violin-playing scion of an ancient and distinguished American family —is clearly reminiscent of the picaresque tradition. But when Henderson journeys into the heart of a symbolic Africa, the novel—while maintaining all the elements of a picaresque—also moves into what might be called the grail tradition. In bringing rain to the dry land Henderson has lifted the curse from the realm of the Fisher King, and he flees to safety with the risen King. The wasteland which he cleanses is Biblical and Shakesperian as well as contemporaneous with the wasteland of T. S. Eliot. The novel is filled with references to fertility myths, and Henderson is a pilgrim in progress. In the faithful guide Romilayu, he has his Sancho Panza, Queequeg, Virgil, and Hopeful. While all of these ingredients are significant to the structure of the novel, it is well to heed Bellow's own advice to "symbol hunters"[7] and to avoid taking such obvious analogies too seriously. Henderson *is* a questing figure, a clumsy knight-errant, and finally a Rain King, but Bellow repeatedly urges us to see him as a human being rather than the embodiment of myths. We can, and invariably must, approach his character through the mythological suggestions which surround him, but we must always see Henderson as an archetype in

[6] Richard Lehan, "Existentialism in Recent American Fiction," *TSLL* 1 (Summer, 1959), pp. 181–202.

[7] See Saul Bellow, "Deep Readers of the World, Beware!" *New York Times Book Review* (February 15, 1959), pp. 1, 34. Bellow's statements on symbolism recall Nathaniel Hawthorne's desire to write a novel "that should evolve some deep lesson and should possess physical substance enough to stand alone" (Nathaniel Hawthorne, *Mosses from an Old Manse* [Boston: Houghton Mifflin Co., 1882], p. 18). Bellow's article reflects one aspect of his prejudice against the novel "of literary derivation"; it is also a modern corollary to Twain's ironic notice at the beginning of *The Adventures of Huckleberry Finn*.

his own right, a character with sufficient substance and importance to stand alone. The comic turn which Bellow often introduces should remind us of the danger of becoming overly serious when dealing with his work. Henderson himself keeps us aware of the ridiculousness of the serious when, as the "Sungo," he runs about an African village in great ballooning green silk pants and sprinkles water on the grateful natives; everyone awaited this blessing from the Sungo. The women were especially eager for the dole of water, Henderson comments, "as the Sungo was also in charge of fertility; you see, it goes together with moisture" (*HRK*, 242). By lacing Henderson's picaresque voyage with suggestions of grail legends, Bellow suggests the former as a comic inversion of the latter, and emphasizes not only the ridiculousness of the serious, but the seriousness of the ridiculous.

Bellow warns us that the quest myth does not totally explain Henderson's experience, and it in large part fails to do so because Henderson does not have recourse to the same spiritual absolutes available to the grail-seeking knight; just as Updike showed us a saint without God, so Bellow shows us a knight without God. To emphasize this quality of the hero Bellow has interjected into the myth and fantasy of his novel tones of what one critic has called *dire realism* and *significant modernity*.[8] Henderson's modernity is emphasized in the opening chapters of the novel, when we see him blundering through the contemporary frustrations and enigmas faced by all Bellow heroes. Trying to explain why he suddenly left for Africa, Henderson comments that "Things got worse and worse and pretty soon they were too complicated."

When I think of my condition at the age of fifty-five when I bought the ticket, all is grief. The facts begin to crowd around me and soon I get a pressure in the chest. A disorderly rush begins—my parents, my wives, my girls, my children, my farm, my animals, my habits, my money, my music lessons, my drunkenness, my prejudices, my brutality, my teeth, my face, my soul! I have to cry, "No, no, get back, curse you, let me alone!" But

[8] Richard Chase, "The Adventures of Saul Bellow: Progress of a Novelist," *Commentary*, 27 (April, 1959), 323.

how can they let me alone? They belong to me. They are me. They are mine. And they pile into me from all sides. It turns to chaos. (*HRK*, 3)

His trip to Africa, Henderson assures us, at last provided an end to this chaos. But it is not merely his dislocation and frustrations which make Henderson a questing man; for inside him is a voice—much like that which haunts Rabbit Angstrom—which says "*I want*," and it is through his voyage into the Africa of his own soul that he will finally satisfy this cry.

Like many absurd heroes, Henderson considers suicide as a salvation from the pains of his life, but suicide must be rejected as a denial of one of the essential terms of the absurd confrontation. After several painful months in Paris, when he tries to adjust to new dental work and a disintegrating marriage, Henderson meets Lily, an eccentric American opportunist with whom he had once had an affair. He runs away with her to visit the famous cathedrals of France, but becomes so disgusted with her sloppiness and lying that he sends her back to Paris alone. He has threatened her with suicide unless she ceases to annoy him, and his threat is not wholly comic. After leaving Lily, he drives to Banyules, and in a marine station there he has a vision of death which he instinctively rejects. Pressing his head against the glass of an aquarium, he looks in at an octopus,

and the creature seemed also to look at me and press its soft head to the glass, flat, the flesh becoming pale and granular—blanched, speckled. The eyes spoke to me coldly. But even more speaking, even more cold, was the soft head with its speckles, and the Brownian motion in those speckles, a cosmic coldness in which I felt I was dying. The tentacles throbbed and motioned through the glass, the bubbles sped upward, and I thought, "This is my last day. Death is giving me notice." (19)

Repulsed by this vision of death, Henderson devotes himself even more intensely to life. The savage, loony gusto with which he attempts to live is certainly unparalleled in contemporary literature; the nearest approximation is Papa Cue Ball, the tormented, rumbustious hero of John Hawkes' *Second Skin*. Everything which he does—including raising pigs in all the handsome old buildings on the estate which he has inherited—is executed with a fierce energy compatible with his enormous body, but every life-seizing gesture seems to end in destruction or frustration. Even the pigs warn him of his alienation from life, as he continually recalls Daniel's admonishment to King Nebuchadnezzar, " 'They shall drive thee from among men, and thy dwelling shall be with the beasts of the field' " (21). While his ponderous body often makes his aloneness seem comical, it also frequently gives his isolation a poignant significance. Such is the case in the crossroads incident which Henderson recalls from the war. After reporting that he has crabs, Henderson is stripped, soaped, and shaved by four army medics, who leave the naked, hairless man standing in the middle of a crossroads near the waterfront at Salerno.

They ran away and left me bald and shivering, ugly, naked, prickling between the legs and under the arms, raging, laughing, and swearing revenge. These are things a man never forgets and afterwards truly values. That beautiful sky, and the mad itch of the razors; and the Mediterranean, which is the cradle of mankind; the towering softness of the air; the sinking softness of the water, where Ulysses got lost, where he, too, was naked as the sirens sang. (22)

Even after he has divorced his first wife and married Lily, Henderson is still naked and alone in the world, and as well as the significant physical pains which he suffers from dental work, fights, and accidents, he is continually and increasingly tormented by the voice which cries "*I want.*" He tries every kind of cure he can think of, meanwhile realizing that "in an age of madness, to expect to be untouched by madness is a form of madness. But the pursuit of sanity can be a form of madness, too" (25). Henderson's particular "mad" pursuit of sanity will eventually reveal itself as the pursuit of order or meaning lying behind the madness and suffering of the world. He attempts to ease the strangulation in his heart by learning to play his father's violin, hoping also to make spiritual contact with a man whose life was one of quiet order and whose beard was "like a protest that gushed from his very soul" (25). "I played," he says, "with dedication, with feeling, with longing, love—played to the point of emotional collapse. Also down there in my studio I sang as I played, 'Rispondi! Anima bella' (Mozart). 'He was despised and rejected, a man of sorrows and acquainted with grief' (Handel)" (30). But the violin and the singing do not relieve his frustrated feeling that he is only another of the countless displaced persons without a station in life.

Henderson opposes reality, which reveals itself to him as suffering, loneliness, madness, with the intention that human life can be made meaningful, that the spirit can be satisfied. He never hides from reality and is in fact, as he argues to Lily, "'on damned good terms with reality'" (36), but it offers no fulfillment of his spiritual needs, a fulfillment which will be consummated only through what King Dahfu will reveal to him as a "higher reality." Like Tommy Wilhelm's frustrations, many of Henderson's stem from pride. It is pride which leads him to a pig-raising career and which also causes him to commit "an offense against my daughter" (37) by parting her from the abandoned Negro baby which she finds and brings home to raise. When he sees the despair in his daughter's eyes, he realizes that he has helped to displace at least one other person in the world, and that Ricey's belief that she is the baby's mother is a corollary to his own desire to love man. Bound home after leaving the inconsolable Ricey with an aunt in Providence, Henderson sits alone playing solitaire and is in such a state of nervous exhaustion when he leaves the train that he has to be carried off, swearing continually, "'There is a curse on this land. There is something bad going on. Something is wrong. There is a curse on this land!'" (38). Henderson will lift this curse when he raises up the ponderous figure of Mummah in an African rain ceremony.

Horrified by what he has done to Ricey and by his possible involvement in the death of the old woman who helped Lucy in the kitchen, Henderson leaves for Africa. The dedication with which he attacks this new mission is indicated by the fact that he buys only a one-way ticket, and in fact, the Henderson who leaves Idlewild Airport never returns—but is sloughed off somewhere in the heart of an imaginary Africa. His break with civilization is not complete, however, so long as he merely accompanies the honeymooning friends who have formed the photographic expedition he joins. Promising him a jeep in return for his services, Henderson convinces the often laughably dedicated native guide, Romilayu, to take him to places "off the beaten track," and in the primitive, isolated villages which they visit Henderson stills the voice that cries inside him. His long trek into the heart of Africa begins with a kind of purification in which he leaves his old troubles behind him:

. . . it was all simplified and splendid, and I felt I was entering the past—the real past, no history or junk like that. The prehuman past. And I believed that there was something between the stones and me. The mountains were naked, and often snake-like in their forms, without trees, and you could see the clouds being born on the slopes. (46)

Henderson's first peccadillo in Africa occurs among the Arnewi, a cattle-worshipping people whose gods are dying because of the drought and whose emergency water system, a cistern, is poisoned by "unholy" frogs. One of Henderson's first announcements to these people is that " 'I am really kind of on a quest' " (65). As he comes to grips with an Arnewi warrior in a wrestling match that is intended to introduce strangers to the tribe, Henderson thinks, " 'I do remember well the hour which burst my spirit's sleep' " (67). And this breaking of his spirit's sleep—like the absurd man's shaking off the routine of "Rising, streetcar, four hours in the office or the factory"—is the beginning of consciousness and identification. Confronted by the Arnewi queen Willatale, Henderson is compelled to review his own life before telling these people who he is:

Who—who was I? A millionaire wanderer and wayfarer. A brutal and violent man driven into the world. A man who fled his own country, settled by his forefathers. A fellow whose heart said, *I want, I want*. Who played the violin in despair, seeking the voice of angels. Who had to burst the spirit's sleep, or else. So what could I tell this old queen in a lion skin and raincoat . . .? (76–77)

He is at last able to confess to someone about the voice inside him, and Willatale helps him to break his spirit's sleep by describing that voice as "grun-tu-molani," the desire to live as a whole man. Henderson becomes convinced that the Queen can show him the mysteries of life and determine precisely what his voice wants. She understands that Henderson has " 'never been at home in life' " (84), and is therefore in many respects still a child. Overcome with the discovery of someone who can understand him, Henderson raises his helmet in salute to all the members of the court. " 'Grun-tu-molani'," he shouts. " 'God does not shoot dice with our souls, and therefore grun-tu-molani' " (85).

In hopes of striking a kind of exchange with the Arnewi through which they will lead him into the secrets of grun-tu-molani, Henderson sets about ridding their cistern of frogs. Using his wartime training, he rigs a bomb out of gunpowder and a flashlight case, but the bomb destroys the cistern as well as the frogs, and Henderson leaves the Arnewi in disgrace. While it might prove interesting to speculate on the degree to which Bellow intended to parody American lend-lease programs in this episode, the real significance rests in the fact that as soon as Henderson calls upon the devices of "civilized" man, he blunders into the same blind alleys that characterized his life in America.

After weary days of walking, Henderson and Romilayu reach the Wariri, a more aggressive tribe whose first act is to strip the white man of all his civilized possessions, leaving him only the clothes he wears as a reminder of the world he has come from. Like the Arnewi, the Wariri are troubled by drought, and it is Henderson's special privilege to be given a seat of honor by their king in order to watch the rainmaking proceedings. His longing to do something for people prompts him to volunteer to try to move the giant wooden goddess Mummah, who must be propitiated if rain is to come, and whose bulk has overwhelmed all contestants. Henderson moves the statue even though, as the unbeliever, he has made a bet with the king that the ceremony will not produce rain. The contest offers Henderson an opportunity to demonstrate his physical power and therefore to make some payment to nature for the gift of strength which he feels he has abused. The challenge of the stolid wooden goddess becomes his opportunity to make a gesture against the "law of decay" (190) by which he has always lived, and his success in lifting the idol fills him with joy:

I stood still. There beside Mummah in her new situation I myself was filled with happiness. I was so gladdened by what I had done that my whole body was filled with soft heat, with soft and sacred light. The sensations of illness I had experienced since morning were all converted into their opposites . . . And so my fever was transformed into jubilation. My whole spirit was awake and it welcomed life anew. Damn the whole thing! Life anew! I was still alive and kicking and I had the old grun-tu-molani. (192–193)

As if to remind us that Henderson's zeal for living and the freeing of his spirit are not the consummation of his quest—that he must also learn *how* to live—Bellow follows this ecstatic monologue with a farcical tour of the village in which the new Sungo or Rain King, stripped naked by the native women, is chased through the village, dropped into muddy water holes that they may be blessed with water, and finally overwhelmed by a shouting, whip-flailing group of his worshippers. But rain does come from what had only a few hours before been a cloudless sky, and Henderson at last has a "sign."

Only one character in this novel is untouched by the comic sense which emerges in Bellow whenever there is danger of overseriousness, and that is King Dahfu, the elegant, graceful, resplendent, slightly rebellious monarch who tries to show Henderson how he can move from what appears to be an arrested state of "becoming" into a state of "being." Dahfu is charmed by Henderson's almost childlike in-

sistence that the world can and should be something other than a
location for suffering.

Henderson's fascination with Daniel's prophecy to Nebuchadnezzar comes back to him when he agrees to become a pupil of Dahfu's
philosophy, for this means entering the den of a massive lion impris-
oned beneath the palace and, through emulation of the lion's movements and sounds, recapturing the dignity and humility which nature
intended her higher creatures to demonstrate. Weakened by fever,
by his duties as Rain King, by trying to understand palace intrigues
and Dahfu's intricate philosophy, Henderson begins again to think
of reality as an unbearable complex of pressures. His point of view is
understandable to the king, who argues that

"Men of most powerful appetite have always been the ones to doubt reality
the most. Those who could not bear that hopes should turn to misery, and
loves to hatreds, and deaths and silences, and so on. The mind has a right
to its reasonable doubts, and with every short life it awakens and sees and
understands what so many other minds of equally short life span have left
behind. It is natural to refuse belief that so many small spans should have
made so glorious one large thing. That human creatures by pondering
should be *correct*. That is what makes a fellow gasp. Yes, Sungo, this same
temporary creature is a master of imagination. And right now this very
valuable possession appears to make him die and not to live. Why? It is
astonishing what a fact that is." (232)

Through his contact with the vital and sympathetic king, Henderson comes to believe with increasing strength that there is a force
which rules the world and to which man can appeal in his need. He
appeals to that still undefined force when he prays for Dahfu's safety,
for the young king must capture the soul of his father wandering the
bush in the form of a massive lion. Each night since his arrival in
Africa, Henderson has watched, with increasing interest, Romilayu
kneeling at his prayers; carried away by his anxiety for the king's
safety, Henderson kneels beside the native and prays:

"Oh, you . . . Something," I said, "you Something because of whom there is not Nothing. Help me to do Thy will. Take off my stupid sins. Untrammel me. Heavenly Father, open up my dumb heart and for Christ's sake preserve me from unreal things. O, Thou who tookest me from pigs, let me not be killed over lions. And forgive my crimes and nonsense and let me return to Lily and the kids." (253)

This appeal to a supernatural power is not, of course, consistent with Camus's description of the absurd man, but insofar as Henderson's prayer emphasizes an order to the universe in opposition to almost everything which reality has revealed to him, its substance correlates with the absurd stance he has begun to take; the successful conclusion of his quest will eliminate Henderson's need for such appeals.

Through the influences of Dahfu, the lion, and Romilayu, Henderson is being purified and prepared for the consummation of his vision. Dahfu tells him of all the things which he can now learn from the lion: " 'She will make consciousness to shine. She will burnish you. She will force the present moment upon you . . . You fled what you were. You did not believe you had to perish. Once more, and a last time, you tried the world. With a hope of alteration' " (260). The lion's den now becomes the scene of a massive and often comical therapy, in which Henderson renounces the tendency of his consciousness " 'to isolate self' " (267). When he roars he gives up everything in his soul which has ever wanted to come forth, and at last he even brings forth, as a "hot noise," all of his human longing. His most supreme moment of roaring summarizes the entire course of his life, "from birth to Africa; and certain words crept into my roars," he says, "like 'God,' 'Help,' 'Lord have mercy,' only they came out 'Hoolp!' 'Moooorcy!' It's funny what words sprang forth. 'Au secours,' which was 'secooooooooor' and also 'De profooooondis,' plus snatches from the 'Messiah' (He was despised and rejected, a man of sorrows, etcetera)" (274).

Despite his fear of the lion and the fever which makes his "exercises" painful and draining, Henderson's persistence in the ritual to which Dahfu has introduced him is not simply the result of his feeling of friendship for the king. The ritual of the lion's den is part of the larger picture of man's search for hope, of his insistence that the world can be changed for the better.

Part of the wisdom that Henderson finds is in the knowledge that he cannot raise himself into any other world, that no matter how much a prison his life and his deeds seem, he must live in the world, and while he admits, *"I don't think the struggles of desire can ever be won"* (285), he continues to reap the profits of the struggle itself. Dahfu has warned him that there is no issue from the dreary circles of fear and desire unless man is willing to take life into his own hands. Freed by his new realizations, he concludes, "I must begin to think how to live," and among other things he knows that he "must break Lily from blackmail and set love on a true course" (288). Despite the apparent ridiculousness of his decision—its *social* absurdity—he determines to enter medical school and learn to serve humanity by healing. The role of healer (like that of Dr. Rieux in *The Plague*) seems to be a logical one for the absurd man who has returned to society.

The most dramatic expression of Henderson's opposition to reality comes when he witnesses Dahfu's attempts to capture the savage lion that presumably bears the soul of his father. The voice of this monstrous beast threatening his friend jars Henderson's mind from any hope of escape from reality through dreams or "unreal" constructs. When Dahfu falls from his slight perch above the enclosure into which the lion has been driven, Henderson leaps down with him. As the king lies dying, Henderson throws himself on the "bitch" of reality and makes it fast with a rope. But when he escapes from the scheming Wariri politicians who plan to make him their puppet king, he takes with him the small lion cub decreed to contain the soul of the dead Dahfu; as the feverish Henderson stumbles his way back to civilization, he also has a reminder that life is not always harsh or cheap. The cub reminds him that something is promised to man, that he is intended, at least occasionally, to have justice.

Henderson's voice has demanded reality, and there is no doubt to what accomplishments its demands have driven him. His "quest is a successful one since he returns from his symbolic Africa in presumed possession of the selfhood he went to seek. But what success means here and how he has achieved it can best be understood by what his symbolic adventures and misadventures achieve. An actual process and method, akin to a religious experience, must be undergone."[9] Through the symbolic prophet Dahfu, Henderson enters a new world of the self, and after becoming naked before the Wariri he is re-clothed in Rome. On the journey home he is attracted by a small orphan who is being sent to live with relatives in Nevada. When the plane lands in Newfoundland to refuel, he gathers the boy up in his arms, trying to give him something of the warmth and joy which he now feels for life. Slipping on the ice, he runs around the plane exultantly:

I held him close to my chest. He didn't seem to be afraid that I would fall with him. While to me he was like medicine applied, and the air, too; it also was a remedy. Plus the happiness that I expected at Idlewild from meeting Lily. And the lion? He was in it, too. Laps and laps I galloped around the shining and riveted body of the plane . . . The great, beautiful propellers were still, all four of them. I guess I felt it was my turn now to move, and so went running—leaping, leaping, pounding, and tingling over the pure white lining of the gray Arctic silence. (*HRK*, 341)

Ihab Hassan has appropriately commented that "for once the American hero does go back home again," and he goes home with the knowledge that "chaos does not run the whole human show."[10]

What Henderson has found is the way back to the world and to a life of service, and his victory comes suddenly after he has dedicated himself to a struggle which seems hopeless but which he must maintain in order to be true to himself. Camus described happiness and the absurd as inseparable, for the absurd teaches "that all is not, has not been, exhausted. It drives out of this world a god who had come

[9] Daniel Hughes, "Reality and the Hero: *Lolita* and *Henderson the Rain King*," *Modern Fiction Studies*, VI (Winter, 1960–1961), 357–358.
[10] Hassan, "Saul Bellow," *Critique*, III, 35.

into it with dissatisfaction and a preference for futile sufferings. It makes of fate a human matter, which must be settled among men."[11] Out of an absurd, chaotic, fragmentary world in which loneliness and pain seem the only constants, Henderson achieves a vision which permits him to take hold of his own fate. In this process he becomes a model for what Leslie Fiedler regards as the most successful contemporary hero, the man who learns that "it is the struggle itself which is his definition."[12]

At first glance, Saul Bellow's *Herzog* would appear to be a return to an earlier narrative mode, recalling Joseph's digressive journal and his long dialogues with self, or even the tormented but essentially static trials by conscience to which Asa Leventhal is subjected. *Herzog* owes much to those early exercises in what Bellow himself has called "victim literature," but it owes an equal debt to the picaresque structures and optimistically assertive conclusions of *The Adventures of Augie March* and *Henderson the Rain King*. Moses Herzog is both victim and victimizer, whose own worst enemy is his "narcissistic, masochistic, anarchic personality" (*H*, 4), but he is also the comic hero—bumptious, often self-contradictory, occasionally roguish. Like Augie March, he is "a sentimental s.o.b." in an unsentimental and selfish world; like Henderson, a dedicated opponent of the wasteland mystique and a comic champion of extreme emotional versatility. Augie's picaresque wanderings through Montreal, Chicago, Mexico, Rome, and Paris were presented in a realistic manner which owes much to the American naturalists who have influenced Bellow; Henderson's voyage was the stuff of romance—more fantastic and more highly charged with symbolic nuances. Like Conrad's Marlowe or Hemingway's African hunters, Henderson moved into an Africa of the heart which exists without relationship to time and space. Herzog is a wanderer in the mind as well as the heart—the picaro flat on his back; his actual travels to Europe, the abortive trips to Martha's

[11] Camus, *The Myth of Sisyphus*, pp. 90–91.
[12] Leslie Fiedler, "No! In Thunder," *Esquire*, 54 (September, 1960), 79.

Vineyard and Chicago, the retreat to the ruined house in the Berk-
shires—these are sharply detailed and memorable episodes, but the
real pilgrimage is more internalized even than that of Henderson, for
whom Africa was a subsuming metaphor. In *Herzog* there is no metaphorical representation of the quest; there is only the quest itself.

Thus, Bellow unites the two traditions in which he had formerly
worked—the meditative, highly ratiocinative but essentially impotent
victim, and the comic, instinctual rebel. Though the fusion is not entirely successful, the effort itself makes *Herzog* Bellow's most ambi-
tious novel to date. He himself has described the process as

a break from Victim literature . . . As one of the chieftans of that school I
have the right to say this. Victim literature purports to show the im-
potence of the ordinary man. In writing *Herzog* I felt I was completing a
certain development, coming to the end of a literary sensibility. This sensibility implies a certain attitude toward civilization—anomaly, estrange-
ment, the outsider, the collapse of humanism. What I'm against is a novel
of purely literary derivation—accepting the canon of Joyce and Kafka.
With Dostoevsky, at least, his eyes are turned freshly to the human scene.
This view of life as literature is the modern disease—a French infection.
Inevitably, it puts all hope into the performance, into virtuosity.[13]

Herzog becomes the extreme extension of all Bellow's earlier themes
and devices—beginning with the victim, morose, almost paranoid,
consumed by self-pity, tottering on the brink of nihilism and alienation, but clinging (like Augie and Henderson) to a transcendent
view of man's fate, though all life seems to negate that vision; and
finally mastering the courage to live in terms of the resulting tension.
If there is fault in the execution, it is that Herzog's determination to
fasten himself to the real in life-giving combat is heavily dependent
on that very "virtuosity" which Bellow ironically cites as a false source
of hope.

Augie's quest was pre-eminently emotional, despite his philosophi-

[13] David Boroff, "Saul Bellow," *Saturday Review*, 47 (September 19, 1964),
38–39.

cal reverence for "axial lines," and it was often supported chiefly by
the rhetoric which Bellow admits he did not have under consistent
control in that book. For Henderson the quest began with a sense
of emotional vacancy, gradually and dynamically—especially in the
dialogues with Dahfu—assuming an enriched spiritual significance.
What Herzog calls "my vague pilgrimage" (H, 17) is charted not
only in emotional and spiritual terms, but in intellectual terms as
well. Though the final form of his resolution seeks its references in
the heart, Herzog must also do battle with the windmills of philosophy, law, psychology, biology, and political theory.

Bellow is the only contemporary novelist who can speak repeatedly of sincerity (indeed, he rarely speaks about anything else) without sounding maudlin, clichéd, or merely irrelevant. The subject is
given flesh in Moses Elkhanah Herzog, the man of "Herz (n., neut.),
heart; breast, bosom; feeling, sympathy; mind, spirit; courage; center; vital part; marrow; pith; core, kernel . . ." He is "Herzog (n.,
masc.), duke"—as one critic has suggested,[14] the man of "noble heart,"
who has given his adult life to a study of "the importance of the 'law of
the heart' in Western traditions, the origins of moral sentimentalism
and related matters" (H, 119). But he studies these laws in vacuo, detached from the objective external world, a profound dilettante at last
undermined and "awakened" by the unfaithfulness of his wife and his
best friend. Thus, Herzog's "stage sets" collapse; when they do so
he samples various alternatives of conduct—indiscriminate "potato
love," the nihilism of Reality Instructors, the final and unredeemable
retreat into self, only to find each one lacking. Herzog must learn to
live with reality without sacrificing heart, without crippling the "vital
part," without denying "Spirit; courage; center." Only contact and
engagement can keep the law of the heart alive; only brotherhood
can legitimatize feeling. In a world dominated by "actors" who de-
press and exploit and distort this law, such an intention is as absurd
as loving Seymour Glass's Fat Lady; it is also as essential.

[14] James Dean Young, "Bellow's View of the Heart," Critique, 7 (Spring,
1965), 12.

Herzog's compulsive letter writing offers a brilliantly versatile conceit for the absurd predicament: these letters are the calling cards by which he attempts to revisit the world from which he had once abdicated, and they also chronicle the absurd conflict of his intention (heart) with the hostile reality which he encounters. Nonetheless, so long as Herzog maintains the conflict only on paper, until he is willing to engage it fully and consciously in life, he is only an absurd man—not an absurd hero. Only when he has learned to live in terms of the conflict does he earn the name Moses, archetype of prophets, or Elkhanah, the one whom "god possesses." The names are, of course, richly allusive. Tony Tanner displayed acrobatic zeal in suggesting a possible relationship between the hero of Bellow's novel and Maurice Herzog, who led a famous mountain-climbing expedition into the French Himalayas; Maurice is a possible derivative of the Biblical name Moses. Discussing his dangerous expedition, Maurice Herzog argued that

in overstepping our limitations, in touching the extreme boundaries of man's world, we have come to know something of its splendour. In my worst moments of anguish I seemed to discover the deep significance of existence of which till then I had been unaware . . . The marks of my ordeal are apparent on my body. I was saved and I had won my freedom. This freedom, which I shall never lose, has given me the assurance and serenity of a man who has fulfilled himself. It has given me the rare joy of loving that which I used to despise. In this narrative . . . we bear witness.[15]

So broad and sensitive is Bellow's literary experience that his knowledge of Maurice Herzog's narrative is not unlikely, and indeed, the passage which Mr. Tanner cites might almost have been drawn from the concluding pages of *Herzog*. But even if Bellow is acquainted with this source, its discovery would have been little more than coincidence, for Herzog's final peace, in which he too can accept that which he used to despise, and in which he wins his freedom despite

[15] Quoted in Tony Tanner, "Saul Bellow: The Flight from Monologue," *Encounter,* 24 (February, 1965), 65.

the marks of ordeal etched in his face, is the logical conclusion of the quest on which all the author's earlier heroes have embarked.

Indeed, if there is a specific literary source for Bellow's intense hero, it is to be found in Joyce's *Ulysses*, though here, too, any possible literary derivation must be thought of in terms of syntactic convenience—at best, a reinforcement of Bellow's own nominal shorthand—rather than as a direct source of imitation or even of inspiration. The sole reference to the Jewish merchant Moses Herzog occurs near the beginning of the Cyclops episode in *Ulysses*. The unnamed, garrulous narrator encounters Joe Hynes "dodging along Stony Batter," and the following is part of the dialogue between them before they decide to visit Barney Kiernan's:

—What are you doing round those parts? says Joe.
—Devil a much, says I. There is a bloody big foxy thief beyond by the garrison church at the corner of Chicken Lane—old Troy was just giving me a wrinkle about him—lifted any God's quantity of tea and sugar to pay three bob and said he had a farm in the country. Down off a hop of my thumb by the name of Moses Herzog over there near Heytesberg street.
—Circumcised! says Joe.
—Ay, says I. A bit off the top.[16]

Then follows shortly a statement of Michael Geraghty's legal transaction with Herzog, who is clearly fated never to collect that debt, due to be repaid in weekly installments of three shillings; similarly, Joe Hynes is unlikely to repay the three shillings borrowed from Leopold Bloom.

The opening section of the Cyclops episode contains various parodies of public rhetoric, of which Herzog's legal agreement (quoted in full) is the first example—and singularly appropriate to a public house favored by the legal profession. In examining the possible significance which this passage in *Ulysses* may have had for Saul Bellow, however, it is necessary to note the degree to which Bloom himself is not only a complex, but also a composite character; he is

[16] James Joyce, *Ulysses*, p. 277.

every older man (ultimately every man) in search and in need of mature resolution; he is many-sided and, as Homer said of Odysseus, "polytropic." Thus, in Bloom, Joyce fuses a complex set of literary and historical personalities in addition to Ulysses: "Jesus, Elijah, Moses, Dante, Shakespeare, Hamlet, and Don Giovanni" are among the antecedents noted by Tindall.[17] Similarly, many of the occasional figures who appear or are referred to in *Ulysses* also represent aspects of Bloom's polytropic experience. Thus, in light of Bellow's novel, Tindall's analysis of the parallel figures incorporated in Bloom takes on enriched significance: "That Jesus gets along with Ulysses is not so surprising as it seems; for allegorical fathers of the Church had found Ulysses a moral prototype of Jesus, who is, of course, a kind of Everyman. Moses is another exile seeking home and leading others there. Jesus and Moses are analogues for Bloom, and, since Stephen is a potential Bloom, for Stephen, too." Tindall then settles on an examination of the four most significant parallels: "Ulysses, Jesus, Moses, and Bloom again."[18] The text of *Ulysses* contains many references to Moses, usually in association with Bloom himself, though occasionally with Stephen. Thus, Bloom's thematic relationship to Moses Herzog is strongly reinforced: both are aliens, Jewish exiles in Irish Dublin, and both are owed "debts" by society which it is therefore unlikely they will ever collect.

In speculating about the Moses/Leopold Bloom/Moses Herzog parallel, one finds in Joyce's Cyclops episode numerous arguments and devices which would seem to foreshadow the method and the themes of Bellow's novel. One must, to be sure, keep in mind Bellow's own prejudice against the novel of literary derivation and his warning to "symbol hunters," although the latter is essentially a contemporary translation of Mark Twain's famous notice to critical poachers in *Huckleberry Finn*. The critic would perhaps be well advised to think of Moses E. Herzog as a collateral descendant (via the force of Bellow's imagination) of Joyce's Herzog-Bloom. Cer-

[17] William York Tindall, *A Reader's Guide to James Joyce*, p. 130.
[18] *Ibid.*, p. 130.

tainly Bellow is familiar with *Ulysses*, whereas his knowledge of Maurice Herzog's story—however tantalizing to the critic—is highly speculative, and would, in any event, have proved far less germinal than the Cyclops episode in Joyce's novel. While an understanding of *Herzog* is in no way dependent upon literary sources and hence not what Bellow would condemn as "the novel of literary derivation," the reader, without violating Bellow's belief in the independent integrity of the work of art, can look to *Ulysses* for the themes and motifs which would have reinforced his own examination of the limitations, the strengths, and the significance of the contemporary hero. In terms of the Cyclops episode, the major reinforcement would seem to rest in three closely related areas: Bloom (the composite hero) as an outcast whom society greets with stony incomprehension, dramatized by the characters who surround him at Barney Kiernan's bar; Bloom's external lassitude, contrasted with his vitally active attempts to understand the world about him—woman, the Citizen, friendship; and Bloom's statements about love, which Bellow's Herzog occasionally seems to be echoing. To his cynical fellow drinkers (Reality Instructors, all), Bloom responds,

—But it's no use . . . Force, hatred, history, all that. That's not life for men and women, insult and hatred. And everybody knows that it's the very opposite of that that is really life.
—What? says Alf.
—Love, says Bloom. I mean the opposite of hatred.[19]

We know that Bloom maintains this belief despite his own failed marriage, and even though his literal-minded companions make him an object of grotesque ridicule. In addition to such thematic parallels to Joyce, there are stylistic correspondences in Bellow's skillful juxtaposition of legal terminology, philosophical jargon, and historical formulations with a vigorous, often bawdy conversational tone, as well as in his kaleidoscopic narrative manner.

The immediate and present action of Bellow's novel describes the

[19] Joyce, *Ulysses*, p. 317.

period of extreme crisis when Moses E. Herzog's fears that he is not only unable but unworthy to live according to "the law of the heart" which he has expounded; though his withdrawn condition can be psychologically described as depressive and occasionally paranoid, he himself best identifies it as "Heartsore" (H, 17). This intellectualized Leopold Bloom sums up his despair when, after temporarily losing radio contact while on maneuvers with the Army, he manages to croak asthmatically (and so that the entire fleet hears him), " 'We're Lost! Fucked!' " Dressing to visit Ramona, Herzog summarizes for himself the factors which collaborate to give him this profound feeling of alienation:

Well, for instance, what it means to be a man. In a city. In a century. In transition. In a mass. Transformed by science. Under organized power. Subject to tremendous controls. In a condition caused by mechanization. After the late failure of radical hopes. In a society that was no community and devalued the person. Owing to the multiplied power of numbers which made the self negligible. Which spent military billions against foreign enemies but would not pay for order at home. Which permitted savagery and barbarism in its own great cities . . . On top of that, an injured heart and raw gasoline poured on the nerves. (H, 201)

The description is a microcosm of the absurd world in which many modern heroes are compelled to function, but to the harshness and impersonality of external reality is added "an injured heart," injured not only by those who have betrayed him, but injured by its very owner, for "he, Herzog, had committed a sin of some kind against his own heart, while in pursuit of a grand synthesis" (H, 207). That heart is finally healed by Ramona's love and by the self-analysis which Herzog undergoes while writing his interminable, unmailed letters.

Herzog's violation consisted in believing that life was a "subject" which could be looked at with intellectual detachment (hence his apparent indifference to his mother's death) and counted on to yield itself to logical principles, to be encompassed in "systems." This fault is not simply the result of misguided and overstimulated intellect; it also grows from Herzog's fear of "the depths of feeling he would eventually have to face, when he could no longer call on his eccentricities for relief" (*H*, 10). Like most of Bellow's heroes, Herzog must learn to face both inner and external reality; he must rejoin the world. The result of his failure to do so is spiritual, emotional, and intellectual sickness. In the critical interim, he becomes masochistic and depressive; he experiences "the sickness *unto* death" (*H*, 105); he is " 'no better than any other kind of addict—sick with abstractions' " (*H*, 123); and in this condition, when an airlines stewardess offers him a drink, he feels "incapable of looking into the girl's pretty, healthful face" (*H*, 241).

Herzog chronicles this agonized man's attempt to rejoin the world without sacrificing the principles of heart for which his integrity demands defense. This entails not only a new understanding of the world which surrounds him, but a purification and revaluation of self. Herzog's most immediate parallel in this regard is Bellow's Bummidge, the hero of *Last Analysis*, whose comical autotherapy is similarly motivated though executed with a greater flair for the burlesque. As Bummidge's harassed agent describes this self-analysis, "He recaptures the emotions. He fits them into a general framework. He thinks and thinks, and talks and talks, and the girl takes it all down, and types it in triplicate, in leather binders." Herzog's syndrome is not unlike Bummidge's "Humanitis": "It isn't that I don't like people. I need 'em, I even love 'em. So why can't I bear 'em?"[20] And Bummidge's lament is precisely that of Herzog: "Oh, how can I pull the plug and let the dirty water out of my soul. Value, value, give me value. Oh, for some substance."[21]

With a variety of intentions—most of them selfish—Herzog's friends suggest therapy for his condition, offering two major alternatives to his intellectual retreat. Sandor Himmelstein is a part-time exponent of Potato Love, that "Amorphous, swelling, hungry, indis-

[20] Saul Bellow, "Scenes from Humanitis—A Farce," *Partisan Review*, 29 (Summer, 1962), 345. (Excerpts from an earlier draft of *Last-Analysis*).
[21] *Ibid.*, p. 349.

criminate, cowardly potato love" (*H*, 91) which shields man from
reality by enveloping him in emotional fantasies. Far more insidious
are the Reality Instructors, whom Sandor himself joins with brutal
intensity when the irrational potato love fails him. The teacher of
reality denies heart entirely, emphasizing that " 'We're all whores in
this world, and don't you forget it' " (*H*, 85). Simkin is another of
the Reality Instructors who love "to pity and poke fun at the same
time" (*H*, 30), and all of them point the way to a pessimism, even a
nilhilism, which Herzog cannot in honesty accept, however much
such a principle might simplify his own dilemma. He must come to
terms with reality, but first he is compelled to understand it, and for
Herzog (as for Bellow's other heroes) reality cannot be encompassed
by *"the commonplaces of the Wasteland outlook, the cheap mental
simulants of Alienation, the cant and rant of pipsqueaks about Inau-
thenticity and Forlornness. I can't accept this foolish dreariness. We
are talking about the whole life of mankind. The subject is too great,
too deep for such weakness, cowardice . . ."* (*H*, 75). Similarly, he
writes testily to Heidegger: *"I should like to know what you mean
by the expression 'the fall into the quotidian.' When did this fall occur?
Where were you standing when it happened?"* (*H*, 49). He is repulsed
that "The very Himmelsteins, who had never even read a book of
metaphysics, were touting the Void as if it were so much salable real
estate" (*H*, 93), that despair is almost a voting requirement, that an
entire generation imagines "that nothing faithful, vulnerable, fragile
can be durable or have any true power" (*H*, 290), and that *"com-
fortable people playing at crisis, alienation, apocalypse and desperation"* dominate the fashionable magazines (*H*, 316–317).

Herzog searches not for rest or escape or illusion, but for that state
in which he can exercise the intentions of his heart in full knowledge
and presence of reality—however antagonistic the latter may seem.
He can deny neither term—unlike the Potato Lovers, who deny reality, and the Reality Instructors, who deny heart. Herzog himself has
been an intellectual Potato Lover, and the results of this sort of ab-
stracted humanism include an unhealthy absorption with the past,

to which the scholar looks "with an intense need for contemporary relevance" (*H*, 5), writing many of his letters to the dead because "He lived with them as much as the living—perhaps more . . ." (*H*, 181). Herzog's intellectualized emotionalism, without anchor in reality, is shown at its most perverted extreme in Lucas Asphalter, who humanizes his animals to a grotesque degree: "Now Herzog had to consider some strange facts about Asphalter. It's possible I influenced him, my emotionalism transmitted itself to him . . . I suspect Luke may be in a bad way" (*H*, 45–46).

Through his meetings with Asphalter, the sordid courtroom trials which he observes, the bizarre automobile accident, the healing love of Ramona, and his questioning, argumentative letters, Herzog finally achieves an objective view of his absurd predicament: "He too could smile at Herzog and despise him. But there still remained the fact. *I am Herzog. I have to be that man. There is no one else to do it*. After smiling he must return to his own Self and see the thing through" (*H*, 67). Herzog learns to "be," and his progress is recorded in the letters, through which he phrases his lover's quarrel with an essentially unloving world; he is schooled in the absurd tension between intention and reality and is at last content to exist in terms of the tension: " '*But what do you want, Herzog?*' " he asks himself at the conclusion of the book. " '*But that's just it—not a solitary thing. I am pretty well satisfied to be, to be just as it is willed, and for so long as I may remain in occupancy*' " (*H*, 340). Thus, he is prepared to renew what he calls "universal connections," the equivalent of Augie's "axial lines," but defined now in more specific humanistic terms. First, he conceives of his struggle as being significant in terms of "the human condition" (*H*, 107) as a whole: "The progress of civilization—indeed, the survival of civilization—depended on the successes of Moses E. Herzog" (*H*, 125). This is not simply narcissism or a distinctive lunacy; it is an index of Herzog's struggle for a stance which will allow him existence in terms of mankind—not merely in terms of intellect, of the exacerbated self, or of a hostile, external reality. Without this broader significance Herzog loses all sense of time and space: he glances at his watch without being able to fix the time in his mind; he tries to orient himself in space, but from his apartment window he can see "Nothing in particular. Only a sense of water bounding the overbuilt island" (*H*, 159), and all he can fix firmly in his mind is his own face in the mirror.

The central paradox of Herzog's experience is that only through self can man renew universal connections, but too much involvement in self may cancel out the universal: "If ever Herzog knew the loathsomeness of a *particular* existence, knew that the *whole* was required to redeem every separate spirit, it was then, in his terrible passion, which he tried, impossibly, to share, telling his story" (*H*, 157). Thus, he becomes increasingly aware of the grotesquerie of his own peccadilloes, and becomes the subject not only of the author's comic sense, but of his own as well. As comic detachment grows, Herzog becomes aware that the letters themselves, though crucial in helping him to resist the Potato Lovers and the Reality Instructors, are a means to an end which can be fully experienced only when he no longer needs to write them. As he explains to Asphalter with grim humor: " 'I must be trying to keep tight the tensions without which human beings can no longer be called human. If they don't suffer, they've gotten away from me. And I've filled the world with letters to prevent their escape. I want them in human form, and so I conjure up a whole environment and catch them in the middle. I put my whole heart into these constructions. But they are constructions' " (*H*, 272). Herzog sees the average intellectual as a "Separatist"—hence he himself has hoarded food in the Ludeyville house in a scheme for solitary self-sufficiency, which seems ludicrous to him once he has become "a specialist in spiritual self-awareness" (*H*, 307), for that very awareness teaches him that no definition of the self is complete unless it embraces other people—even such actors as Gersbach and Madeleine.

Madeleine is essential in forcing the crisis through which Herzog comes to terms with reality, and Ramona is the crucial counterbalance which saves him from insanity and gives him strength to keep

his absurd intention alive. He confesses to Simkin that he is not a
realist (convinced now of the necessity of confronting reality but
uncertain how to interpret it), and his ultimate vision embraces all
the ambiguities of the world about him, resisting both romanticism
and nihilism:

The air from the west was drier than the east air. Herzog's sharp senses de-
tected the difference. In these days of near-delirium and wide-ranging
disordered thought, deeper currents of feeling had heightened his per-
ceptions, or made him instill something of his own into his surroundings.
As though he painted them with moisture and color taken from his own
mouth, his blood, liver, bowels, genitals. In this mingled way, therefore,
he was aware of Chicago, familiar ground to him for more than thirty
years. And out of these elements, by this peculiar art of his own organs, he
created his version of it. Where the thick walls and buckled slabs of pave-
ment in the Negro slums exhaled their bad smells. Farther West, the in-
dustries; the sluggish South Branch dense with sewage and glittering with
a crust of golden slime; the Stockyards, deserted; the dullness of bungalows
and scrawny parks; and vast shopping centers; and the cemeteries after
these—Waldheim, with its graves for Herzogs past and present; the Forest
Preserves for riding parties, Croatian picnics, lovers' lanes, horrible murders; airports; quarries; and, last of all, cornfields. And with this, infinite
forms of activity—Reality. (H, 278)

Madeleine had hampered such an inclusive vision by driving him,
through her own ambition, further onto the shoals of intellectualism,
and by giving him additional evidence to support the nihilists' conclusion that man is by nature whorish. As a bitch goddess who coolly
applies lipstick after a meal by looking at herself in a knife blade,
Madeleine has a polite and morally rigid ancestress in James' Ma-
dame de Mauves, a frivolous one in Fitzgerald's Daisy Fay Buch-
anan, and a serious competitor in West's Faye Greener, with her
"long, sword-like legs." Herzog's spirit is too active, too resilient, to
be completely dominated by this woman (though she does give him
cause to question his own potency); she appropriately chooses a
one-legged lover named Valentine: a paper imitation of the real man

of heart, an *ersatz* Herzog, though physically more powerful, as his name implies.

Ramona, on the other hand, offers regeneration through love:

> She, Ramona, wanted to add riches to his life and give him what he pursued in the wrong places. This she could do by the art of love, she said—the art of love which was one of the sublime achievements of the spirit . . . What he had to learn from her—while there was still time; while he was still virile, his powers substantially intact—was how to renew the spirit through the flesh (a precious vessel in which the spirit rested). (*H*, 185)

And Ramona can succeed because she knows not only how to produce sensual gratification (as cook, florist, lover), but because she, too, has been tested and tempered: ". . . she knew the bitterness of death and nullity, too" (*H*, 185). In the conclusion of the novel Herzog offers Ramona not one of the letters he has written for months, but a bouquet of wildflowers.

Ramona, the friendship of Asphalter, his two children, the rich memories of Napoleon Street—all reinforce the man of heart as he passes through this crisis of consciousness. They reaffirm his belief that man only *seems* lost, remains alienated only when he blindly accepts the fashionable stance of alienation as a condition of existence. Despite the new barbarisms of a machine age, well known to Herzog as a moral historian, he can reaffirm that "*Civilization and even morality are implicit in technological transformation*" (*H*, 165); that ". . . *there are moral realities*" as well as physically unstable, destructive ones (*H*, 178); and even as he scents the odor of decay rising through a waste pipe, he notes "Unexpected intrusions of beauty" (*H*, 218).

Herzog's Jewishness, a matter on which many reviewers of the novel peremptorily turned their backs, seems a vital factor insofar as it gives Herzog a sense of the significance of family ("He could be a patriarch, as every Herzog was meant to be. The Family man, transmitter of life, intermediary between past and future, instrument of mysterious creation . . ." [*H*, 202]); a richness and complexity of experience, heavy with love as well as deprivation, which causes him to rebel against the simplistic clichés of popular nihilism ("much heavy love in Herzog; grief did not pass quickly, with him" [*H*, 119]); and an almost dauntless compassion (". . . we had a great school-ing in grief. I still know these cries of the soul" [*H*, 148]). It is true that he possesses these traits in greater degree than the other members of his family; that he himself feels that modern experience has made much of the traditional Jewish experience inapplicable; and that other backgrounds might have resulted in a constitution similarly resistant to nihilism, dedicated to children and the prin-ciple of family. Nonetheless, the relevant fact remains that such values as Herzog embodies are not, at least in this degree, the com-mon stock of modern industrialized America. Herzog *is* a Jew, and many of his values grow directly from his Jewish-immigrant back-ground rather than from his adult experiences as a liberal intellec-tual. Though he was brought up in an eccentric and only erratically "religious" family, he himself repeatedly refers to his Jewishness. The critic who urges that this "Jewishness" is unimportant to the novel is correct to the same degree that Leopold Bloom's Jewishness is un-important; he is right if he intends to suggest that the character is a symbolic alien whose struggle has significance for all of us. But he is clearly wrong if he intends to suggest that a Jewish background is irrelevant in terms of the particular character's dramatic develop-ment. Similar arguments apply to all of Bellow's Jewish heroes.

In Moses E. Herzog, Saul Bellow presents the richest and most diverse of his band of questing men who dissipate their powers and energies in fruitless, often comic quests for salvation which are re-solved only through the character's realization that man's triumph comes when he has learned to sustain the vital equilibrium between intention and reality. One need only recall Joseph's remarks in *Dang-ling Man* to observe the consistency of Bellow's heroes while, at the same time, appreciating the mature development which these con-cepts are given in the person of Herzog:

We are all drawn to the same craters of the spirit—to know what we are
and what we are for, to know our purpose, to seek grace. And, if the quest
is the same, the differences in our personal histories, which hitherto meant
so much to us, become of minor importance. (*DM*, 154)

In every case the Bellow hero is aggravated into self-awareness and
into revaluation of the world around him as preparation for engaging the vital tensions in the most fruitful manner. The hero shouts
"Hurray for regular hours!" he develops conscience, orients himself
to the axial lines of life, learns to confront death, returns to society,
renews "universal connections." Bellow's knights progress in orderly
file from one novel to the next—increasing in complexity of treatment if not, consistently, in depth. If Bellow has, in effect, only written one book from six different points of view, the book has constantly improved, although it would seem to have reached its most
extreme extension in *Herzog*. Further elaboration on the theme might
well force the novelist to yield to the rhetorician—a danger already
apparent in the concluding pages of both *Henderson the Rain King*
and *Herzog*. Bellow may have had such dangers in mind when he
noted that "In writing *Herzog* I felt I was completing a certain development, coming to the end of a literary sensibility."[22] It is, perhaps,
the end of monologue as well, for the technique comes to a crisis in
Herzog. Here the struggle to externalize, to escape the trap of self
and renew universal connections, depends on Herzog's seeing his
own dilemma in an objective light: that he cannot do so consistently is indicated by the shifting narrative voice, which moves erratically between first and third persons until at last, after Herzog has
made his resolution that "*I am pretty well satisfied to be, to be just
as it is willed, and for as long as I remain in occupancy*," the third-
person voice takes over entirely; with the exception of the opening
sentence the first section of the novel, which similarly describes Herzog at the end of his ordeal, is also in the third person. It is almost
as though the objective narrative voice were a further indication of

[22]Boroff, "Saul Bellow," p. 39.

Herzog's restoration to life, a proof that he is now "confident, cheerful, clairvoyant, and strong" (*H*, 1), just as significant as his "weirdly tranquil" face and the "radiant line . . . from mid-forehead over his straight nose and full, silent lips" (*H*, 2). The alternating voices in the remainder of the book constitute monologue despite the constantly shifting person; there is dialectic but not dialogue. If *Herzog* seems Joycean in its circular structure (though it is a formal, not a thematic circularity), in narrative manner it also owes a debt to *Tristram Shandy*, that "history book . . . of what passes in a man's mind."

Perhaps Herzog's victory is only temporary, but we leave him in the conclusion of the novel a far wiser man than any of Bellow's earlier heroes, one who has now affirmed and legitimatized the absurd struggle on all levels of experience—emotional, spiritual, and intellectual. Perhaps now Bellow has prepared himself for the novel of dialogue, which can begin with the engagement toward which his diverse knights have struggled—in short, perhaps he can move beyond affirmation of the absurd experience to examine the consequences of those "tensions" which he has detailed with such skill and integrity.

THE *Love* ETHIC

Few heroes of contemporary literature have aroused so much devotion, imitation, or controversy as J. D. Salinger's Holden Caulfield, the disaffiliated adolescent whose lost weekend in New York is chronicled in *The Catcher in the Rye*. As an impressionable adolescent making his first tentative movements into an adult world, Holden becomes a sensitive register by which the values of that world can be judged. From the opening pages of this novel the world is seen to be fragmentary, distorted, and absurd—in Holden's own special vernacular, "phony." It is an environment in which real communication on a sensitive level is impossible, and when Holden unsuccessfully tries to explain his spiritual pain to Sally Hayes, there is certainly more than a coincidental suggestion of Eliot's "J. Alfred Prufrock" in the frustrated cry, " 'You don't see what I meant at all' " (*CR*, 173).

Holden does not refuse to grow up so much as he agonizes over the state of being grown up. The innocent world of childhood is amply represented in *The Catcher in the Rye*, but Holden, as a frustrated, disillusioned, anxious hero, stands for modern man rather than merely for the modern adolescent. He is self-conscious and often ridiculous, but he is also an anguished human being of special sensitivity. Even though he is often childishly ingenuous, and his language is frequently comic, Holden must be seen as both a representative and a critic of the modern environment, as the highly subjective tone of the novel suggests.

As a misfit Holden has literary predecessors in such early Salinger stories as "The Hang of It," "The Varioni Brothers," "Soft-Boiled Sergeant," "This Sandwich Has no Mayonnaise," and "The Stranger." Holden is not unlike Rabbit Angstrom or Augie March in seeking the environment in which he can perform at his best, and the result is a painful contemporary odyssey. As the novel opens, Holden is in the process of rejecting yet another uncongenial environment, Pencey Prep. There he feels surrounded by phonies, just as he had felt surrounded by them at Elkton Hills, his previous school: "One of the biggest reasons I left Elkton Hills was because I was surrounded by phonies. That's all. They were coming in the goddam window" (19). That "Goddam Elkton Hills" is far more than an example of the social snobbery of an Eastern prep school. It comes to stand for a world in which values and perspectives have become so distorted that there seems little if any room for the sensitive individual who attempts to order the flux of human existence or to bring it into the light of a consistent aesthetic perspective. To this significant degree, the milieu in which Salinger heroes function is "absurd." Like Camus's absurd man, the Salinger hero tries to live by ethical standards in an indifferent, often nihilistic universe. An important distinction, however, must be drawn between Camus's absurd man and the absurd man in Salinger's fiction. This distinction is primarily one of consciousness, for Camus's heroes consciously acknowledge the absurdity of their struggle against reality. While the reader is in a position to see the absurdity of Holden's quixotic gestures and of Zooey's ultimate, transcendent "love" stance, he is never entirely certain that the characters themselves see their own struggles as absurd, though Zooey at least approaches this essential awareness. These characters, however, do demonstrate "disproportions" on the level of values which make the myth of the absurd applicable to their struggles. The context of the absurd does not perhaps explain as much about Salinger as it did about Updike, Styron, or Bellow, but it does help us to see what Salinger has tried to accomplish in his writing and to understand his relationship to other contemporary novelists.

Few areas of modern life escape Holden Caulfield's indictment. Among those most severely challenged are the movies (to which his brother D. B., a writer, has prostituted himself) and religious enthusiasm. Holden explains that the children in his family are all "atheists" because his parents are of different religious persuasions (foreshadowing the Irish-Jewish Glass family). Thus Holden's biting but revealing point of view is not clouded by specific religious commitments, and he can love the nuns whom he meets in Grand Central Station even though he feels that Catholicism usually throws up insurmountable barriers to communication. Just as he loves the nuns for their simplicity and honesty, he sees through the selfish religious pose of "this guy Ossenburger," an undertaker who contributes a dormitory wing to Pencey.

The phoniness of Hollywood and of religion as it is often practiced in the contemporary world come together to form a dramatic whole in the Christmas pageant which Holden attends at Radio City. Following the Rockettes and a man who roller-skated under tables, "they had this Christmas thing they have at Radio City every year":

All these angels start coming out of the boxes and everywhere, guys carrying crucifixes and stuff all over the place, and the whole bunch of them—*thousands* of them—singing "Come All Ye Faithful!" like mad. Big deal. It's supposed to be religious as hell, I know, and very pretty and all, but I can't see anything religious or pretty, for God's sake, about a bunch of actors carrying crucifixes all over the stage. (178)

The blatant, graceless *kitsch* of the movie which follows the stage show (and which has been identified as James Hilton's *Random Harvest*) is an equally commercial deception, an artificial substitute for the love and generosity which Americans have forgotten how to express. After his experience with a Radio City Christmas, Holden feels yet more agonizingly frustrated and alone. "I'm sort of glad they've got the atomic bomb invented," he comments. "If there's ever another war, I'm going to sit right the hell on top of it. I'll volunteer for it, I swear to God I will" (*CR*, 183).

Wherever Holden turns, his craving for truth seems to be frustrated by the phoniness of the world. From his hotel window he looks out upon scenes of perversion and distortion; in bars and night clubs he hears only the laconic accents of shallow supersophisticates or self-satisfied intellectuals. When he finds innocence or purity it is always jeopardized by evil or apathy, and he searches desperately for something to sustain him. An answer seems to come from Mr. Antolini, a former English teacher who explains to Holden that the fall he is riding for is " 'a special kind of fall, a horrible kind. The man falling isn't permitted to feel or hear himself hit bottom. He just keeps falling and falling. The whole arrangement's designed for men who, at some time or other in their lives, were looking for something their own environment couldn't supply them with. So they gave up looking' " (243–244). Mr. Antolini urges Holden to continue to search in humility for a cause worth living for. Such a search, he assures Holden, has been chronicled by educated and scholarly men, and he promises to guide the boy into an intellectual channel that will both stimulate and comfort him. Whatever consolation there may have been in this message is destroyed when Holden awakens to find Mr. Antolini petting him—and he flees from yet another example of the world's perversion.

What prompts Holden's quest is his desire for unity, a desire that is expressed in the comfort and safety which he always felt in the Museum of Natural History:

The best thing, though, in that museum was that everything always stayed right where it was. Nobody'd move. You could go there a hundred thousand times, and that Eskimo would still be just finished catching those two fish, the birds would still be on their way south, the deers would still be drinking out of that water hole, with their pretty antlers and their pretty, skinny legs, and that squaw with the naked bosom would still be weaving that same blanket. Nobody'd be different. (157–158)

That such a reassuringly ordered universe is an impossible dream is emphasized by the fact that, when Holden visits the Museum near the conclusion of his New York odyssey, he sees the words " 'Fuck you' . . . written with a red crayon or something, right under the glass part of the wall, under the stones" (264). Holden wishes to erase the interminable "Fuck you's" on all the alley walls and school corridors and sidewalks in the world, and this intention to cancel out vulgarity and phoniness is a poignant if naive example of the absurd.

  The Catcher in the Rye is an important articulation of one of the possible responses which man may make to an essentially destructive life experience. Since, Holden reasons, there is no fulfillment in the adult world, since all it can offer man is frustration or corruption, the only worthwhile task to which he can devote himself is that of the protector who stops children before they enter the world of destruction and phoniness and keeps them in a state of arrested innocence:

"Anyway, I keep picturing all these little kids playing some game in this big field of rye and all. Thousands of little kids, and nobody's around—nobody big, I mean, except me. And I'm standing on the edge of some crazy cliff. What I have to do, I have to catch everybody if they start to go over the cliff—I mean if they're running and they don't look where they're going I have to come out from somewhere and *catch* them. That's all I'd do all day. I'd just be the catcher in the rye and all. I know it's crazy, but that's the only thing I'd really like to be. I know it's crazy." (224–225)

Holden's reiteration of the word "crazy" reminds us that his ambition is also "absurd," for his Christ-like intention (suffering the little children to come unto him) is opposed to the reality in which children like his own sister, Phoebe, are carted off to the Lister Foundation to see movies on euthanasia and move along grimy school corridors which flaunt the words "Fuck you!" at them. While Holden has a vision of his role in the world, he is unable either to live the absurdity he has outlined or to develop an absurd faith. The reasons for this failure on his part are simple and obvious. First, even though we are clearly intended to see him as a representative of modern man, Holden is an adolescent, and both his experience and his perspectives are too limited for him to offer any kind of finalized "answer" to the phoniness of the world. Second, and perhaps most important, his vision carries within itself a destructive contradiction. While Holden's intention is absurd in its opposition to reality, the goal of his intention is to help innocent children to *avoid* reality. His conclusion negates his premise insofar as it eliminates one of the two crucial terms of the absurd confrontation and offers no formula by which man can live in and with his world. Holden's intention is moving and vaguely saintly, but it involves a nostalgia which, according to Camus, the absurd man must reject. (Indeed, Holden himself rejects it when he decides that he must not attempt to protect Phoebe during her final ride on the carousel.)

What Salinger leaves us with in this novel is an often biting image of the absurd contemporary milieu. The idea of perpetuating the innocence of childhood is a philosophically untenable position, and the only other unrejected proposals in the novel are so vague that their full importance can be seen only in Salinger's later work. The first of these proposals for a stance at once self-protective and humanistically fulfilling is made by Carl Luce, who suggests a vague mystical discipline derived from Eastern philosophy as a solution to Holden's spiritual agony, but Luce's approach to this discipline seems supersophisticated and "phony." In the epilogue to the novel Holden suggests the possibility of re-entering society when he says, "I sort of *miss* everybody I told about. Even old Stradlater and Ackley, for instance. I think I even miss that goddam Maurice" (277). Holden misses even the phonies of the world because his experience has taught him something about the necessity of loving, and here Salinger sounds what is to become his major and most complex theme.

After *The Catcher in the Rye* Salinger wrote several stories examining the mystical process, and even though his mystically inclined heroes are engaging and at times inspiring, their stance must be rejected, too, in favor of a position that leads man to the world rather than to an intense but isolating subjective experience. Like efforts to recapture the innocence of childhood, mysticism (which Salinger usually considers in terms of Zen Buddhism) is finally seen as an evasion and contradiction of Western man's spiritual quest. In Zen Buddhism, the life of the mystic is only temporarily one of isolation, for after the achievement of *satori,* the state of total enlightenment and consciousness that is the goal of Zen Buddhism, the enlightened man re-enters the world to perform good works. Thus, Salinger's rejection of the transitory, unearned mystical *experience* is understandable in terms of its failure to provide a program which the individual can follow in order to give his life meaning, but his rejecton of mysticism itself is more difficult to understand—especially in light of his own involvement with Zen Buddhism. Mysticism is treated as a "fever" in Salinger's writings, an isolating and therefore unfruitful discipline that inevitably leads Western man away from the paths of significant human involvement. Furthermore, while *satori* may eventually guide the Buddhist back into his world, the good works which he is prepared to perform are not necessarily those works which a spiritually enlightened Westerner should be prepared to perform. It is not through mysticism but through love that the Salinger hero at last re-enters the world.

From 1945 until 1951, J. D. Salinger published sixteen short stories, several of the same slick, predictable character as the stories he wrote for popular magazines during the Second World War. Five of those stories, however, were concerned with Holden Caulfield and his family, and three of them represented the beginning of his largest and most serious body of work—the "saga" of the Glass family. The first of these stories centers on an elusive character named Seymour Glass, whose suicide is the subject of the first story in Salinger's second book,

Nine Stories. Little in this brief account indicates the scope of the Glass series, but it sets the stage for the rejection of mysticism as a solution to the contemporary spiritual dilemma. In order to appreciate the strength of Salinger's rejection, one must understand his fascination with the mystical process itself. Two of Salinger's *Nine Stories*, "De Daumier-Smith's Blue Period" and "Teddy," chronicle, respectively, the mystical vision and the mystical faith.

De Daumier-Smith is the fanciful pseudonym adopted by a somewhat typical Salinger *isolatoe* who brashly attempts to create a new image of himself with which he can confront a world from which he suddenly feels disaffiliated. De Daumier-Smith's rebellion resembles Holden's in that he too is hypersensitive to the phoniness of the world, but the origin of his disaffiliation is more specifically identified as the absence of love. Jean narrates his own story, and the most pertinent fact about his childhood is that he had never truly loved anyone but his mother. Shortly after her death, he moves to New York with his stepfather. Having drawn some slight attention as an artist when his family lived in Paris, Jean embroiders his experiences, draws up an imaginary list of professional credentials and friends (including Picasso) and applies for a job as an instructor at "Les Amis des Vieux Maîtres," a correspondence art school in Montreal. What prompts him to make this sudden "quixotic gesture" is the realization that he and his father "were both in love with the same deceased woman" (*NS*, 98). This knowledge forces him out of the innocent private world in which he had formerly lived, and the very telling of his story is an attempt to give order to the experiences which greet him in the public world—a world which at first seems no more complete or fulfilling than the Oedipally narrow world in which he had previously functioned. The isolation which De Daumier-Smith suffers is underscored by the fact that we never learn his real name; he adopts a bogus identity and a preposterously contrived set of credentials in order to teach students whom he will never see in a French art school run by two Japanese. When Jean reveals to the Yoshotos

that he is a student of Buddhism, they inform him that they are Pres-
byterians. However ambitiously ingratiating he becomes to his em-
ployers, his loneliness only increases.

What seems to offer Jean consolation is his discovery of naive
beauty in the crude but talented paintings of Sister Irma of the Order
of St. Joseph. In Jean's wild daydreams about the nun, she comes to
represent his last chance to communicate with another sensitive
spirit, and he yearns for a moment of truth and love with her which
will make him spiritually whole and effect his conversion into a great
healer.

When her Superior severs Sister Irma's relationship with the art
school after reading Jean's passionate letter to her, the boy is cast
into a painful and almost total despair; but from that dark night of
the soul he passes into a period of illumination. Like the precocious
members of the Glass family, Jean has been a student of comparative
religions, and his study has at least partially prepared him for the
epiphany which greets him and flashes like the sun into his dark
night. Les Amis des Vieux Maîtres is located over an orthopedic ap-
pliances shop, and as Jean pauses before the window, he seems to
see it as a *collage* representing all of the crippling inhumanity of the
world: "The thought was forced on me that no matter how coolly or
sensibly or gracefully I might one day learn to live my life, I would
always at best be a visitor in a garden of enamel urinals and bedpans,
with a sightless, wooden dummy-deity standing by in a marked-down
rupture truss" (116). Later, however, he has what he calls an "Experience," in which everything in the window is transformed:

Suddenly (and I say this, I believe, with all due self-consciousness), the
sun came up and sped toward the bridge of my nose at the rate of ninety-
three million miles a second. Blinded and very frightened—I had to put my
hand on the glass to keep my balance. The thing lasted for no more than a
few seconds. When I got my sight back, the girl had gone from the window,
leaving behind her a shimmering field of exquisite, twice-blessed flowers.
(121)

"De Daumier-Smith's Blue Period" offers a strong suggestion that a mystical experience may help man to alter his vision of the world so significantly that he will be able to live in it. Jean de Daumier-Smith does return to the world after his dark night of despair to spend a "normal" summer of girl-watching on the beach. While Jean has something closely related to a mystical revelation, he is not a mystic: "I'd like, if possible, to avoid seeming to pass it off as a case, or even a borderline case, of genuine mysticism" (120). While his experience offers the promise of a degree of spiritual fulfillment he had not known before, his story suggests no code by which the individual can oppose a world made up of "enamel urinals and bedpans" and ruled over by a "wooden dummy-deity." His discovery of an order and transcendent meaning in a sterile and hostile world is rather a product of chance, than the climax of experience. This situation is typical for the modern hero, to whom revelation or epiphany comes as a sudden intuitive flash, suggesting in part that visions of order or meaning are not available through reason.

In "Teddy" Salinger concerned himself with the realized mystic Teddy McArdle, a precocious ten-year-old who has achieved the enlightened consciousness of *satori*. Teddy's mysticism frees him from the grossness of his parents, but Salinger treats his mystic lyrically and impressionistically, never attempting to describe the process by which Teddy arrives at *satori*, other than by referring to the boy's intense periods of meditation, but in "A Perfect Day for Bananafish" he allegorically demonstrates that mysticism is not a solution to man's dilemma.

As we learn from later stories about the Glass family, Seymour Glass has travelled to Florida with his wife in order to "recover" from a state of acute depression. In the first half of "A Perfect Day for Bananafish," through a telephone conversation between his wife and her mother, we are given some insight into the causes of his depression. Muriel comes from a world whose main concerns are with "normalcy" and whose emotional outlets are found in the kind of melo-

dramatic movie which to Holden Caulfield seemed a puerile commercial sham. The hotel room in which Seymour commits suicide is
characterized by the smell "of new calfskin luggage and nail-lacquer
remover" (*NS*, 18). Without the bananafish allegory the reader might
see Seymour's suicide as merely a rejection of this world of crass
superficiality, but it is also—and more significantly—a rejection of
the mystical life itself.

While Muriel is talking to her mother and trying to reassure her
that Seymour has had no more destructive urges, Seymour is on the
beach with Sybil Carpenter. He catches the young girl's attention
with a variety of fantasies, the most complex of which involves the
bananafish. Pushing Sybil out into the water on a rubber float, he
explains to her the inherent fatalism of bananafish:

> "Well, they swim into a hole where there's a lot of bananas. They're very
> ordinary-looking fish when they swim *in*. But once they get in, they behave
> like pigs. Why, I've known some bananafish to swim into a banana hole
> and eat as many as seventy-eight bananas." He edged the float and its
> passenger a foot closer to the horizon. "Naturally, after that they're so fat
> they can't get out of the hole again. Can't fit through the door." (16)

Seymour's life has been filled with erratic spiritual experiences,
and to his brothers and sisters he stands as a kind of Christ-figure.
Like the bananafish, however, he has become so glutted with this
experience that he can no longer participate in the real world outside himself. This inability, which accounts for what he calls the
"very tragic life" which the bananafish leads, is emphasized by the
fact that he cannot bear the eyes of the world. After leaving Sybil on
the beach, Seymour walks into the hotel elevator along with a young
woman:

> "I see you're looking at my feet," he said to her when the car was in
> motion.
> "I beg your pardon?" said the woman.
> "I said I see you're looking at my feet."

"I *beg* your pardon. I happened to be looking at the floor," said the woman, and faced the doors of the car.

"If you want to look at my feet, say so," said the young man. "But don't be a God-damned sneak about it." (17)

Following this episode, Seymour enters his hotel room, takes a pistol from his suitcase, and fires a bullet through his head.

Salinger rejects the mystic's experience as a solution to man's alienation in an absurd universe because mysticism ("banana fever") removes man from reality. While Seymour is never a fully realized mystic like Teddy, it is inconsistent to explain away his suicide as despair over the idea of achieving *satori*. Seymour has already rejected *satori* because it leads him out of the world in which he feels he must live, and his rejection is overt and conscious. His life has been filled with one transcendent experience after another, with visions and intense spiritual moments which affirm his ability to achieve *satori*. Among the reminders of such experiences, Seymour notes, "I have scars on my hands from touching certain people."

"Once, in the park, when Franny was still in the carriage, I put my hand on the downy pate of her head and left it there too long. Another time, at Lowe's Seventy-second Street, with Zooey during a spooky movie. He was about six or seven, and he went under the seat to avoid watching a scary scene. I put my hand on his head. Certain heads, certain colors and textures of human hair leave permanent marks on me. Other things, too. Charlotte once ran away from me, outside the studio, and I grabbed her dress to stop her, to keep her near me. A yellow cotton dress I loved because it was too long for her. I still have a lemon-yellow mark on the palm of my right hand. Oh, God, if I'm anything by a clinical name, I'm a kind of paranoiac in reverse. I suspect people of plotting to make me happy." (*RHRB*, 88)

As we learn in "Raise High the Roof Beam, Carpenters," Seymour was so happy over his marriage to Muriel that he was unable to attend his own wedding. Seymour's wedding-day happiness came from the thought that he might at last emerge from the spiritual "hole" into which he had begun swimming as a child. Unable to resign a quest for a miraculous spiritual perfection, and simultaneously un-equipped to join the world of mere possibility, Seymour chose suicide. As Dan Wakefield has noted, suicide and miracle are the extremes between which many of Salinger's characters fluctuate, but the author's primary concern is with the alternatives which exist between those extremes. No appeal to a spiritual absolute (and no transcendent spiritual experience) is a wholly successful alternative. In his later stories Salinger turns his attention to other stances which man can make in an absurd world to give his life meaning.

Salinger would certainly agree with Dan Wakefield's observation that ours is a time in which men are " 'no longer feeling within themselves the idol but still feeling the altar,' and the questions of what replaces the idol which once provided a set of answers for human conduct; the question of how men act with morality and love if there is no idol which prescribes the rules, is a central and vital question."[1] Salinger begins to define his answer in "For Esmé—with Love and Squalor." The narrator of this story—who is never more fully identified than as "Sergeant X"—writes his story as a kind of epithalamium after receiving an invitation to Esmé's wedding. He had met the girl while stationed in England for special D-Day training, and the loneliness which he experienced before their meeting is idiomatic to the Salinger hero.

On a free Saturday afternoon at the end of his training course Sergeant X walks into Devon and almost by accident enters a church in which a children's choir is rehearsing. There he becomes enchanted by Esmé, a young girl of "about thirteen, with straight, ash-blond hair of ear-lobe length, an exquisite forehead, and blasé eyes that, I thought, might very possibly have counted the house" (NS, 68). Later Sergeant X meets the girl in a tea room, and Esmé tries to comfort and entertain the lonely G.I. When she leaves the tea room, it is with the request that X someday write her a story "about love and squalor."

[1] Dan Wakefield, "Salinger and the Search for Love," New World Writing, 14 (1958), 79–80.

X's experience with squalor comes in Bavaria, where he is trying unsuccessfully to recover from his encounter with undefined battle-field horrors. His recovery is not aided by the loutish insensitivity of his companion, Clay, or by his own brother's request for wartime souvenirs: "'How about sending the kids a couple of bayonets or swastikas . . .?'" (79). X is quartered in a house recently confiscated from a family whose daughter was an official in the Nazi party; among the books which she has left behind is Goebbel's *Die Zeit Ohne Beis-piel*, a title ironically descriptive of X's condition. He opens the book to find the words "'Dear God, life is hell'" written on the flyleaf. With a sudden energy X writes under this a passage from Dostoev-ski, "'Fathers and teachers,' I ponder, 'What is hell?' I maintain that it is the suffering of being unable to love'" (79). It is in this inscrip-tion that the inability to love is specifically articulated as the curse that visits Salinger's pilgrims. Later X is saved by a small package lying among the clutter of his desk, for the package represents a ges-ture of love which directly opposes the squalor of his world. In the package is an "extremely water-proof and shock-proof" watch which had belonged to Esmé's dead father, and which she now sends X as a lucky talisman. X sits for a long while with the watch in his hand, and "Then, suddenly, almost ecstatically, he felt sleepy. You take a really sleepy man, Esmé, and he *always* stands a chance of again becoming a man with all his fac—with all his f-a-c-u-l-t-i-e-s intact" (85). The story which X writes for Esmé is itself a gesture of love (similarly, Salinger wrote one of his most important stories, "Franny," as a wedding present for his wife). The love which saves Sergeant X comes from an innocent child, but the idea of love as man's salvation, unlike the suggestion of mysticism, is not rejected, and it finally be-comes developed into an absurd gesture which Salinger offers as the answer to an idol-less altar.

The absurd love gesture is chronicled in the two interrelated stories, "Franny" and "Zooey," which were originally published in *The New Yorker* and later combined and published as a book. Franny and Zooey are the youngest brother and sister of Seymour Glass, and part of the urban menagerie of sensitiveness and titanesque idiosyncrasy around which Salinger is constructing his contemporary saga. To understand how Franny and Zooey offer a resolution which Seymour and other mystically inclined heroes could not accomplish, it is necessary to know something of the relationships of this sprawling family.

There are seven Glass children—in order of birth, Seymour, Buddy, Boo Boo, the twins Walt and Waker, Zachary (Zooey), and Franny. Les and Bessie Glass, the parents, were once a famous vaudeville team (billed as "Gallagher and Glass") on the old Pantages and Orpheum circuits. Les is Jewish and Bessie Irish, and they are descended "from an astonishingly long and motley double file of professional entertainers." The public life of their parents has helped to give the Glass children an especially acute sense of the public world, and this sense is accented by the fact that all seven children began life as child prodigies on a radio quiz program called "It's a Wise Child." (Salinger is almost certainly aware of Telemachus' consciously cryptic reply to Athena when she questions him about Odysseus: "It's a wise child that knows its own father." This oblique reference to *The Odyssey* emphasizes the quest for identity on which each of the Glass children has at some point embarked.)

The story of Seymour Glass (1917–1948) is told directly through "A Perfect Day for Bananafish" and indirectly through "Raise High the Roof Beam, Carpenters," "Seymour: An Introduction," and "Zooey." Buddy Glass is a shy, sardonic creative-writing teacher who occasionally takes upon himself the task of narrating his family's spiritual history. In "Seymour: An Introduction" he emerges as a *persona* for Salinger himself. In spiritual training Buddy was closer to Seymour than any other member of the family, and while he hardly seems well adjusted, he is less clearly psychotic than Seymour. Boo Boo first appears in the Glass saga as Boo Boo Tannenbaum, the mother of Lionel, the sensitive child hero of "Down at the Dinghy." In this story Salinger suggested the brutality of the world in the specific guise of anti-Semitism. Lionel has isolated himself from the world because he has overheard the family cook refer to his father as a "kike." Even though Lionel believes that a kike is " 'One of those things that go up in the air' " (*NS*, 65), he is horrified that his father should be considered such an obscurely unnatural phenomenon. Boo Boo's involvement with Zen Buddhism does not seem significant, and she is perhaps more down-to-earth than any of the other children, preferring to be thought of as a "Tuckahoe homemaker." Our only other encounter with Boo Boo is through the Sapphic scrawl which she leaves on a bathroom mirror on the day of Seymour's wedding: " 'Raise high the roof beam, carpenters. Like Ares comes the bridegroom, taller far than a tall man. Love, Irving Sappho, formerly under contract to Elysium Studios Ltd. Please be happy happy *happy* with your beautiful Muriel. This is an order. I outrank everybody on this block' " (*RHRB*, 76).

Of Waker we know no more than the fact that he has presumably found peace through becoming a Roman Catholic priest. In "Zooey," however, we learn that his answer offers no promise to the other children in the family. Walt never directly enters any of the Glass stories, although he seems to have certain qualities in common with an earlier Salinger creation, Sergeant Babe Gladwaller, the hero of "The Last Day of the Furlough" and the friend of Vincent Caulfield, Holden's older brother. We do learn, however, that Walt was killed in the Army of Occupation in Japan following the explosion of a Japanese stove which he was packing for his commanding officer. Walt is a symbol of innocence and tenderness for the heroine of "Uncle Wiggily in Connecticut." When she thinks of the innocence she has lost, Eloise has an alcoholic vision of the sophisticated squalor of her life and a moment of visionary love with her escapist daughter, Ramona. Eloise, who was once engaged to Walt, feels she has been destroyed by the exurbanite world her husband Lew represents (and when she refers to his favorite author as the unheard-of L. Manning Vines, she identifies him as the company commander who grudgingly gave Buddy leave to attend Seymour's wedding in "Raise High the Roof Beam, Carpenters"). Through the innocent love of a child Eloise achieves a moment of salvation similar to that which Sergeant X achieved, and, while like his salvation, hers is temporary and unstable, it nonetheless suggests the future development of Salinger's love theme.

When Salinger first introduces Franny Glass, she is a twenty-year-old college girl and summer-stock actress; and her older brother Zooey, who guides her through a religious crisis to the absurd love stance, is a television actor in his late twenties who suffers from an ulcer and, like Holden Caulfield, from profound disgust with the world of shams in which he lives. It is Zooey who gives the final *coup de grâce* to the idea of mysticism as an answer to the absurd universe.

"Franny" opens on a brilliantly lit Yale-game Saturday with Lane Coutell, Franny's date for the weekend (and her sometime lover, as we later learn), waiting on a railroad-station platform. He is rereading a letter from Franny which creates for the reader the impression of a typical college girl enthusiastically if somewhat vaguely in love. She hopes there will be an opportunity for dancing, that the weekend will not involve tiresome receiving lines, and that her spelling is improving. When Franny steps from the train the picture given by her letter seems to be elaborately confirmed:

> Franny was among the first of the girls to get off the train, from a car at the far, northern end of the platform. Lane spotted her immediately, and despite whatever it was he was trying to do with his face, his arm that shot up into the air was the whole truth. Franny saw it, and him, and waved extravagantly back. She was wearing a sheared raccoon coat, and Lane, walking toward her quickly but with a slow face, reasoned to himself, with suppressed excitement, that he was the only one who really *knew* Franny's coat. He remembered that once, in a borrowed car, after kissing Franny for a half hour or so, he had kissed her coat lapel, as though it were a perfectly desirable, organic extension of the person herself. (*FZ*, 7–8)

Lane pilots his date to a fashionable French restaurant, and it is only there that we see Franny as another of the Glass family suffering from "banana fever." She has begun to retreat into a world of mysticism, but like Seymour, she realizes the importance of an answer which will permit her to live in the real world. Her efforts at presenting a typical girl-on-a-football-weekend appearance are part of a last stand in which she tries to face the public world. Lane Coutell, the slick, falsely sophisticated representative of that world, is reminiscent of Muriel Fedders and her mother, and of Eloise's husband Lew. Franny is obviously on the verge of a nervous breakdown after a sudden depressing vision of the insignificance of the world around her that is emphasized by Lane's chatter about an "A" paper on Flaubert that he has written for a professor who lacks " 'testicularity'." His chief interest in Franny rests in being seen with "an unimpeachably right-looking girl—a girl who was not only extraordinarily pretty but, so much the better, not too categorically cashmere sweater and flannel skirt" (11).

In the beginning of the story Lane's own "phoniness" only encourages Franny to try more earnestly to fulfill the role he has outlined for her, but it gradually becomes clear that Franny suffers from an acute and oversensitive weariness with all that is phony in the world. Her mind wanders, and her lack of interest in Lane's distinctly "publishable" paper angers him. When he challenges her disinterestedness, she apologizes but adds that he is " 'talking just like a section man'," and in her description of this Eastern-college phenomenon, Franny begins to outline her disillusionment.

When Lane interrupts her frenzied dissection of the junior faculty member Franny confesses not only that she has felt *"destructive"* all week, but that she had to strain to write the "natural" letter to him. Listening to Lane's description of the events of the weekend, Franny becomes progressively depressed and begins to ridicule Wally Campbell, the person giving the inevitable cocktail party. But Wally is only a symbol of Franny's disgust with those individuals who resign themselves to the phoniness of the world:

"I don't mean there's anything horrible about him or anything like that. It's just that for four solid years I've kept seeing Wally Campbells wherever I go . . . It's *everybody*, I mean. Everything everybody does is so—I don't know—not *wrong*, or even mean, or even stupid necessarily. But just so tiny and meaningless and—sad-making. And the worst part is, if you go bohemian or something crazy like that, you're conforming just as much as everybody else, only in a different way." (25–26)

Franny's description of her illness—or at least of one of its major manifestations—is reminiscent of Celia's description of her "perplexing" illness in T. S. Eliot's "The Cocktail Party":

> An awareness of solitude.
> But that sounds so flat. I don't mean simply
> That there's been a crash: though indeed there has been.
> It isn't simply the end of an illusion
> In the ordinary way, or being ditched.
> Of course that's something that's always happening
> To all sorts of people, and they get over it
> More or less, or at least they carry on.
> No. I mean that what has happened has made me aware
> That I've always been alone. That one always is alone.
> Not simply the ending of one relationship,
> Not even simply finding that it never existed—
> But a revelation about my relationship
> With *everybody*. Do you know—
> It no longer seems worth while to *speak* to anyone![2]

Indeed, one of the first details we learn about Franny in "Zooey" is that, following her weekend with Lane, she no longer wants to speak to anyone.

The only thing that Franny can think of worth concerning herself over is something which interests Lane only superficially—a small, pea-green book entitled *The Way of a Pilgrim*. The book has presumably been suggested to her by a professor, and she comes increasingly to see its message as her answer. When she almost loses control in the restaurant, she goes to the ladies' room and sits down with the book on her knees. "After a moment, she picked up the book, raised it chest-high, and pressed it to her—firmly, and quite briefly"

---

[2] T. S. Eliot, "The Cocktail Party," *The Complete Poems and Plays of T. S. Eliot*, pp. 359–360.

(*FZ*, 22). The book seems momentarily to restore her control. The book which Franny clutches so zealously describes the search of a Russian peasant for the meaning of the Biblical commandment to "pray incessantly." The peasant learns the solution from a "starets"— "'some sort of terribly advanced religious person'" (33), who tells him to repeat the "Jesus Prayer" ("Lord Jesus Christ, have mercy on me") so often that the prayer becomes an automatic response of his heart. When the peasant has perfected his mystical prayer he walks all over Russia teaching people how to pray "'by this incredible method'" (34). "'He says'," Franny adds, "'that any name of God—any name at all—has this peculiar, self-active power of its own, and it starts working after you've sort of started it up'" (37). As Franny's excited description of the book continues, Lane's comments become as irrelevant ("'I hate to mention it, but I'm going to reek of garlic'" [34]) as the comments with which Franny had interrupted his discussion of Flaubert. Franny makes a final effort to adjust to Lane's idea of the "unimpeachably right-looking girl," but as she rises to leave, she faints, and when she awakens she is lying in a back room of the restaurant. The final satiric touch to Lane's insensitivity is given when he wonders if Franny does not simply need to go to bed with him.

"Zooey" begins on the Monday morning following Franny's weekend date with Lane; she has taken refuge on the couch in the Glass living room, where she clutches *The Way of the Pilgrim* and strokes the family cat, Bloomberg. Only two other members of the family are in the apartment, but the spirits of all the other brilliant Glass children crowd around Franny, "like so many Banquo's ghosts," threatening first to destroy her but suddenly offering her salvation. Just as Salinger warned us in "De Daumier-Smith's Blue Period" that he was not describing genuine mysticism, so he warns us in "Zooey" that what is to follow is not a mystical story but a love story which will take the form of a home movie (which in its close-ups, its attention to quotidian detail, and its casualness, it does).

Pointing out that Nick Carraway in *The Great Gatsby* recognizes his cardinal virtue as honesty, the narrator says, "*Mine*, I think, is that I know the difference between a mystical story and a love story. I say that my current offering isn't a mystical story, or a religiously mystifying story, at all. I say it's a compound, or multiple, love story, pure and complicated" (49).

We are introduced to Zooey Glass at ten-thirty in the morning as he sits in "a very full bath" rereading a four-year-old letter from his brother Buddy. Among other things, the letter relates Buddy's arrival in Florida on the day following Seymour's suicide, but other than its value in filling in details in the ever-growing Glass legend, the letter from Buddy is important for the emphasis which it puts on the religious training which Franny and Zooey had received from their eldest brothers. Rather than urging the classics on the youngest children in the family, as they had urged them on the twins and Boo Boo, Buddy and Seymour decided to direct Franny and Zooey toward what is known in Zen as

"no-knowledge. Dr. Suzuki says somewhere that to be in a state of pure consciousness—*satori*—is to be with God before he said, Let there be light. Seymour and I thought that it might be a good thing to hold back this light from you and Franny (at least as far as we were able), and all the many lower, more fashionable lighting effects—the arts, sciences, classics, languages—till you were both able at least to conceive of a state of being where the mind knows the source of all light. We thought it would be wonderfully constructive to at least (that is, if our own 'limitations' got in the way) tell you as much as we knew about the men—the saints, the arhats, the bodhisattvas, the jivanmuktas—who knew something or everything about this state of being." (65)

The description of this training for a state of pure consciousness is reinforced by a Taoist tale which Buddy (as narrator) repeats at the beginning of "Raise High the Roof Beam, Carpenters." The story had been read to Franny when she was an infant, but she always maintained that she could remember Seymour's reading it. In this brief Taoist allegory, Chiu-fang Kao has recently been retained by his Duke as a horse buyer, and he returns with the news that he has found a superlative horse—a dun-colored mare. When the animal turns out to be a coal-black stallion, the Duke is displeased, but his former horse-buyer exclaims with satisfaction,

"Has he really got as far as that? . . . Ah, then, he is worth ten thousand of me put together. There is no comparison between us. What Kao keeps in view is the spiritual mechanism. In making sure of the essential, he forgets the homely details; intent on the inward qualities, he loses sight of the external. He sees what he wants to see, and not what he does not want to see. He looks at the things he ought to look at, and neglects those that need not be looked at. So clever a judge of horses is Kao, that he has it in him to judge something better than horses." (*RHRB*, 5)

Chiu-fang Kao had achieved the state of pure consciousness which Buddy and Seymour envisioned for Franny and Zooey, and which Teddy McArdle possessed. Teddy's proposals represented Salinger's first consideration of Zen-oriented education. Teddy believed that the first thing to be done with children was to bring them together "'and show them how to meditate'." His primary interest was in teaching children "'who they *are*, not just what their names are and things like that . . . I'd get them to empty out everything their parents and everybody ever told them. I mean even if their parents just told them an elephant's big, I'd make them empty *that* out. An elephant's big only when it's next to something else—a dog or a lady, for example'." If the children wanted to learn other "stuff"—colors, names, categories—"'they could do it, if they felt like it, later on when they were older. But I'd want them to *begin* with all the real ways of looking at things . . .'" (*NS*, 142–143). Teddy's death prevents him from implementing his scheme of education, but Franny and Zooey are the products of controlled, intelligent experiments aimed at making them buyers who can always distinguish a "superlative horse." Franny's crisis, like Zooey's cynicism, is a result of this training, and her final victory is a throwing off of the banana fever of Buddhism, which for all its beauty and hope, is not a solution for modern Western man.

Zooey's private reverie over Buddy's letter is broken by the entrance of his mother, and there follows a forty-seven–page dialogue in which we not only glimpse Zooey's cynicism (toward television, the theatre, writers, almost anyone who asks him to lunch), but also realize that beneath his cynical surface is a strong core of love. His bantering attitude toward Bessie is largely a "routine" which they have played so often that it is completely natural to them. Buddy does not understand this attitude, and in his letter had somewhat patronizingly requested, " 'Be kinder to Bessie, Zooey, when you can. I don't think I mean because she's our mother, but because she's weary' " (57). At times Zooey's conversation with his mother seems no better integrated than Franny's conversation with Lane, but his preoccupied manner is largely the result of his own efforts to maintain an undistorted spiritual perspective. Bessie accuses Zooey of demonstrating a family failing, an inability to be " 'any help when the chips are down' " (84). He scoffs at the idea of being asked to live Franny's life for her, and especially at the inevitable chicken broth Bessie offers as a cure-all. Bessie is right when she says " 'You can't live in the world with such strong likes and dislikes' " (99), but she does not realize that Zooey is coming to a realization about love which will not only teach him that chicken broth is sacred, but will permit him to help Franny. Buddy (who, symbolically, can never be reached in a crisis) offers no help with his mysticism; Waker, the Catholic priest, is out of the question because, as Zooey urges, " 'This thing with Franny is strictly non-sectarian' " (94); and Boo Boo is never considered.

Zooey makes the first important step toward relieving Franny's "fever" as well as his own when he realizes that *The Way of the Pilgrim* was not, as Franny told Lane, checked out of her school library, but was taken from the desk in Seymour and Buddy's old room. When he sees the pain which the mention of Seymour's name gives his mother, Zooey apologizes. "His apology had been genuine, and Mrs. Glass knew it, but evidently couldn't resist taking advantage of it, perhaps because of its rarity" (102), to compare him unfavorably with

Buddy. It is in his violent reaction to Bessie's reprimand that we first learn that Zooey is conscious of the sickness which he and Franny have inherited:

"Buddy, Buddy, *Buddy*," he said. "Seymour, Seymour, *Seymour*." He had turned toward his mother, whom the crash of the razor had startled and alarmed but not really frightened. "I'm so sick of their names I could cut my throat." His face was pale but very nearly expressionless. "This whole goddam house stinks of ghosts. I don't mind so much being haunted by a dead ghost, but I resent like *hell* being haunted by a half-dead one. I wish to *God* Buddy'd make up his mind. He does everything else Seymour ever did—or tries to. Why the hell doesn't he kill himself and be done with it?"

Mrs. Glass blinked her eyes, just once, and Zooey instantly looked away from her face. He bent over and fished his razor out of the wastebasket. "We're *freaks*, the two of us, Franny and I," he announced, standing up. "I'm a twenty-five-year-old freak and she's a twenty-year-old freak, and both those bastards are responsible . . . The symptoms are a little more delayed in Franny's case than mine, but she's a freak, too, and don't you forget it. I swear to you, I could murder them both without even batting an eyelash. The great teachers. The great emancipators. My God. I can't even sit down to lunch with a man any more and hold up my end of a decent conversation. I either get so bored or so goddam preachy that if the son-of-a-bitch had any sense, he'd break his chair over my head." (102–103)

When Zooey cites the fact that Franny's own symptoms are more "delayed" than his, we are able to see her revulsion and its crisis as a concentrated example of Zooey's own spiritual experience. Franny herself notes, after talking with Zooey from her couch-retreat, " 'We're not bothered by exactly the same things, but by the same kind of things, I think, and for the same reasons' " (143). In his efforts to bring Franny back into the world Zooey achieves final definition for his own struggle. Together they are able to scuttle out of the banana hole, achieving a victory important not only for its rejection of isolation but for its emphasis on participation in the world.

In arguing against Franny's withdrawal, Zooey emphasizes her misuse of the Jesus prayer, for instead of resisting a world whose emphasis is on piling up " 'money, property, culture, knowledge, and so on and so on' " (147), she is attempting to pile up another kind of treasure, less material, but just as negotiable. " 'Ninety per cent of all the world-hating saints in history,' " Zooey argues, " 'were just as ac*quis*itive and unattractive, basically, as the rest of us are' " (147–148). Because he was brought up on the same perfectionist principles, Zooey understands Franny's mystical retreat from the world and her hope for some kind of miracle that will provide salvation. Her insistence on a mystical salvation, however, is only another example of the way in which they have been " 'side-tracked. Always, always, always referring every goddam thing that happens back to our lousy little egos' " (151). Zooey does not oppose the Jesus prayer itself so much as "why and how and *where*" Franny is using it. Franny is not fulfilling any duty in life through the prayer but merely substituting it for her real duty. It is this fatal tendency to leave the realities of life behind which makes Franny and Zooey "freaks." " 'You don't face any facts. This same damned attitude of not facing facts is what got you into this messy state of mind in the first place, and it can't possibly get you out of it' " (168). If Christ has a real function, it is not to take man up in his arms and relieve him of all his duties and make all his "nasty *Weltschmerzen*" go away.

In her dedication to the Jesus prayer Franny has tried to make what Albert Camus regarded as the suicidal leap into faith. Franny's real crisis is not the result of the fact that she has reached an acute depth of despair, but that she is on the brink of becoming, like Seymour, a misfit who can never accept or be accepted by society. Franny is consequently in danger of joining the other Salinger heroes who refuse to come to terms with reality, confusing the life of isolation with the life of the spirit. Despite his disgust with stereotyped scripts and the "phonies" with whom he is so often cast, Zooey has fought to maintain a contact with reality. His realization of the danger of fleeing to the deceptive private world gives him an insight which the rest of the family lacks, and hence he is the only member to have forgiven Seymour his suicide because he is the only one who fully

understands it. So anxious is Zooey to maintain his contact with
reality—however painful it may be—that he is hesitant about the idea
of going to Paris to make a movie. Any movement away from the
specific world in which he has suffered seems distinctly suspect. To
Franny the idea of making a movie in Paris is exciting, but Zooey
counters her,

"It is not exciting. That's exactly the point. I'd enjoy doing it, yes. *God*, yes.
But I'd hate like hell to leave New York . . . I was *born* here. I went to
school here. I've been *run over* here—twice, and on the same damn *street*.
I have no business acting in Europe, for God's sake." (136)

After trying unsuccessfully to convince Franny that the Jesus
prayer offers her no answer, Zooey enters Seymour and Buddy's old
room. Picking up the phone still listed in Seymour's name, Zooey calls
his sister and, disguising his voice, pretends to be Buddy. This is not
the call from Seymour which Franny had said she wanted, but Buddy
is so much the dead man's spiritual counterpart that there is little
difference. Although Zooey's impersonation finally rings false, he has
captured Franny's attention, and she is more prepared to listen than
she was when he stretched out on the living room floor and lectured
her. The absurd vision which Zooey is finally able to impart to Franny is that everything in the world, no matter how base or corrupt, is
sacred. Salinger has continually reiterated the fact that "reality" has
presented both young people impressions of deceit, pettiness, and insensitivity. The intention to see the world as sacred is, therefore, in
total opposition to reality and a profound example of metaphysical
absurdity. Until she adopts this vision, Zooey argues, she will never
have the religious satisfaction she craves: "'You don't even have
enough sense to *drink* when somebody brings you a cup of consecrated chicken soup—which is the only kind of chicken soup Bessie
ever brings to anybody around this madhouse'" (194–195). Franny
begins to be persuaded when Zooey argues that

"The only thing you can do now, the only religious thing you can do, is *act*.
Act for God, if you want to—be God's actress, if you want to . . . One other

thing. And that's all. I promise you. But the thing is, you raved and bitched
. . . about the stupidity of audiences. The goddam 'unskilled laughter' coming from the fifth row. And that's right, that's right—God knows it's depressing. I'm not saying it isn't. But that's none of your business, really.
That's none of your business, Franny. An artist's only concern is to shoot
for some kind of perfection, and *on his own terms,* not anyone else's. You
have no right to think about those things. I swear to you. Not in any real
sense, anyway. You know what I mean?" (258)

Franny's realization—and now also Zooey's own—can come
through dedication to her art. Camus saw art as the most complete
and successful form of rebellion, since the artist reconstructs the
world according to his own plan (his concern "to shoot for some
kind of perfection"). "Art is the activity that exalts and denies simultaneously," and it therefore "should give us a final perspective on the
content of rebellion." While Camus agrees with Nietzsche's dictum
that " 'No artist tolerates reality'," he also argues that "no artist can
get along without reality."[3] A lack of toleration and an escape are two
different things; "art disputes reality, but does not hide from it."[4]
Nietzsche had argued that all forms of transcendence were slanders
against this world and against life, but Camus envisions a nonsuper-
natural but "living transcendence, of which beauty carries the promise, which can make this mortal and limited world preferable to and
more appealing than any other. Art thus leads us back to the origins
of rebellion to the extent that it tries to give its form to an elusive
value which the future perpetually promises, but of which the artist
has a presentiment and wishes to snatch from the grasp of history."[5]
Art is a paramount quixotic gesture by which man attempts to give
order (at least an order in the same sense of making statements about
individual experience or a state of being) to a disordered world. In
support of his arguments, Camus cites Van Gogh's complaint as "the
arrogant and desperate cry of all artists. 'I can very well, in life and

[3] Albert Camus, *The Rebel,* p. 253.
[4] *Ibid.,* p. 258.
[5] *Ibid.*

in painting, too, do without God. But I cannot, suffering as I do, do without something that is greater than I am, that is my life—the power to create'."[6]

Zooey has shown his tormented sister the absurd gesture which she can make, and suggests that in making it she will not only affirm her intention to find order and meaning in life, but also realize the goal of "The Wise Child," whose obligation it is both to know and be himself. Franny recognizes the validity of this gesture, but Zooey goes on to infuse her with the absurd belief that will give the gesture its final meaning. He recalls that when as a child he had rebelled against having to polish his shoes for the "moronic" audience and sponsors of "It's a Wise Child," Seymour had taken him aside and asked him to shine them for the Fat Lady. " 'He never did tell me who the Fat Lady was, but I shined my shoes for the Fat Lady every time I ever went on the air again . . . ' " (FZ, 199). Zooey always pictured Seymour's Fat Lady sitting on her porch listening to the radio, swatting flies, and dying of cancer. He then learns that Seymour had once told Franny to be funny for the Fat Lady, and the blaring radio and cancer were part of the fantasy Franny had created just as they were part of Zooey's. In the final moments of this "pure and complicated love story," Zooey explains the Fat Lady's identity:

"I don't care where an actor acts. It can be in summer stock, it can be over the radio, it can be over *tele*vision, it can be in a goddam Broadway theater, complete with the most fashionable, most well-fed, most sunburned looking audience you can imagine. But I'll tell you a terrible secret—Are you listening to me? *There isn't anyone out there who isn't Seymour's Fat Lady.* That includes your Professor Tupper, buddy. And all his goddam cousins by the dozens. There isn't anyone *any*where who isn't Seymour's Fat Lady. Don't you know that? Don't you know that goddam secret yet? And don't you know—*listen* to me now—*don't you know who that Fat Lady really is?* . . . Ah, buddy. Ah, buddy. It's Christ Himself. Christ Himself, buddy." (200)

[6] *Ibid.*, p. 257.

For a moment all Franny can do—"for joy, apparently"—is cradle the phone in her hands, but at the conclusion of the story she falls "into a deep, dreamless sleep" (201), like the sleep of Sergeant X in "For Esmé—with Love and Squalor." While neither mysticism nor religion in its traditional sense "provides an answer to the search of any of the members of the Glass family, a concern for mystic and religious experience provides a path to Zooey's and Franny's conception of perfect love . . . That conception includes, embraces, and goes beyond the ordinary conceptions of religion and morality (and in its humanness, stops short of mysticism) and can properly be called by no other name than the simple and profound name of love."[7] To love the mercenaries, the butchers, the deceivers, the phonies of the world with the idea that each of them is Christ is to assume a preponderantly absurd stance. Zooey's message is not to love man as Christ would have loved him, but to love man *as* Christ. There is no appeal to a final supernatural authority, no desire for mystical transcendence, no hope that a better world awaits man as a reward for his struggle. Zooey is at last able to convince Franny that, as Sherwood Anderson's Dr. Parcival stated, "everyone in the world is Christ and they are all crucified."

To act with morality and love in a universe in which God is dead (or, at least, in which historical preconceptions of God frequently seem invalid) is perhaps the most acute problem of our age. Salinger's intense consideration of that problem in large part accounts for the fact that, while he is one of the least prolific authors writing today, he is the most popular. The progression from early stories in which the misfit hero can find genuine love only in children to the later stories in which mysticism is rejected in favor of an absurd love stance is a progression whose scope is perhaps not fully measured in the stories which Salinger has written, but more specifically in the personal struggle he has undergone in arriving at this philosophical position. There is no question that the author loves Seymour, and it is

[7] Wakefield, "Salinger and the Search for Love," *New World Writing,* 14, 82.

with an uneasy feeling that the reader is compelled to reject this Christ-like man. Salinger began the Glass saga with Seymour's suicide, and since that time has been writing his way around and back to that day in 1945 in order to show where Seymour failed. Seymour is at least partly exonerated for making "freaks" of Franny and Zooey when we note that it was his death (and its admission of failure) which saved the youngest Glass children; in a metaphorical sense in no way foreign to Salinger's intention, Seymour (who could, in fact, *see more* than his contemporaries) died that Franny and Zooey might live, and it is in this sense of his almost ritualistic death, rather than in the deluding mysticism of his life, that one seizes on the essence of this character's saintliness. Through Seymour's death, Zooey learns that the Fat Lady, the eternal vulgarian, must not be passed over for any mystical discipline. As Ihab Hassan has observed, "Zooey's message constitutes high praise of life. It is the sound of humility, calling us to *this* world. The vulgarian and the outsider are reconciled, not in the momentary flash of a quixotic gesture, nor even in the exclusive heart of a mystical revelation, but in the constancy of love."[8] And in this light it can, no doubt, be safely conjectured that "the sound of one hand clapping" is precisely, triumphantly, the commonplace sound of the Fat Lady swatting flies.

[8] Ihab Hassan, *Radical Innocence: Studies in the Contemporary American Novel*, p. 283.

EPILOGUE

In articles, lectures, and interviews Saul Bellow has frequently attempted to assess and to defend the cultural relevance of the contemporary novel, which—like so many traditional aesthetic forms—seems repeatedly undermined by what he terms our "eschatological age," where the metaphysics of a mass society is common dinner-table talk and the fashions of alienation presuppose a world both shallow and centerless. When so many beliefs, attitudes, and attachments which once seemed impregnable now appear obsolete or merely irrelevant, it is only logical that the legitimacy of older art forms like the novel should also be questioned. The justification for yet "another" novel, Bellow concludes, is simply that someone has cared to turn his imagination to the world around him: ". . . this caring or believing or love alone matters. All the rest, obsolescence, historical views, manners, agreed views of the Universe, is simply nonsense and trash."[1] Bellow bases his plea for the modern novel on Simone Weil's statement that "To believe in the existence of human beings as such

[1] Saul Bellow, "Distractions of a Fiction Writer," in *The Living Novel*, ed. Granville Hicks, p. 20.

is love," and for Bellow the serious, significant novelist is always one whose aim is to express a belief in the existence of human beings *as such*, for this manifestation of concern and involvement can never be superfluous. The novelist's greatest challenge, however, comes in presenting this concern in such a manner that it establishes relevance without recourse to the distortions of romanticism or nihilism; for Bellow as (more tentatively) for Camus, the anti-novel embodies a fundamental aesthetic contradiction.

In light of the absurd hero as he has been seen in this study, Bellow's emphasis on the manifestation of love is of particular significance, for that hero's great concern has been either with learning how to love or with finding an environment in which love can be constructively expressed. Rabbit Angstrom, Cass Kinsolving, Augie March, Henderson, and Franny and Zooey Glass all embark on love quests. Like the saint, Rabbit desires to love one thing absolutely. Cass Kinsolving learns through his fall the significance of other human beings, and through a new humility and love for mankind he becomes a social reformer. In suddenly realizing his own inadequacies in ministering to his diseased friend Michele, Cass concluded that "Hell is not giving"; that conclusion is a close parallel, if not simply a paraphrase, of Sergeant X's hasty scrawl on the flyleaf of Goebbels' *Die Zeit Ohne Beispiel*: "Fathers and teachers, I ponder 'What is hell?' I maintain that it is the suffering of being unable to love." When Bellow's Henderson turns his attention to an implementation of the absurd vision, he decides first of all to "set love on a true course"; and Herzog's ultimate spiritual ease owes a major debt to Ramona's frank and uncomplicated love. The most intense statement of the humanizing love theme comes, of course, in Zooey's final, lyrical message to Franny.

These heroes all begin their quests with a vision of the apparent lack of meaning in the world, of the mendacity and failure of ideals, but they conclude with gestures of affirmation derived explicity from their realization of the significance of love. Albert Maquet has argued that, placed in the context of the absurd world as Camus envisioned it, man is in a position "to edify, without God, a humanism of high nobility."[2] The love stance edifies because it reaffirms a belief in human beings *as such*, and it is this belief which promises to generate values to replace those which are lost as the traditional sacred society disappears. Such belief goes beyond the absurd, but it is important to remember that Camus considered the myth of the absurd as descriptive, not conclusive or programmatic, a provisional statement which was not intended to exclude a value system which might eventually transcend the absurd sensitivity.

Salinger's Teddy McArdle lamented the fact that "it's very hard to meditate and live a spiritual life in America," and the efforts of absurd heroes to achieve any recognizable degree of spiritual fulfillment are frequently painful and chaotic. As the absurd man's desire for unity and meaning increases, so too does his consciousness of the walls which enclose and trap him, but his struggle sheds light on what Camus called "the step taken by the mind when, starting from a philosophy of the world's lack of meaning, it ends by finding a meaning and depth in it."[3] The four writers discussed here share with Camus the paradoxical belief that, while the role of the individual undergoes ruthless diminishment in the modern world, only individual will and responsibility, only the sincere private gesture, can redeem the general existence and make it tenable.

Updike, Styron, Bellow, and Salinger suggest a patterning of attitudes and tensions fundamental to any discussion of the nature of the contemporary hero. Their initial response is to distrust conventional values and orthodox systems, and this profound skepticism in large part accounts for the irony which so frequently characterizes their work. That this irony is not a reflection of nihilism is indicated by the fact that each author has envisioned his most compelling hero as a sympathetic "knight" in search of order and value. Camus's absurd man, too, is involved in a quest, although he is a knight without God. In beginning with such a *tabula rasa*, Camus's knight sets a course which his counterparts in the American novel do not, of course, fol-

---

[2] Albert Maquet, *Albert Camus: The Invincible Summer,* p. 109.
[3] Albert Camus, *The Myth of Sisyphus,* p. 31.

low with exact precision. In the work of Salinger, for example, the spiritual quest takes a more familiar form, one which at least acknowledges the possibility of Christ as a representative of absolute values. To attempt to reconcile this tendency in Salinger's writing by reference to Camus's statement that "It is possible to be Christian and absurd,"[4] is merely to take advantage of the frequently ubiquitous treatment of absurdity in Camus's work; for it is impossible to be both absurd and Christian in any conventional sense. The failure of recourse to spiritual absolutes is strongly emphasized in Salinger's work, but their failure as values is not total. Similarly, Henderson's appeal to the "Something because of whom there is not Nothing" is one of Bellow's most memorable passages.

Such distinctions and divergences must be kept in mind if the reader is to avoid that *lèse majesté* by which critical formulation becomes academic dogma. While the myth of the absurd may serve as a useful critical tool in the study of many contemporary novels, it is as unwise to demand rigidity from such criticism as it is to demand of Camus's meditations the logic and consistency of a finalized philosophical system. Camus's investigation of the absurd is itself impressionistic and often lyrical, and as his own diverse fiction amply illustrates, even less finality can be demanded of the work of imagination which explores the dimensions of the absurd experience. Like the absurd hero himself, absurd fiction must have sufficient substance to stand apart from the myths and metaphysics which help to give it definition. The absurd sensitivity does not account for the artistic accomplishments of the authors considered here; but hopefully it does help to clarify their vision, to isolate the attitudes which ultimately shape their view of the life-enhancing alternatives which man may adopt when confronted by the dark, fragmented, absurd night of despair which colors so much of the modern imagination.

[4] *Ibid.*, p. 83.

WORKS CITED

(with abbreviations used in parenthetical textual notes)

Bellow, Saul. *The Adventures of Augie March*. New York: Viking Press, 1953. *AAM*

——. *Dangling Man*. New York: Vanguard Press, 1944. *DM*

——. "Deep Readers of the World, Beware!" *New York Times Book Review* (February 15, 1959), 1, 34.

——. "Distractions of a Fiction Writer," in *The Living Novel*, ed. Granville Hicks (New York: The Macmillan Company, 1957), 1–20.

——. *Henderson the Rain King*. New York: Viking Press, 1959. *HRK*

——. *Herzog*. New York: Viking Press, 1964. *H*

——. *Seize the Day*. New York: Viking Press, 1956. *SD*

——. *The Victim*. New York: Viking Press, 1956. *V*

Boroff, David. "Saul Bellow," *Saturday Review*, 47 (September 19, 1964), 38–39.

Brée, Germaine. *Camus*. New Brunswick: Rutgers University Press, 1959.

Camus, Albert. *The Myth of Sisyphus*, trans. Justin O'Brien. New York: Vintage Books, 1959.

——. *The Rebel*, trans. Anthony Bower. New York: Vintage Books, 1960.

Chase, Richard. "The Adventures of Saul Bellow: Progress of a Novelist," *Commentary*, 27 (April, 1959), 323–330.

Cruickshank, John. *Albert Camus and the Literature of Revolt*. New York: Galaxy Books, 1960.

Eliot, T. S. "The Cocktail Party," in *The Compete Poems and Plays of T. S. Eliot* (New York: Harcourt, Brace, and Co , 1950), 295–387.

Fiedler, Leslie. "No! In Thunder," *Esquire*, 44 (September, 1960), 79–82.

176 THE ABSURD HERO

Frye, Northrop. *Anatomy of Criticism*. Princeton: Princeton University Press, 1957.

Galloway, David D. "Absurd Art, Absurd Men, Absurd Heroes," in *The Literature of the Western World*, vol. VI, ed. David Daiches and A. J. Thorlby (London: Aldus Books, 1970).

Geismar, Maxwell. *American Moderns: From Rebellion to Conformity*. New York: Hill and Wang, 1958.

——. "The Postwar Generation in American Arts and Letters," *Saturday Review*, 36 (March 15, 1953), 11–12, 60.

Glicksberg, Charles A. "Camus's Quest for God," *Southwest Review*, 44 (Summer, 1959), 240–252.

Hassan, Ihab. "Saul Bellow: Five Faces of a Hero," *Critique*, 3 (September, 1960), 28–36.

Joyce, James. *Ulysses*. London: The Bodley Head, 1937.

Lehan, Richard. "Existentialism in Recent American Fiction: The Demonic Quest," *Texas Studies in Literature and Language*, I (Summer, 1959), 181–202.

Levine, Paul. "Saul Bellow: The Affirmation of the Philosophical Fool," *Perspective*, 10 (Winter, 1959), 163–176.

Lewis, R. W. B. *The Picaresque Saint*. Philadelphia: J. P. Lippincott, 1959.

Maquet, Albert. *Albert Camus: The Invincible Summer*, trans. Herma Briffault. New York: George Braziller, 1958.

Matthiessen, Peter, and George Plimpton. "William Styron," in *Writers at Work: The Paris Review Interviews*, ed. and with an introduction by Malcolm Cowley (New York: Viking Press, 1958), 268–282.

Salinger, J. D. *The Catcher in the Rye*. New York: The Modern Library, 1951. *CR*

——. *Franny and Zooey*. Boston: Little, Brown and Co., 1961. *FZ*

——. *Nine Stories*. New York: The New American Library, 1954. *NS*

——. *"Raise High the Roof Beam, Carpenters," and "Seymour: An Introduction."* Boston: Little, Brown and Co., 1963. *RHRB*

Sartre, Jean Paul. "Réponse à Albert Camus," *Les Temps Modernes* (August, 1952), 345.

Styron, William. *The Confessions of Nat Turner*. New York: Random House, 1967.

———. *Lie Down in Darkness*. Indianapolis: Bobbs-Merrill, 1951. *LDD*

———. "The Long March," in *Best Short Stories of World War II*, ed. Charles A. Fenton (New York: Viking Press, 1957). *LM*

———. "The Prevalence of Wonders," *Nation*, 176 (May 2, 1953), 370–371.

——— *Set This House on Fire*. New York: Random House, 1959. *STHF*

Tanner, Tony. "Saul Bellow: The Flight from Monologue," *Encounter*, 24 (February, 1965), 58–70.

Thelwell, Mike. "Back with the Wind: Mr. Styron and the Reverend Turner," in *William Styron's Nat Turner: Ten Black Writers Respond*, ed. John Henrik Clarke. (Boston: Beacon Press, 1968).

Tindall, William York. *A Reader's Guide to James Joyce*. London: Thames and Hudson, 1959.

Updike, John. *The Carpentered Hen and Other Tame Creatures*. New York: Harper and Bros., 1954. *CH*

———. *The Centaur*. New York: Alfred A. Knopf, 1963. *C*

———. *Couples*. New York: Alfred A. Knopf, 1968.

———. *Pigeon Feathers*. New York: Alfred A. Knopf, 1962. *PFe*

———. *The Poorhouse Fair*. New York: Alfred A. Knopf, 1959. *PFa*

———. *Rabbit, Run*. New York: Alfred A. Knopf, 1960. *RR*

———. "Reflection," *The New Yorker*, 33 (November 30, 1957), 216.

———. *The Same Door*. New York: Alfred A. Knopf, 1959. *SD*

———. "The Sea's Green Sameness," *New World Writing*, No. 17 (1960), 54–59.

Young, James Dean. "Bellow's View of the Heart," *Critique*, 7 (Spring, 1965), 5–17.

APPENDIX: FOUR CONTEMPORARY CHECKLISTS

FOUR CONTEMPORARY CHECKLISTS

Anyone who has attempted to prepare a checklist for a contemporary writer is no doubt aware that a high degree of serendipity is as significant a prerequisite as patience or meticulousness. It is unfortunate that no annual indexes give more than rudimentary coverage to the increasing number of articles on contemporary American literature printed in languages other than English. More difficult to comprehend is the incompleteness of the traditional journals which are primarily concerned with indexing English-language articles, though the proliferation of new and often short-lived little magazines and journals must endlessly complicate the task of even the most professional bibliographer.

The following checklists are offered for the convenience of readers who may wish to explore in more detail the work of the four writers who are the subject of this book. I should point out, however, that I have not been concerned to list translations of the authors' work, editions beyond the first, photographs, simple news items, or brief references in books and articles not concerned in significant part with one of the authors treated here. I have, on the other hand, endeavored to list all primary sources (novels, collections, short stories, articles, reviews, poetry, published letters)—however brief; all available English-language reviews; and all critical articles and books making important reference to any of the four writers.

Each checklist has been treated independently, so that an article or book referring to more than one of the four authors is listed separately under each relevant heading. Some omissions are inevitable, but within the stated limits I have worked for as much completeness as the annual indexes permitted and as serendipity and eagle-eyed graduate students and friends were able to provide.

In preparing the Bellow and Styron checklists I made use of the two bibliographies prepared by Harold W. Schneider for the Summer, 1960, issue of *Critique*. I have made some additions and corrections for the period covered by Mr. Schneider's bibliographies, but my chief contribution has been in bringing his work up to date. I have also had technical assistance from Mrs. Beverly Logan, who is currently preparing a thesis on Styron's critical reputation. My own original Salinger checklist was considerably amplified by Donald M. Fiene's impressive bibliography in *Wisconsin Studies in Contemporary Literature* (Winter, 1963); at the time of publication, his bibliography (printed in slightly abridged form) contained more than 2,000 entries, including foreign-language reviews and news items not cited in my bibliography. As with Mr. Schneider's bibliographical work, my chief contribution has consisted in attempting to bring the list up to date.

As yet only Salinger has prompted book-length critical work, although books are currently in preparation on Bellow, Styron, and Updike as well. Thus, like most conventional techniques, a division of secondary sources into books and articles was irrelevant, and yet the quantity of criticism has encouraged something more than simple alphabetical arrangement. Hence, both primary and secondary sources are divided on a chronological basis, with entries for each year arranged alphabetically; reviews immediately follow the books to which they have reference. The chronological division incidentally offers a kind of history of each author's work and of his critical reception, and even the casual reader may be interested to note the increasing amount of critical attention which Updike, Styron, Bellow, and Salinger have received.

In the interest of economy the names of publishers have been cited in as brief a form as possible (e.g., *Atlantic* for *The Atlantic Monthly*), and to the same end, the following abbreviations have been used throughout:

MFS	*Modern Fiction Studies*
NY	*The New Yorker*
NYHTBR	*The New York Herald Tribune Book Review* (now *Book Week*)
NYRB	*The New York Review of Books*
NYT	*The New York Times* (weekly edition)
NYTBR	*The New York Times Book Review*
REL	*Review of English Literature*
SRL	*The Saturday Review of Literature*
TLS	*Times Literary Supplement (London)*
TSLL	*Texas Studies in Literature and Language*
WHR	*Western Humanities Review*
WSCL	*Wisconsin Studies in Contemporary Literature*

NOTE TO THE REVISED EDITION

So many readers have commented on the usefulness of the following checklists that I have brought them up to date. In the interest of economy, however, I have had to refrain from including the occasional items published prior to 1965 that did not appear in the original checklists and to revise only in terms of items published since 1965. Miss Marie Oemler and Miss Susan Tom were of invaluable assistance to me in locating new entries.

A JOHN UPDIKE CHECKLIST

I. PRIMARY SOURCES

A. Books

The Carpentered Hen and Other Tame Creatures. New York: Harper and Brothers, 1958.
   Reviews:
      Booklist, 54 (April 15, 1958), 470.
      Bookmark, 17 (April, 1958), 169.
      Dorn, N. K. San Francisco *Chronicle* (November 23, 1958), 13.
      Kirkus, 26 (January 15, 1958), 59.
      McCord, David. *SRL,* 41 (August 9, 1958), 32.
      McDonald, G. D. *Library Journal,* 83 (June 15, 1958), 1938.

The Poorhouse Fair. New York: Alfred A. Knopf, 1959.
   Reviews:
      Adams, Phoebe. *Atlantic,* 203 (February, 1959), 100.
      Balliett, Whitney. *NY,* 34 (February 7, 1959), 138.
      Barr, Donald. *NYTBR* (January 11, 1959), 4.
      Buchanan, Leigh M. *Epoch,* 9 (Spring, 1959), 252–254.
      Butcher, Fanny. Chicago *Sunday Tribune* (January 11, 1959), 4.
      Chase, M. E. *NYHTBR* (January 11, 1959), 3.
      Coleman, John. *Spectator* (March 13, 1959), 58.
      Gilman, Richard. *Commonweal,* 69 (February 6, 1959), 499–500.
      Hicks, Granville. *SRL,* 42 (January 17, 1959), 58.
      Hughes, Riley. *Catholic World,* 189 (May, 1959), 162.
      Johnson, J. H. *New Statesman,* 57 (March 28, 1959), 453.
      Kirkus, 26 (November 1, 1958), 830.
      Murchland, B. G. *Commonweal,* 69 (February 27, 1959), 581.
      Price, Martin. *Yale Review,* 48 (March, 1959), 464.
      Salmon, Peter. *New Republic,* 140 (January 12, 1959), 20.
      Serebnick, Judith. *Library Journal,* 84 (January 1, 1959), 123.
      Time, 73 (January 19, 1959), 92.
      TLS (March 20, 1959), 157.

The Same Door. New York: Alfred A. Knopf, 1959.
   Reviews:
      Cassidy, T. E. *Commonweal,* 70 (September 11, 1959), 499.

Christian Science Monitor (August 20, 1959), 7.
Crane, Milton. Chicago *Sunday Tribune* (August 16, 1959), 3.
Flory, Claude R. *English Journal*, 44 (February, 1960), 143.
Healey, R. C. *NYHTBR* (August 16, 1959), 3.
Keown, Eric. *Punch*, 242 (May 2, 1962), 697.
Lodge, David. *TLS* (June 21, 1962), 10.
Mayne, Richard. *New Statesman*, 63 (April 27, 1962), 607.
Peden, William. *NYTBR* (August 16, 1959), 5.
Serebnick, Judith. *Library Journal*, 84 (August, 1959), 2376.
Spectorsky, A. C. *SRL*, 42 (August 22, 1959), 15.
Time, 74 (August 17, 1959), 90.
TLS, (April 27, 1962), 277.
Tindall, Gillian. *Time and Tide*, 43 (April 26, 1962), 30.

Rabbit, Run. New York: Alfred A. Knopf, 1960.
  Reviews:
    Balliett, Whitney. *NY*, 36 (November 5, 1960), 222–224.
    Booklist, 57 (November 15, 1960), 180.
    Boroff, David. *NYTBR* (November 6, 1960), 4, 43.
    Crane, Milton. Chicago *Sunday Tribune* (November 13, 1960), 6.
    Edelstein, J. M. *New Republic*, 142 (November 21, 1960), 17.
    Galloway, David D. *Night Watch*, 1 (May, 1961), 20.
    Gilman, Richard. *Commonweal*, 73 (October 28, 1960), 128–129.
    Gorn, Lester H. San Francisco *Chronicle* (November 20, 1960), 28.
    Hicks, Granville. *SRL*, 43 (November 5, 1960), 28.
    Hutchins, John K. *NYHTBR* (November 6, 1960), 7.
    Miller, Nolan. *Antioch Review*, 21 (Spring, 1961), 118.
    Rugoff, Milton. *NYHTBR* (November 6, 1960), 7.
    Serebnick, Judith. *Library Journal*, 85 (November 1, 1960), 4009.
    Southern, Terry. *Nation*, 191 (November 19, 1960), 380.
    Time, 76 (November 7, 1960), 108.

The Magic Flute by Wolfgang Amadeus Mozart. John Updike and Warren
Chappell (adaptors and illustrators). New York: Alfred A. Knopf, 1962.
  Reviews:
    Graves, E. M. *Commonweal*, 77 (November 16, 1962), 214.
    Lask, Thomas. *NYTBR* (November 11, 1962), 62.
    Library Journal, 87 (October 15, 1962), 3896.
    SRL, 45 (December 15, 1962), 28.

Pigeon Feathers. New York: Alfred A. Knopf, 1962.
  Reviews:
    Booklist, 58 (April 1, 1962), 522.
    Chase, Mary Ellen. *NYHTBR* (March 18, 1962), 4.
    Chester, Alfred. *Commentary,* 39 (July, 1962), 77–80.
    Cook, B. A. *Commonweal,* 76 (May 11, 1962), 184.
    Crane, Milton. Chicago *Sunday Tribune* (April 1, 1962), 4.
    Didion, Joan. *National Review,* 12 (June 19, 1962), 419.
    Edelstein, J. M. *New Republic,* 146 (May 14, 1962), 30.
    Hicks, Granville. *SRL,* 45 (March 17, 1962), 21.
    Hogan, William. San Francisco *Chronicle* (March 22, 1962), 39.
    Kirkus, 30 (January 15, 1962), 71.
    Maddocks, Melvin. *Christian Science Monitor* (March 22, 1962), 11.
    Mizener, Arthur. *NYTBR* (March 18, 1962), 1, 29.
    Morse, J. Mitchell. *Hudson Review,* 15 (Summer, 1962), 302.
    Newsweek, 59 (March 19, 1962), 120.
    Novak, Michael. *Commonweal,* 77 (February 22, 1963), 577.
    Poore, Charles. *NYTBR* (March 24, 1962), 23.
    Rowland, Stanley J. *Christian Century,* 79 (July 4, 1962), 840–841.
    Serebnick, Judith. *Library Journal,* 87 (February 15, 1962), 786.
    Slavitt, D. R. *Book-of-the-Month-Club News* (April, 1962), 15.
    Time, 79 (March 16, 1962), 86.
    Wisconsin Library Bulletin (July, 1962), 240.

The Centaur, New York: Alfred A. Knopf, 1963.
  Reviews:
    Adams, Phoebe. *Atlantic,* 211 (February, 1963), 134–135.
    Adler, Renata. *NY,* 39 (April 13, 1963), 182, 184–188.
    Buitenhuis, Peter. *NYTBR* (April 7, 1963), 4, 26.
    Cook, Eleanor. *Canadian Forum,* 43 (August, 1963), 113.
    Curley, Thomas. *Commonweal,* 78 (March 29, 1963), 26–27.
    Davenport, Guy. *National Review,* 66 (September 27, 1963), 406.
    Gardiner, H. C. *America,* 108 (March 9, 1963), 340–341.
    Gilman, Richard. *New Republic,* 148 (April 13, 1963), 25–27.
    Grauel, G. E. *Best Sellers,* 22 (February 15, 1963), 423.
    Hicks, Granville. *SRL,* 46 (February 2, 1963), 27.
    Hill, W. B. *America,* 108 (May 11, 1963), 678–679.
    Kluger, Richard. *NYHTBR* (April 7, 1963), 8.
    Lacourse, Guerin. *Commonweal,* 77 (February 8, 1963), 512–514.
    Murray, J. G. *Critic,* 21 (February, 1963), 72.
    Newsweek, 61 (February 11, 1963), 91–92.

Nordell, Roderick. *Christian Science Monitor* (February 7, 1963), 7.
Pickrel, Paul. *Harper's,* 226 (April, 1963), 92–93.
Podhoretz, Norman. *Show,* 3 (April, 1963), 49–50, 52. Reprinted in
  Norman Podhoretz, *Doings and Undoings* (New York: Farrar,
  Straus, and Giroux, 1964), pp. 251–257.
Price, Martin. *Yale Review,* 52 (June, 1963), 601.
Roberts, Preston. *Christian Century,* 80 (April 10, 1963), 463–464.
Serebnick, Judith. *Library Journal* (January 15, 1963), 238.
Steiner, George. *Reporter,* 28 (March 14, 1963), 52–54.
Stern, Richard G. *Spectator,* 211 (September 27, 1963), 389.
Taubman, Robert. *New Statesman,* 66 (September 27, 1963), 406.
Time, 81 (February 8, 1963), 86–87.
TLS (September 27, 1963), 728.
Virginia Quarterly Review, 39 (Spring, 1963), xlviii.

Telephone Poles and Other Poems. New York: Alfred A. Knopf, 1963.
  Reviews:
    Burns, R. K. *Library Journal,* 88 (October 1, 1963), 3628.
    Kennedy, X. J. *NYTBR* (September 22, 1963), 10.
    Simpson, Louis. *Book Week* (October 27, 1963), 10.
    Spector, R. D. *SRL,* 47 (February 1, 1964), 37.
    Time, 82 (November 1, 1963), 112.

The Ring, by Richard Wagner. John Updike and Warren Chappell (adaptors and illustrators). New York: Alfred A. Knopf, 1964.
  Reviews:
    Christian Science Monitor (November 5, 1964), 8.
    Dagliesh, Alice. *SRL,* 47 (November 7, 1964), 52.
    Lask, Thomas. *NYTBR* (November 1, 1964), 63.
    Morse, J. C. *Horn Book,* 41 (February, 1965), 71.
    Sheehan, Ethna. *America,* 111 (November 21, 1964), 671.

Assorted Prose. New York: Alfred A. Knopf, 1965. (This collection contains a number of incidental pieces originally published anonymously, and not listed elsewhere in this checklist.)
  Reviews:
    Binns, F. W. *Library Journal,* 90 (May 15, 1965), 2264.
    Booklist, 61 (June 15, 1965), 982.
    Coleman, J. *Observer* (January 30, 1966), 27.
    Davis, D. M. *National Observer,* 4 (June 21, 1965), 19.
    Fremont-Smith, Eliot. *NYT* (June 23, 1965), 43M.

Galloway, David. *Spectator* (February 4, 1966), 142.
Hicks, Granville. *SRL*, 48 (May 15, 1965), 25–26.
Kay, J. H. *Christian Science Monitor* (June 26, 1965), 9.
Kirkus, 33 (March 15, 1965), 353.
Mayne, Richard. *New Statesman*, 71 (February 4, 1966), 169.
Moraes, Dom. *Listener*, 75 (February 3, 1966), 180.
Morgan, Thomas B. *NYTBR* (June 13, 1965), 10.
Nettell, S. *Books and Bookmen*, 11 (April, 1966), 30.
Newsweek, 65 (May 17, 1965), 107.
Petersen, C. *Books Today* (May 7, 1965), 9.
SRL, 50 (January 21, 1967), 40.
Time, 85 (May 21, 1965), 113.
TLS (February 17, 1966), 124.

A Child's Calendar: A Poem for Each Month. New York: Alfred A. Knopf, 1965.
Reviews:
Bulletin of the Center for Children's Books, 19 (February, 1966), 107.
Christian Science Monitor (November 4, 1965), 2B.
Dickey, James. *NYTBR* (November 7, 1965), 6.
Eaton, A. T. *Commonweal*, 83 (November 5, 1965), 157.
Haviland, Virginia. *Horn Book*, 42 (February, 1966), 64.
Kirkus, 33 (October 1, 1965), 1038.
Library Journal, 91 (February 15, 1966), 1058.
Lurie, Allison. *NYRB* 5 (December 9, 1965), 39.
Maxwell, Emily. *NY*, 41 (December 4, 1965), 232.
Pryce-Jones, A. *Book Week* (October 31, 1965), 7.
SRL, 49 (January 22, 1966), 45.

Of the Farm. New York: Alfred A. Knopf, 1965.
Reviews:
Aldridge, J. W. *Book Week* (November 21, 1965), 5.
Berolzheimer, H. F. *Library Journal*, 90 (December 1, 1965), 5303.
Best Sellers, 25 (February 1, 1966), 420.
Booklist, 62 (December 1, 1965), 355.
Buitenhuis, Peter. *NYTBR* (November 14, 1965), 4.
Burgess, Eve. *Punch*, 250 (April 13, 1966), 556.
Casey, Florence. *Christian Science Monitor* (November 18, 1965), 15.
Choice: Books for College Libraries, 2 (February, 1966), 862.
Cook, Roderick. *Harper's*, 232 (January, 1966), 100.
Davenport, John. *Spectator* (April 29, 1966), 537.

Davis, D. M. *National Observer*, 4 (November 22, 1965), 24.

Enright, D. J. *Holiday*, 38 (November, 1965), 162. Reprinted in D. J. Enright, *Conspirators and Poets* (Chester Springs, Pennsylvania: Dufour, 1966), 134–140.

Epstein, Joseph. *New Republic*, 153 (December 11, 1965), 23–25.

Fleischer, Leonore. *Publisher's Weekly*, 190 (November 21, 1966), 77.

Hicks, Granville. *SRL*, 48 (November 13, 1965), 41–42.

Kirkus, 33 (September 1, 1965), 937.

Klein, Marcus. *Reporter*, 33 (December 16, 1965), 54.

Kort, Wesley. *Christian Century*, 83 (January 19, 1966), 82.

Lindroth, J. R. *America*, 113 (November 27, 1965), 692.

L'Heureux, John. *Critic*, 24 (December, 1965–January, 1966), 64.

Nettell, S. *Books and Bookmen*, 11 (June, 1966), 39.

Newsweek, 66 (November 15, 1965), 129.

Nightingale, B. *Manchester Guardian*, 94 (April 28, 1966), 11.

Petersen, C. *Books Today* (January 29, 1967), 11.

Poore, Charles. *NYT* (November 20, 1965), 37.

Sale, Roger. *Hudson Review*, 19 (Spring, 1966), 124.

Sams, H. W. *Journal of General Education*, 18 (July, 1966), 146.

Samuels, C. T. *Kenyon Review*, 28 (March, 1966), 268.

Sullivan, Walter. *Sewanee Review*, 74 (Summer, 1966), 709.

Taubman, Robert. *New Statesman*, 72 (August 12, 1966), 233.

Time, 86 (November 12, 1965), 118.

TLS (April 14, 1966), 321.

Virginia Quarterly Review, 42 (Winter, 1966), ix.

Wardle, Irving. *Observer* (April 17, 1966), 27.

Weeks, Edward. *Atlantic*, 216 (December, 1965), 138.

The Music School. New York: Alfred A. Knopf, 1966.

Reviews:

Adams, R. M. *NYTBR* (September 18, 1966), 4.

Bergonzi, Bernard. *NYRB* (February 9, 1967), 28–30.

Booklist, 63 (October 15, 1966), 238.

Bradbury, Malcolm. *Manchester Guardian*, 96 (June 29, 1967), 10.

Braybrooke, Neville. *Spectator* (June 23, 1967), 744.

Casey, Florence. *Christian Science Monitor* (September 22, 1966), 11.

Choice: Books for College Libraries, 3 (February, 1967), 1130.

Cook, Roderick. *Harper's*, 233 (September, 1966), 113.

Critic, 25 (October, 1966), 116.

Gray, Simon. *New Statesman,* 71 (June 16, 1967), 840.
Haworth. *Listener,* 77 (June 29, 1967), 861.
Hicks, Granville. *SRL,* 49 (September 24, 1966), 31.
Hill, W. B. *America,* 116 (May 6, 1967), 702.
Jacobsen, Josephine. *Commonweal,* 85 (December 9, 1966), 299.
Kauffman, Stanley. *New Republic,* 155 (September 24, 1966), 15–17.
Kirkus, 34 (July 15, 1966), 708.
Kitching, Jessie. *Publisher's Weekly,* 190 (July 11, 1966), 227.
Light, C. M. *Best Sellers,* 26 (October 1, 1966), 240.
Macauley, Robie. *Book Week* (September 25, 1966), 4.
McNamara, Eugene. *America,* 115 (October 15, 1966), 462.
Meinke, Peter. *Christian Century,* 83 (December 7, 1966), 1512.
Minerof, Arthur. *Library Journal,* 91 (September 15, 1966), 4137.
Morse, J. M. *Hudson Review,* 19 (Winter, 1966–1967), 673.
Newman, C. *Books Today* (September 11, 1966), 8.
Newsweek, 68 (September 26, 1966), 116.
Price, R. G. *Punch,* 252 (June 21, 1967), 924.
Publisher's Weekly, 192 (October 16, 1967), 59.
Samuels, C. T. *Nation,* 203 (October 3, 1967), 328.
Time, 88 (September 23, 1966), 105.
TLS (August 24, 1967), 757.
Wardle, Irving. *Observer* (August 6, 1967), 16.
Weeks, Edward. *Atlantic,* 218 (November, 1966), 154.

Couples. New York: Alfred A. Knopf, 1968.
Reviews:
Archer, W. H. *Best Sellers,* 28 (April 15, 1968), 32.
Booklist, 64 (June 1, 1968), 1129.
Broyard, Anatole. *New Republic,* 158 (May 4, 1968), 28–30.
Cayton, R. F. *Library Journal,* 93 (March 15, 1968), 1164.
Fremont-Smith, Eliot. *NYT* (March 25, 1968), 39.
Fuller, E. *Wall Street Journal* (May 13, 1968), 16.
Gass, W. H. *NYRB,* 10 (April 11, 1968), 3.
Greenfield, Josh. *Commonweal,* 88 (April 26, 1968), 185–187.
Griffin, C. W. *Reporter,* 38 (May 30, 1968), 43–44.
Hicks, Granville. *SRL,* 51 (April 6, 1968), 21–22.
Hill, W. B. *America,* 118 (May 4, 1968), 622, 757.
Hyman, Stanley E. *New Leader,* 31 (May 20, 1968), 20.
Kazin, Alfred. *Book World* (April 7, 1968), 1.
Kennedy, William. *National Observer,* 7 (April 15, 1968), 19.

Kirkus, 36 (February 1, 1968), 143.
Maddocks, Melvin. *Life,* 64 (April 5, 1968), 8.
Novak, Michael. *Critic,* 26 (June, 1968), 72–74.
Publisher's Weekly, 193 (February 12, 1968), 70.
Sheed, Wilfrid. *NYTBR* (April 7, 1968), 1, 30–33.
Sokolov, R. A. *Newsweek,* 171 (April 8, 1968), 125–126.
Thompson, John. *Commentary,* 45 (May, 1968), 70–73.
Time, 91 (April 26, 1968), 66.
Trilling, Diana. *Atlantic,* 221 (April, 1968), 129–131.
Yglesias, José. *Nation,* 206 (May 13, 1968), 637–638.

B. Briefer Writings

1. *Short Fiction*

1954
"Friends from Philadelphia," *NY,* 30 (October 30, 1954), 29–32. Collected in *The Same Door.*

1955
"Ace in the Hole," *NY,* 31 (April 9, 1955), 92–98. Collected in *The Same Door.*
"Dentistry and Doubt," *NY,* 31 (October 29, 1955), 28–30. Collected in *The Same Door.*
"The Kid's Whistling," *NY,* 31 (December 3, 1955), 127–128, 130, 132, 134. Collected in *The Same Door.*
"Tomorrow, and Tomorrow, etc.," *NY,* 31 (April 30, 1955), 80, 82, 85–91. Collected in *The Same Door.*

1956
"His Finest Hour," *NY,* 32 (November 17, 1956), 50. Collected in *The Same Door.*
"Snowing in Greenwich Village," *NY,* 32 (January 21, 1956), 30–33. Collected in *The Same Door.*
"Sunday Teasing," *NY,* 32 (October 13, 1956), 46–48. Collected in *The Same Door.*
"A Trillion Feet of Gas," *NY,* 32 (December 8, 1956), 51–56. Collected in *The Same Door.*
"Who made those yellow roses yellow?" *NY,* 32 (April 7, 1956), 28–34.

1957
"Incest," *NY,* 33 (June 29, 1957), 22–27. Collected in *The Same Door.*

1958

"The Alligators," *NY*, 34 (March 22, 1958), 28–31. Collected in *The Same Door*.

"A Gift from the City," *NY*, 34 (April 12, 1958), 45–50, 52, 54, 57–58, 60–64. Collected in *The Same Door*.

"Intercession," *NY*, 34 (August 30, 1958), 24–27. Collected in *The Same Door*.

1959

"Dear Alexandros," *NY*, 35 (October 31, 1959), 40–41. Collected in *Pigeon Feathers*.

"Flight," *NY*, 35 (August 22, 1959), 30–37. Collected in *Pigeon Feathers*.

"The Happiest I've Been," *NY*, 34 (January 3, 1959), 24–31.

"The Persistence of Desire," *NY*, 35 (July 11, 1959), 22–26. Collected in *Pigeon Feathers*.

"Should Wizard Hit Mommy?" *NY*, 35 (June 13, 1959), 38–40. Collected in *Pigeon Feathers*.

"Vergil Moss," *NY*, 35 (June 13, 1959), 99–102.

1960

"Archangel," *Big Table*, 2 (1960), 78–79. Collected in *Pigeon Feathers*.

"Home," *NY*, 36 (July 9, 1960), 26–31. Collected in *Pigeon Feathers*.

"A Sense of Shelter," *NY*, 35 (January 16, 1960), 28–34. Collected in *Pigeon Feathers*.

"Wife-wooing," *NY*, 36 (March 12, 1960), 49–51. Collected in *Pigeon Feathers*.

"You'll never know, dear, how much I love you," *NY*, 36 (June 18, 1960), 39–40. Collected in *Pigeon Feathers*.

1961

"A & P," *NY*, 37 (July 22, 1961), 22–24. Collected in *Pigeon Feathers*.

"The Astronomer," *NY*, 37 (April 1, 1961), 28–30. Collected in *Pigeon Feathers*.

"The Crow in the Woods," *The Transatlantic Review*, 8 (Winter, 1961), 47–50. Collected in *Pigeon Feathers*.

"Lifeguard," *NY*, 37 (June 17, 1961), 28–31. Collected in *Pigeon Feathers*.

"Packed Dirt, Churchgoing, a Dying Cat, a Traded Car," *NY*, 37 (December 16, 1961), 59–62. Collected in *Pigeon Feathers*.

1962

"Blessed Man of Boston, My Grandmother's Thimble, and Fanning Island," *NY*, 37 (January 13, 1962), 28–33. Collected in *Pigeon Feathers*.

"In Football Season," *NY*, 38 (November 10, 1962), 48–49.

"Madman," *NY*, 38 (December 22, 1962), 34–38.

"Unstuck," *NY*, 37 (February 3, 1962), 24–27.

1963

"After the Storm," *Esquire*, 59 (January, 1963), 81, 83–84, 123–126.

"Giving Blood," *NY*, 39 (April 6, 1963), 36–41.

"On the Way to School," *NY*, 38 (January 5, 1963), 32–40.

1964

"At a Bar in Charlotte Amalie," *NY*, 39 (January 11, 1964), 28–32.

"Christian Roommates," *NY*, 40 (April 4, 1964), 44–50.

"Dark," *NY*, 40 (October 31, 1964), 61–62.

"Leaves," *NY*, 40 (November 14, 1964), 52–53.

"Morning," *NY*, 40 (May 23, 1964), 24–26.

"Music School," *NY*, 40 (December 12, 1964), 50–52.

"Twin Bells in Rome," *NY*, 39 (February 8, 1964), 32–35.

1965

"The Bulgarian Poetess," *NY*, 41 (March 13, 1965), 44–51. Reprinted in *Prize Stories, 1966: The O. Henry Awards,* ed. Richard Poirier and William Abrams. Garden City, New York: Doubleday, 1966. Collected in *The Music School.*

"Deus Dixit," *Esquire*, 64 (September, 1965), 100–102.

"The Family Meadow," *NY*, 41 (July 24, 1965), 24–25. Collected in *The Music School.*

"Four Sides of One Story," *NY*, 41 (October 9, 1965), 48–52. Collected in *The Music School.*

"The Hermit," *NY*, 41 (February 20, 1965), 38–46. Collected in *The Music School.*

"My Lover Has Dirty Fingernails," *NY*, 41 (July 17, 1965), 28–31. Collected in *The Music School.*

"The Rescue," *NY*, 40 (January 2, 1965), 28–31. Collected in *The Music School.*

"The Stare," *NY*, 41 (April 3, 1965), 41–43. Collected in *The Music School.*

1966
"Avec la Bébé-sitter" *NY*, 41 (January 1, 1966), 24–27. Collected in
   The Music School.
"Bech in Rumania," *NY*, 42 (October 8, 1966), 54–63.
"During the Jurassic," *Transatlantic Review*, 21 (Summer, 1966), 47–
   50. Collected in *The Music School*.
"Harv Is Plowing Now," *NY*, 42 (April 23, 1966), 46–48. Collected in
   The Music School.
"Marching Through Boston," *NY*, 41 (January 22, 1966), 34–38. Re-
   printed in *Prize Stories, 1967: The O. Henry Awards*, ed. William
   Abrams. Garden City, New York: Doubleday, 1967.
"Pro," *NY*, 42 (September 17, 1966), 53–54.
"Witnesses," *NY*, 42 (August 13, 1966), 27–29.

1967
"Museums and Women," *NY*, 43 (November 18, 1967), 57–61.
"Taste of Metal," *NY*, 43 (March 11, 1967), 49–51.
"Your Lover Just Called," *Harper's*, 234 (January, 1967), 48–51. Re-
   printed in *Prize Stories 1968: The O. Henry Awards*, ed. William
   Abrams. Garden City, New York: Doubleday, 1968.

1968
"Eros Rampant," *Harper's*, 236 (June, 1968), 59–64.
"Bech Takes Pot Luck," *NY*, 44 (September 7, 1968), 28–36.
"Man and Daughter in the Cold," *NY*, 44 (March 9, 1968), 34–36.
"Wait," *NY*, 43 (February 17, 1968), 34–40.

2. *Articles and Reviews*

1957
"American Man: What of Him?" *NY*, 32 (January 12, 1957), 22. Collected in *Assorted Prose*.
"And Whose Little Generation Are You?" *NY*, 33 (October 5, 1957),
   38–39.
"Anywhere Is Where You Hang Your Hat," *NY*, 33 (June 8, 1957),
   97–98, 101. Collected in *Assorted Prose*.

1958
"Outing," *NY*, 34 (June 14, 1958), 28–29. Collected in *Assorted Prose*.

1959

"Drinking from a Cup Made Cinchy," *NY*, 35 (March 21, 1959), 41–42. Collected in *Assorted Prose*.

"On the Sidewalk," *NY*, 35 (February 21, 1959), 32. Collected in *Assorted Prose*.

"What is a Rhyme?" *Contact*, 2 (1959), 57–60. Collected in *Assorted Prose*.

1960

"Confessions of a Wild Bore," *NY*, 35 (February 6, 1960), 34–35. Collected in *Assorted Prose*.

"Hub Fans Bid Kid Adieu" ("Our Far-flung Correspondents"), *NY*, 36 (October 22, 1960), 109–110, 112, 114–116, 121–122, 124, 126–128, 131. Collected in *Assorted Prose*.

"Poetry from Downtrodden," *New Republic*, 142 (May 9, 1960), 11–12. Review of Alan Sillitoe's *The Loneliness of the Long-Distance Runner*; collected in *Assorted Prose*.

"The Sea's Green Sameness," *New World Writing*, 17 (1960), 54–59.

"Snow from a Dead Sky," *New Republic*, 143 (November 28, 1960), 26–27. Review of *The Collected Stories of Conrad Aiken*; collected in *Assorted Prose*.

"Why Robert Frost Should Receive the Nobel Prize," *Audience*, 7 (Summer, 1960), 45–46. Collected in *Assorted Prose*.

1961

"Alphonse Peintre," *NY*, 37 (March 18, 1961), 159–161. Collected in *Assorted Prose*.

"Anxious Days for the Glass Family," *NYTBR* (September 17, 1961), 1, 52. Review of J. D. Salinger's *Franny and Zooey*; collected in *Assorted Prose*.

"Beerbohm and Others," *NY*, 37 (September 16, 1961), 163–164, 166–170, 173–176. Review of *Parodies: An Anthology from Chaucer to Beerbohm—and After*, ed. Dwight MacDonald; collected in *Assorted Prose*.

"Creatures of the Air," *NY*, 37 (September 30, 1961), 161–162, 165–167. Review of Muriel Spark's *The Bachelors*; collected in *Assorted Prose*.

"Mr. Ex-resident," *NY*, 37 (August 5, 1961), 27. Collected in *Assorted Prose*.

"Unread Book Route," *NY*, 37 (March 4, 1961), 28–29. Collected in *Assorted Prose*.

1962

"Briefly Noted," *NY*, 38 (March 24, 1962), 176, 178. Review of Richard Hughes' *The Fox in the Attic* and Catherine Gaskin's *I Know My Love*; the Hughes review collected in *Assorted Prose*.

"Credos and Curios," *NYTBR* (November 25, 1962), 5. Review of James Thurber's *Credos and Curios*; collected in *Assorted Prose*.

"The Dogwood Tree: A Boyhood," *Five Boyhoods*, ed. Martin Levin (New York: Doubleday, 1962), 155–198. Collected in *Assorted Prose*.

"Foreword," *The Young King and Other Fairy Tales by Oscar Wilde* (New York: The Macmillan Co., 1962), iii–v. Collected in *Assorted Prose*.

"No Use Talking," *New Republic*, 147 (August 13, 1962), 23–24. Review of *The Letters of James Agee to Father Flye*; collected in *Assorted Prose*.

1963

"Between a Wedding and a Funeral," *NY*, 39 (September 14, 1963), 192–194. Review of Muriel Spark's *The Girls of Slender Means*; collected in *Assorted Prose*.

"Eclipse," *Saturday Evening Post*, 236 (November 16, 1963), 92. Collected in *Assorted Prose*.*

"Faith in Search of Understanding," *NY*, 39 (October 12, 1963), 203–206, 209–210. Review of Karl Barth's *Anselm: Fides Quaerens Intellectum*; collected in *Assorted Prose*.

"Honest Horn," *American Scholar*, 32 (Autumn, 1963), 660, 662, 664. Review of Harry Levin's *Gates of Horn*; collected in *Assorted Prose*.

"The Indian," *NY*, 39 (August 17, 1963), 24–26.

"Mea Culpa: A Travel Note," *NY*, 39 (November 16, 1963), 137–138, 140. Collected in *Assorted Prose*.

"More Love in the Western World," *NY*, 39 (August 24, 1963), 90–94, 97–104. Review of Denis de Rougemont's *Love Declared*; collected in *Assorted Prose*.

---

* Although "Eclipse," "Mea Culpa," "My Uncle's Death," and "The Lucid Eye in Silver Town" are in the apparent form of short stories or vignettes, and seem no more autobiographical than much of Updike's fiction, they are listed here as nonfiction after the author's own suggestion in including them among the nonfictional selections in *Assorted Prose*.

"My Uncle's Death," *Saturday Evening Post,* 236 (March 2, 1963), 48–50. Collected in *Assorted Prose*

1964

"Books, Briefly Noted," *NY,* 39 (February 1, 1964), 96–100. Fourteen very brief reviews of current books, including Paul Tillich's *Morality and Beyond;* the Tillich review collected in *Assorted Prose.*

"Comment," *TLS* (June 4, 1964), 473.

"Grandmaster Nabokov," *New Republic,* 151 (September 26, 1964), 15–18. Review of Vladimir Nabokov's *The Luzhin Defense;* collected in *Assorted Prose.*

"How *How It Is* Was," *NY,* 39 (December 19, 1964), 165–166. Review of Samuel Beckett's *How It Is.* Collected in *Assorted Prose.*

"The Lucid Eye in Silver Town," *Saturday Evening Post,* 237 (May 23, 1964), 54–55, 58–61. Collected in *Assorted Prose.*

"Rhyming Max," *NY,* 40 (March 7, 1964), 176, 178–181. Review of Max Beerbohm's *Max in Verse;* collected in *Assorted Prose.*

1965

"The Author as Librarian," *NY,* 41 (October 30, 1965), 223–224, 226–228, 231–236, 238, 241–246. Review of Jorge Luis Borges' *Dreamtigers, Other Inquisitions, Ficciones, Labyrinths, and Ana Maria* Barrenechea's *Borges the Labyrinth Maker.*

"Death's Heads," *NY,* 41 (October 2, 1965), 216, 218, 221–222, 224, 226–228. Review of Pierre Drieu La Rochelle's *The Fire Within* and *Selected Works of Alfred Jarry,* ed. Roger Shattuck and Simon Watson Taylor.

1966

"The Fork," *NY,* 42 (February 26, 1966), 115–118, 121–124, 128–130, 133–134. Review of Soren Kierkegaard's *The Last Years: Journals, 1853–1855.*

"Mastery of Miss Warner," *New Republic,* 154 (March 5, 1966), 23–25. Review of Sylvia Townsend Warner's *Swan's on an Autumn River.*

1967

"My Mind Was Without a Shadow," *NY,* 43 (December 2, 1967), 223–224, 227, 230, 232. Review of Knut Hamsun's *Hunger* and *On Overgrown Paths.*

"Nabokov's Look Back: A National Loss," *Life*, 62 (January 13, 1967), 9, 15. Review of Vladimir Nabokov's *Speak, Memory*.

1968
"Indifference," *NY*, 44 (November 2, 1968), 197–201. Review of James Gould Cozzens's *Morning, Noon and Night*.
"Letter from Anguilla," *NY*, 44 (June 22, 1968), 70–80.
"Questions Concerning Giacomo," *NY*, 44 (April 6, 1968), 167–168. 171–174.
"Writers I Have Met," *NYTBR* (August 11, 1968), 2, 23.

1969
"Albertine Disparue," *NY*, 45 (March 15, 1969), 174. Review of Albertine Sarrazin's *The Runaway* and *Astragal*.
"Amor Vincit Omnia Ad Nauseam," *NY*, 45 (April 5, 1969), 33. Parody of Iris Murdoch's *Bruno's Dream*.

3. *Poetry*

1954
"The Clan," *NY*, 30 (December 18, 1954), 119. Collected in *The Carpentered Hen*.
"Duet, with muffled brake drums," *NY*, 30 (August 14, 1954), 66. Collected in *The Carpentered Hen*.
"Player Piano," *NY*, 30 (December 4, 1954), 169. Collected in *The Carpentered Hen*.

1955
"Humanities Course," *NY*, 31 (June 4, 1955), 100. Collected in *The Carpentered Hen*.
"An Imaginable Conference," *NY*, 31 (August 6, 1955), 24. Collected in *The Carpentered Hen*.
"Lament, for Cocoa," *NY*, 31 (May 14, 1955), 163. Collected in *The Carpentered Hen*.
"March," *NY*, 30 (February 12, 1955), 38. Collected in *The Carpentered Hen*.
"Ode Fired into Being by *Life*'s 48-star Editorial," *NY*, 31 (October 15, 1955), 47. Collected in *The Carpentered Hen*.

"Poem," *NY*, 31 (October 1, 1955), 34. Collected in *The Carpentered Hen*.

"Recitative for Punished Products," *Punch*, 228 (February 9, 1955), 97. Collected in *The Carpentered Hen*.

"Shipboard," *NY*, 30 (January 15, 1955), 93. Collected in *The Carpentered Hen*.

"Song of the Open Fireplace," *NY*, (January 8, 1955), 31. Collected in *The Carpentered Hen*.

"Sunflower," *NY*, 31 (September 10, 1955), 136. Collected in *The Carpentered Hen*.

"Sunglasses," *NY*, 31 (July 16, 1955), 65. Collected in *The Carpentered Hen*.

"Superman," *NY*, 31 (November 12, 1955), 56. Collected in *The Carpentered Hen*.

"To an Usherette," *NY*, 31 (December 10, 1955), 190. Collected in *The Carpentered Hen*.

"V. B. Nimble, V. B. Quick," *NY*, 31 (April 2, 1955), 36. Collected in *The Carpentered Hen*.

"Youth's Progress," *NY*, 31 (February 26, 1955), 28. Collected in *The Carpentered Hen*.

1956

"Bitter Life," *NY*, 31 (January 7, 1956), 26.

"Due Respect," *NY*, 32 (November 17, 1956), 50. Collected in *The Carpentered Hen*.

"Little Poems," *NY*, 32 (July 21, 1956), 73. Collected in *The Carpentered Hen*.

"Mr. High-Mind," *NY*, 32 (October 27, 1956), 36. Collected in *The Carpentered Hen*.

"Old Faces of '56," *NY*, 32 (October 27, 1956), 36.

"Publius Virgilius Maro, the Madison Avenue Hick," *NY*, 32 (March 31, 1956), 32. Collected in *The Carpentered Hen*.

"Solid Comfort," *NY*, 31 (February 13, 1956), 93.

"Tao in the Yankee Stadium Bleachers," *NY*, 32 (August 18, 1956), 28. Collected in *The Carpentered Hen*.

"Tsokadzeo, Altitudo," *NY*, 32 (February 25, 1956), 51–56. Collected in *The Carpentered Hen*.

"A Wooden Darning Egg," *Harper's,* 213 (December, 1956), 34. Collected in *The Carpentered Hen.*

1957
"Capacity," *NY,* 32 (January 5, 1957), 29.
"Even Egrets Err," *NY,* 33 (September 7, 1957), 74. Collected in *The Carpentered Hen.*
"Ex-Basketball Player," *NY,* 33 (July 6, 1957), 62. Collected in *The Carpentered Hen.*
"Glasses," *NY,* 33 (April 20, 1957), 139. Collected in *The Carpentered Hen.*
"Jack," *NY,* 33 (October 19, 1957), 134.
"Modest Mound of Bones," *Commonweal,* 66 (April 26, 1957), 92. Collected in *The Carpentered Hen.*
"Notes," *NY,* 32 (January 26, 1957), 28–29.
"Ode III ii: Horace," *Commonweal,* 66 (June 7, 1957), 254. Collected in *The Carpentered Hen.*
"One-year-old," *Ladies Home Journal,* 74 (March, 1957), 172. Collected in *The Carpentered Hen.*
"Philological," *NY,* 33 (April 6, 1957), 109. Collected in *The Carpentered Hen.*
"Planting a Mailbox," *NY,* 33 (May 11, 1957), 109. Collected in *The Carpentered Hen.*
"A Rack of Paperbacks," *NY,* 33 (March 23, 1957), 124. Collected in *The Carpentered Hen.*
"Reflection," *NY,* 33 (November 30, 1957), 200. Collected in *The Carpentered Hen.*
"Room 28, National Gallery, London," *NY,* 33 (November 2, 1957), 40. Collected in *The Carpentered Hen.*
"Scansion from Exalted Heights," *NY,* 32 (February 9, 1957), 28–29.
"Scenic," *NY,* 33 (March 9, 1957), 97. Collected in *The Carpentered Hen.*
"The Sensualist," *NY,* 32 (February 16, 1957), 30. Collected in *The Carpentered Hen.*
"Tune, in American Type," *NY,* 33 (March 30, 1957), 30. Collected in *The Carpentered Hen.*

1958

"Bendix," *NY*, 33 (February 15, 1958), 30. Collected in *Telephone Poles.*

"Blkd," *NY*, 34 (June 21, 1958), 90.

"Caligula's Dream," *Commonweal*, 68 (June 27, 1958), 327.

"The Menagerie at Versailles in 1775," *Harper's*, 226 (May, 1958), 78. Collected in *Telephone Poles.*

"Party Knee," *NY*, 34 (May 3, 1958), 28–29. Collected in *Telephone Poles.*

"Reel," *NY*, 34 (May 3, 1958), 133. Collected in *Telephone Poles.*

"Simple Life," *NY*, 33 (January 18, 1958), 108.

"Toothache Man," *NY*, 34 (November 15, 1958), 58. Collected in *Telephone Poles.*

"Upon Learning That a Bird Exists Called the Turnstone," *NY*, 34 (October 4, 1958), 39. Collected in *Telephone Poles.*

1959

"Deities and Beasts," *New Republic*, 140 (March 30, 1959), 17. Collected in *Telephone Poles.*

"Fritillary," *NY*, 35 (August 15, 1959), 28. Collected in *Telephone Poles.*

"Idyll," *NY*, 35 (October 10, 1959), 50. Collected in *Telephone Poles.*

"In Praise of ($C_{10}H_9O_5$)," *NY*, 35 (May 16, 1959), 44. Collected in *Telephone Poles.*

"Mobile of Birds," *NY*, 35 (December 19, 1959), 32. Collected in *Telephone Poles.*

"The Moderate," *NY*, 34 (January 10, 1959), 103. Collected in *Telephone Poles.*

"Sonic Boom," *NY*, 35 (August 8, 1959), 89. Collected in *Telephone Poles.*

"Suburban Madrigal," *NY*, 35 (April 25, 1959), 100. Collected in *Telephone Poles.*

"Thoughts While Driving Home," *NY*, 35 (September 26, 1959), 180. Collected in *Telephone Poles.*

"Tome-thoughts, from the Times," *New Republic*, 141 (August 10, 1959), 20. Collected in *Telephone Poles.*

1960

"Agatha Christie and Beatrix Potter," *NY*, 36 (November 26, 1960), 52. Collected in *Telephone Poles*.

"B.W.I.," *NY*, 36 (April 20, 1960), 98. Collected in *Telephone Poles*.

"Cosmic Gall," *NY*, 36 (December 17, 1960), 36. Collected in *Telephone Poles*.

"Meditation on a News Item," *NY*, 36 (July 16, 1960), 38. Collected in *Telephone Poles*.

"Modigliani's Death Mask," *NY*, 36 (March 26, 1960), 34. Collected in *Telephone Poles*.

"Mosquito," *NY*, 36 (June 11, 1960), 32. Collected in *Telephone Poles*.

"A Song of Paternal Care," *NY*, 36 (March 19, 1960), 169. Collected in *Telephone Poles*.

"Summer: West Side," *NY*, 36 (July 30, 1960), 26. Collected in *Telephone Poles*.

"Tropical Beetles," *NY*, 36 (April 9, 1960), 154. Collected in *Telephone Poles*.

"Wash," *NY*, 36 (December 3, 1960), 161. Collected in *Telephone Poles*.

"Yonder Peasant," "Martini," "Parable," *Contact*, 1 (February, 1960), 52–53.

1961

"Comparative Religion," *NY*, 37 (April 8, 1961), 51. Collected in *Telephone Poles*.

"February 22," *NY*, 37 (February 18, 1961), 40. Collected in *Telephone Poles*.

"Handkerchiefs of Khaibar Khan," *NY*, 37 (November 25, 1961), 172.

"I missed the book but I read his name," *NY*, 37 (November 4, 1961), 142. Collected in *Telephone Poles*.

"Maples in a Spruce Forest," *Commonweal*, 74 (June 2, 1961), 252. Collected in *Telephone Poles*.

"Old-Fashioned Lightning Rod," *NY*, 37 (November 18, 1961), 171. Collected in *Telephone Poles*.

"Seven Stanzas at Easter," *Christian Century*, 78 (February 22, 1961), 236. Collected in *Telephone Poles*.

"Telephone Poles," *NY*, 36 (January 21, 1961), 36. Collected in *Telephone Poles*.

"Upon learning that a town exists in Virginia called Uppersville," *NY*, 37 (May 20, 1961), 135. Collected in *Telephone Poles.*

"Vermont," *Harper's*, 223 (July, 1961), 67. Collected in *Telephone Poles.*

"Vision," *NY*, 36 (January 7, 1961), 77.

1962

"Bestiary," *NY*, 38 (December 1, 1962), 228. Collected in *Telephone Poles.*

"Calendar," *American Scholar*, 31 (Autumn, 1962), 550. Collected in *Telephone Poles.*

"Earthworm," *NY*, 38 (May 12, 1962), 145. Collected in *Telephone Poles.*

"Exposure," *NY*, 38 (December 8, 1962), 49. Collected in *Telephone Poles.*

"Flirt," *Commonweal*, 77 (November 30, 1962), 253. Collected in *Telephone Poles.*

"The Great Scarf of Birds," *NY*, 38 (November 10, 1962), 48–49.

"Marriage Counsel," *NY*, 37 (January 20, 1962), 71. Collected in *Telephone Poles.*

"Die Neuen Heiligen," *Harper's*, 225 (August, 1962), 44. Collected in *Telephone Poles.*

"Les Saints Nouveaux," *Harper's*, 224 (January, 1962), 59. Collected in *Telephone Poles.*

"Seagulls," *NY*, 38 (August 25, 1962), 28. Collected in *Telephone Poles.*

"Short Days," *NY*, 38 (March 10, 1962), 28. Collected in *Telephone Poles.*

"Stunt Flier," *NY*, 37 (January 6, 1962), 59. Collected in *Telephone Poles.*

"White Dwarf," *NY*, 38 (September 1, 1962), 67. Collected in *Telephone Poles.*

1963

"Azores," *Harper's*, 228 (January, 1964), 37.

"Erotic Epigrams," *Commonweal*, 78 (June 14, 1963), 327. Collected in *Telephone Poles.*

"Exposé," *NY*, 39 (May 25, 1963), 40.

"Farewell to the Shopping District of Antibes," *NY,* 39 (April 20, 1963),
50.
"Fireworks," *NY,* 40 (July 4, 1964), 28.
"Hoeing," *NY,* 39 (April 27, 1963), 142. Collected in *Telephone Poles.*
"Lamplight," *New Republic,* 150 (February 29, 1964), 22.
"Sea Knell," *NY,* 40 (March 28, 1964), 44.
"Some Frenchmen," *NY,* 39 (November 9, 1963), 54.
"Vow," *NY,* 40 (May 23, 1964), 48.

1965
"Decor," *American Scholar,* 34 (Summer, 1965), 412.
"Poem for a Far Land," *New Republic,* 152 (March 13, 1965), 17.
"Postcards from Soviet Cities: Moscow; Kiev; Leningrad; Yerevan," *NY,*
41 (May 29, 1965), 34.
"Roman Portrait Busts," *New Republic,* 152 (February 6, 1965), 21.
"Sunshine on Sandstone," *New Republic,* 152 (April 17, 1965), 26.

1966
"Air Show," *New Republic,* 155 (December 17, 1966), 25.
"Amoeba," *New Republic,* 154 (January 25, 1966), 23.
"Home Movies," *New Republic,* 154 (January 8, 1966), 23.
"Seal in Nature," *New Republic,* 155 (October 15, 1966), 16.

1967
"Antigua," *NY,* 42 (February 11, 1967), 46.
"Memories of Anguilla, 1960," *New Republic,* 157 (November 11,
1967), 21.
"Subway Love," *New Republic,* 156 (May 20, 1967), 26.
Translation of Evgenil Aleksandrovich Evtushenko's "Restaurant for
Two" and "Ballad About Nuggets," *Life,* 62 (February 17, 1967), 33.

1968
"Angels," *NY,* 43 (January 27, 1968), 34.
"Dream Objects," *NY,* 44 (October 26, 1968), 54.
"Naked Ape," *New Republic,* 158 (February 3, 1968), 28.
"Topsfield Fair," *American Scholar,* 37 (Summer, 1968), 419.
Translation (with Albert C. Todd) of Evgenil Aleksandrovich Evtu-
shenko's "America and I Sat Down Together," *Holiday,* 44 (Novem-
ber, 1968), 38–43. Group of seven poems.

1969

"The Dance of the Solids," *Scientific American,* 220 (January, 1969), 130–131.

"Report of Health," *NY,* 45 (February 22, 1969), 40.

"Skyey Developments," *New Republic,* 160 (March 8, 1969), 28.

II. SECONDARY SOURCES (biographical and critical)

1959

Serebnick, Judith. "New Creative Writers," *Library Journal,* 84 (February 1, 1959), 499.

1961

Geller, Evelyn. "Biography," *Wilson Library Bulletin,* 36 (September, 1961), 67.

Klausler, A. P. *Christian Century,* 78 (February 22, 1961), 245–246.

1962

Cimatti, Pietro. "Burroughs e Updike," *Fiera Lettéraria,* 17 (October 28, 1962), 4.

Doner, Dean. "Rabbit Angstrom's Unseen World," *New World Writing,* 20 (1962), 58–75.

Fisher, Richard E. "John Updike: Theme and Form in the Garden of Epiphanies," *Moderna Språk,* 56 (Fall, 1962), 255–260.

Hicks, Granville. "Mysteries of the Commonplace," *SRL,* 45 (March 17, 1962), 21.

Hyman, Stanley Edgar. "The Artist as a Young Man," *The New Leader,* 45 (March 19, 1962), 22–23.

Murphy, Richard W. "John Updike," *Horizon,* 4 (March, 1962), 84–85.

Ward, J. A. "John Updike's Fiction," *Critique,* 5 (Spring-Summer, 1962), 27–40.

1963

Adams, Mildred. "El escritor John Updike: ¿Cuento o novella?" *Revue de Occidente,* 1 (August, 1963), 198–202.

Duncan, Graham H. "The Thing Itself in *Rabbit, Run,*" *English Record,* 13 (April, 1963), 25–27, 36–37.

Hicks, Granville. "Generations of the Fifties: Malamud, Gold, and Up-
    dike," *The Creative Present,* ed. Norma Balakian and Charles Sim-
    mons (New York: Doubleday, 1963), pp. 213–238.
Lacourse, Guerin. "The Innocence of John Updike," *Commonweal,* 78
    (May 10, 1963), 512–514.
Mailer, Norman. "Norman Mailer vs. Nine Writers," *Esquire,* 60 (July,
    1963), 63–69, 105.
Novak, Michael. "Updike's Quest for Liturgy," *Commonweal,* 78 (May
    10, 1963), 192–195.
"Sustaining Stream," *Time,* 81 (February 1, 1963), M24, M26.

1964

Detweiler, Robert. "John Updike and the Indictment of Culture-
    Protestantism," *Spiritual Crises in Mid-Century American Fiction*
    (Gainesville: University of Florida Press, 1964), 14–24.
Doyle, P. A. "Updike's Fiction: Motifs and Techniques," *Catholic
    World,* 199 (September, 1964), 356–362.
Galloway, David D. "The Absurd Man as Saint: The Novels of John
    Updike," *MFS,* 11 (September 24, 1964), 111–127.
Geismar, Maxwell. "The American Short Story Today," *Studies on the
    Left,* 4 (Spring, 1964), 21–27.
Mizener, Arthur. "The American Hero as High-School Boy," *The Sense
    of Life in the Modern Novel* (New York: Houghton Mifflin, 1964),
    pp. 247–266.
O'Connor, William Van. "John Updike and William Styron: The Burden
    of Talent," *Contemporary American Novelists,* ed. Harry T. Moore
    (Carbondale: Southern Illinois University Press, 1964), pp. 205–221.
Tate, Sister Judith M. "John Updike: Of Rabbits and Centaurs," *Critic,*
    22 (February–March, 1964), 44–51.

1965

Enright, D. J. "Updike's Ups and Downs," *Holiday,* 38 (November,
    1965), 162–164, 165. Reprinted in D. J. Enright, *Conspirators and
    Poets* (Chester Springs, Pennsylvania: Dufour, 1966), pp. 134–140.
Finkelstein, Sidney. "Acceptance of Alienation: John Updike and James
    Purdy," *Existentialism and Alienation in American Literature* (New
    York: International Publishers, 1965), pp. 242–252.

Muradian, Thaddeus. "The World of Updike," *English Journal,* 54 (October, 1965), 577–584.

Yates, Norris W. "The Doubt and Faith of John Updike," *College English,* 26 (March, 1965), 469–474.

1966

Arnavon, Cyrille. "Les Romans de John Updike," *Eyrope,* 44 (June, 1966), 193–213.

Aldridge, J. W. "The Private Voice of John Updike," *Time to Murder and Create: The Contemporary Novel in Crisis* (New York: McKay, 1966), pp. 164–170.

Brenner, Gerry. "*Rabbit, Run*: John Updike's Criticism of the Return to Nature," *Twentieth Century Literature,* 12 (April, 1966), 3–14.

Burgess, Anthony. "Language, Myth and Mr. Updike," *Commonweal,* 83 (February 11, 1966), 557–559.

Guyol, Hazel Sample. "The Lord Loves a Cheerful Corpse," *English Journal,* 55 (October, 1966), 863–866.

Howard, J. "Can a Nice Novelist Finish First?" *Life,* 61 (November 4, 1966), 74–74A, 74C–74D, 76, 79–82.

Hyman, Stanley Edgar. "Chiron at Olinger High," *Standards: A Chronicle of Books for Our Time* (New York: Horizon, 1966), pp. 128–132.

1967

Alley, Alvin D. "The Centaur: Transcendental Imagination and Metamorphic Death," *English Journal,* 56 (October, 1967), 982–985.

Brewer, Joseph E. "The Anti-Hero in Contemporary Literature," *Iowa English Yearbook,* 12 (1967), 55–60.

Haas, Rudolf. "Griechischer Mythos in Modernen Roman: John Updikes *The Centaur,*" *Lebende Antike: Symposion für Rudolf Sühnel,* ed. Horst Meller and Hans-Joachim Zimmerman (Berlin: E. Schmidt, 1967), pp. 513–527.

Hainsworth, J. D. "John Updike," *Hibbert Journal,* 65 (Spring, 1967), 115–116.

Hamilton, Kenneth. *John Updike: A Critical Essay.* Grand Rapids, Michigan: Eerdmans, 1967.

———. "John Updike: Chronicler of the Time of the Death of God," *Christian Century,* 84 (June 7, 1967), 745–748.

Harper, Howard M., Jr. "John Updike—the Intrinsic Problem of Human Existence," *Desperate Faith: A Study of Bellow, Salinger, Mailer,*

Baldwin and Updike (Chapel Hill: University of North Carolina
    Press, 1967), pp. 162–190.
Matson, Elizabeth. "A Chinese Paradox, but Not Much of One: John
    Updike in His Poetry," *Minnesota Review*, 7, no. 2 (1967), 157–167.
Rupp, Richard H. "John Updike: Style in Search of a Center," *Sewanee
    Review*, 75 (Autumn, 1967), 693–709.
Standley, Fred L. *"Rabbit, Run:* An Image of Life," *Midwest Quarterly*,
    8 (Summer, 1967), 371–386.
Wyatt, Bryant N. "John Updike: The Psychological Novel in Search of
    Structure," *Twentieth Century Literature*, 13 (July, 1967), 89–96.

1968
Stubbs, S. C. "Search for Perfection in *Rabbit, Run*," *Critique*, 10, no. 2
    (1968), 94–101.
"View from the Catacombs," *Time*, 91 (April 26, 1968), 66–68, 73–75.

A WILLIAM STYRON CHECKLIST

I. Primary Sources

A. Books

Lie Down in Darkness. Indianapolis: Bobbs-Merrill Co., 1951.
    Reviews:
        Aldridge, John W. *NYTBR* (September 9, 1951), 5.
        Breit, Harvey. *Atlantic*, 188 (October, 1951), 76, 78, 79, 80.
        Byam, Milton S. *Library Journal*, 76 (September 15, 1951), 1423–
            1424.
        Canadian Forum, 31 (January, 1952), 239.
        Chapin, Ruth. *Christian Science Monitor* (October 4, 1951), 15.
        Cowley, Malcolm. *New Republic*, 125 (October 8, 1951), 19–20.
        Davis, Robert Gorham. *American Scholar*, 21 (Winter, 1951–1952),
            114, 116.

Derleth, August. Chicago *Sunday Tribune*, Part 4 (September 9, 1951), 3.

Downing, Francis. *Commonweal*, 54 (October 5, 1951), 620.

Geismar, Maxwell. *SRL*, 34 (September 15, 1951), 12–13.

Janeway, Elizabeth. *New Leader*, 28 (January 21, 1952), 25.

Jones, Howard Mumford. *NYHTBR* (September 9, 1951), 3.

Lambert, J. W. *Sunday Times* (London), (March 31, 1952), 3.

Munn, L. S. *Springfield Republican* (September 30, 1951), 10 B.

Newsweek, 38 (September 10, 1951), 106–107.

NY, 27 (September 29, 1951), 118–119.

O'Brien, Alfred, Jr. *Commonweal*, 55 (October 19, 1951), 43–44.

Prescott, Orville. *NYT* (September 10, 1951), 19.

Rubin, Louis D., Jr. *Hopkins Review*, 5 (Fall, 1951), 65–68.

Scott, J. D. *New Statesman and Nation*, n.s. 43 (April 19, 1952), 473.

Swados, Harvey. *Nation*, 173 (November 24, 1951), 453.

Time, 58 (September 10, 1951), 106, 108.

Wallace, Margaret. *Independent Woman* (now *National Business Woman*), 19 (November, 1951), 325.

The Long March. New York: Random House Modern Library (paperback only), 1956. See also entry under "Short Fiction."

Reviews:

Bryden, Ronald. *Spectator* (April 6, 1962), 454.

Maitland, Zane. *Time and Tide* (April 12, 1962), 30.

Punch, 242 (May 9, 1962), 735.

TLS (April 4, 1962), 229.

Set This House on Fire. New York: Random House, 1960.

Reviews:

Adams, Phoebe. *Atlantic*, 206 (July, 1960), 97–98.

Baro, Gene. *NYHTBR* (June 5, 1960), 1, 12.

Borklund, Elmer. *Commentary*, 30 (November, 1960), 452–454.

Breit, Harvey. *Partisan Review*, 27 (Summer, 1960), 561–563.

Dahms, Joseph G. *America*, 103 (June 18, 1960), 380–381.

Fenton, Charles A. *South Atlantic Quarterly*, 59 (Fall, 1960), 469–476.

Fuller, Edmund. *Chicago Sunday Tribune Magazine*, Part 4 (June 5, 1960), 3.

Galloway, David D. *Night Watch*, 1 (May, 1961), 20.
Gentry, Curt. San Francisco *Sunday Chronicle* (June 5, 1960), 22 TW.
Griffin, Lloyd W. *Library Journal*, 85 (June 15, 1960), 2458.
Hicks, Granville. *SRL*, 43 (June 4, 1960), 4.
Highet, Gilbert. *Book-of-the-Month-Club News* (June, 1960), 7.
Hollander, John. *Yale Review*, 50 (Autumn, 1960), 149.
Hutchens, John K. *NYHT* (June 3, 1960), 11.
Kirkus, 28 (April 15, 1960), 333.
Le Clec'h, Guy. *Le Figaro Littéraire* (February 24, 1962), 3.
Malcolm, Donald. *NY*, 36 (June 4, 1960), 152.
Miller, Nolan. *Antioch Review*, 20 (Summer, 1960), 248–256.
Mizener, Arthur. *NYTBR* (June 5, 1960), 5, 26.
Monaghan, Charles. *Commonweal*, 72 (July 22, 1960), 380.
Newberry, Mike. *Mainstream*, 13 (September, 1960), 61–63.
Newsweek, 46 (June 6, 1960), 117–118.
Pickrel, Paul. *Harper's*, 221 (July, 1960), 93.
Prescott, Orville. *NYT* (June 3, 1960), 29.
Rothberg, Abraham. *New Leader* (July 4–11, 1960), 25–27.
Rubin, Louis D., Jr. *Sewanee Review*, 69 (Winter, 1961), 174–179.
Scott, Paul. *New Statesman*, 61 (February 17, 1961), 271.
Southern, Terry. *Nation*, 191 (November 19, 1960), 380–383.
Thompson, Frank H., Jr. *Prairie Schooner*, 37 (Summer, 1963), 183–185.
Time, 75 (June 6, 1960), 98.
TLS (February 17, 1961), 101.

The Confessions of Nat Turner. New York: Random House, 1967.
  Reviews:
      Aptheker, Herbert. *Nation*, 205 (October 16, 1967), 375–376.
      Buckmaster, Henrietta. *Christian Science Monitor* (October 12, 1967), 5.
      Collier, Peter. *Progressive* (December, 1967), 41.
      Cooke, Michael. *Yale Review*, 57 (December, 1967), 273.
      Core, George. *Southern Review*, 4 (July, 1968), 745–751.
      Fremont-Smith, Eliot. *NYT* (October 3, 1967), 49.
      Griffin, L. W. *Library Journal*, 92 (October 1, 1967), 3448–3449.
      Hicks, Granville. *SRL*, 50 (October 7, 1967), 29–31.

Kincaid, Anne. *Library Journal,* 92 (November 15, 1967), 4274.
La Haye, Judson, *Best Sellers,* 27 (November 1, 1967), 308.
Life, 63 (October 13, 1967), 51–52.
Miller, W. L. *Reporter,* 37 (November 16, 1967), 42–46.
Murray, Albert. *New Leader,* 4 (December, 1967), 18.
O'Connell, Shaun. *Nation,* 205 (October 16, 1967), 373–374.
Rahv, Philip. *NYRB,* 9 (October 26, 1967), 6–8.
Schroth, R. A. *America,* 117 (October 14, 1967), 416.
Sheed, Wilfrid. *NYTBR* (October 8, 1967), 1–2.
Sokolov, R. A. *Newsweek,* 70 (October 19, 1967), 65–69.
Steiner, George. *NY,* 43 (November 25, 1967), 236–244.
Thompson, John. *Commentary,* 44 (November, 1967), 81–85.
Time, 90 (October 13, 1967), 110, 113.
Tucker, Martin. *Commonweal,* 87 (December 22, 1967), 388–389.
Virginia Quarterly Review, 44 (Winter, 1968), viii.
Weeks, Edward. *Atlantic,* 220 (November, 1967), 130–132.
Woodward, Charles V. *New Republic,* 157 (October 7, 1967), 25–28.

B. Briefer Writings

1. *Short Fiction*
1945
"Autumn," *One and Twenty: Duke Narrative and Verse, 1924–1945,* ed.
William M. Blackburn (Durham, North Carolina: Duke University
Press, 1945), pp. 36–53.

1948
"A Moment in Trieste," *American Vanguard, 1948,* ed. Don M. Wolfe
(Ithaca, New York: Cornell University Press, 1948), pp. 241–247.

1950
"The Enormous Window," *American Vanguard, 1950,* ed. Charles I.
Glicksberg (New York: New School for Social Research, 1950).

1953
"[The] Long March," *discovery No. 1,* ed. John W. Aldridge and Vance
Bourjaily (New York: Pocket Books, 1953), 221–283. Reprinted as
a Random House Modern Library paperback, 1956; and in *Best Short
Stories of World War II,* ed. Charles A. Fenton (New York: Viking
Press, 1957), 361–421.

1960

"The McCabes," *Paris Review*, No. 22 (Autumn-Winter, 1960), 12–28. Part of Chapter VI of *Set This House on Fire*.

1966

"Runaway," *Partisan Review*, 33 (Fall, 1966), 574–582. Excerpt from *The Confessions of Nat Turner*.
"Virginia: 1831," *Paris Review*, 9 (Winter, 1966), 13–45. Excerpt from *The Confessions of Nat Turner*.

2. *Articles and Reviews*

1953

"Letter to an Editor," *Paris Review*, No. 1 (Spring, 1953), pp. 9–13.
"The Paris Review," *Harper's Bazaar*, 87 (August, 1953), 122, 173.
"The Prevalence of Wonders," *Nation*, 176 (May 2, 1953), 370–371.

1955

"What's Wrong with the American Novel?" *American Scholar*, 24 (Autumn, 1955), 464–503. A panel discussion with William Styron, Hiram Haydn, Ralph Ellison, *et al.*

1959

"If You Write for Television . . .," *New Republic*, 140 (April 6, 1959), 16.
"Introduction," *Best Short Stories from The Paris Review* (New York: E. P. Dutton, 1959), pp. 9–16.

1961

"Mrs. Aadland's Little Girl, Beverly," *Esquire*, 56 (November, 1961), 142, 189–191. Review of Florence Aadland's *The Big Love*; reprinted in *First Person Singular*, ed. Herbert Gold (New York: Dial Press, 1963), pp. 209–216.

1962

"Aftermath of Benjamin Reid," *Esquire*, 58 (November, 1962), 79, 81, 158, 160, 164.
"As He Lay Dead, a Bitter Grief," *Life*, 53 (July 20, 1962), 39–42.
"Death-in-life of Benjamin Reid," *Esquire*, 57 (February, 1962), 114, 141–145.

1963

"An Elegy for F. Scott Fitzgerald," *NYRB*, 1 (November 28, 1963), 1–3. Review of Andrew Turnbull's edition of *The Letters of F. Scott Fitzgerald.*

"The Habit," *NYRB*, 1 (December 26, 1963), 13–14. Review of *The Consumers' Union Report on Smoking and the Public Interest.*

"Overcome," *NYRB*, 1 (September 26, 1963), 18–19. Review of Herbert Aptheker's *American Negro Slave Revolts*

"Two Writers Talk it Over," *Esquire*, 60 (July, 1963), 57–59. Tape-recorded discussion between James Jones and William Styron.

1964

"MacArthur's Reminiscences," *NYRB*, 3 (October 8, 1964), 3–5. Review of General Douglas MacArthur's *Reminiscences.*

"A Southern Conscience," *NYRB*, 2 (April 2, 1964), 3. Review of Lewis H. Blair's *A Southern Prophecy.*

"Tootsie Rolls," *NYRB*, 2 (May 14, 1964), 8. Review of Terry Southern and Mason Hoffenberg's *Candy.*

1965

"This Quiet Dust," *Harper's*, 230 (April, 1965), 134–146.

1966

"John Fitzgerald Kennedy . . . As We Remember Him," *Hi Fi*, 16 (January, 1966), 38.

1968

"My Generation," *Esquire*, 70 (October, 1968), 122–124.

"Oldest America," *McCall's*, 95 (July, 1968), 94.

"William Styron Replies: An Answer to Herbert Aptheker," *Nation*, 206 (April 22, 1968), 544–547.

"The Vice That Has No Name," *Harper's*, 236 (February, 1968), 97–100. Review of Jefferis' and Nichols' *Light On Dark Corners.*

II. SECONDARY SOURCES (biographical and critical)

1951

Dempsey, David. "Talk with William Styron," *NYTBR* (September 9, 1951), 27.

1952

Hazard, Eloise Perry. "Eight Fiction Finds," *SRL*, 35 (February 16, 1952), 17.

1953

Cowley, Malcolm. "American Novels Since the War," *New Republic*, 129 (December 28, 1953), 17.

Geismar, Maxwell. "The Post-War Generation in Arts and Letters," *SRL*, 36 (March 14, 1953), 11–12, 60.

1954

Cambon, Glauco. "Faulkner fa scoula," *La Fiera Lettéraria* (March 7, 1954), 5.

Davis, Robert Gorham. "In a Ravelled World Love Endures," *NYTBR* (December 26, 1954), 1, 13.

Matthiessen, Peter, and George Plimpton. "The Art of Fiction V" (interview with William Styron), *Paris Review*, No. 5 (Spring, 1954), pp. 42–57. Reprinted in *Writers at Work: The* PARIS REVIEW *Interviews*, ed. with an introduction by Malcolm Cowley (New York: Viking, 1958), pp. 268–282.

1955

Mohrt, Michel. "Le Renouveau du Roman Psychologique," *Le Nouveau Roman Américain* (Paris: Gallimard, 1955), 171–174.

TLS (August 5, 1955), ii–iii.

1956

Aldridge, John W. "The Society of Three Novels," *In Search of Heresy* (New York: McGraw-Hill, 1956), pp. 126–148.

1957

Friedman, Joseph J. "Non-Conformity and the Writer," *Venture*, 2 (Winter, 1957), 23–31.

Hazard, Eloise Perry. "William Styron," *SRL*, 34 (September 15, 1951), 12.

1958

Geismar, Maxwell. "William Styron: The End of Innocence," *American Moderns: From Rebellion to Conformity* (New York: Hill and Wang, 1958), pp. 239–250.

Lichtenstein, Gerald. "The Exiles," *New Statesman and Nation*, n.s. 49 (September 6, 1958), 320, 322.

Stevenson, David L. "Fiction's Unfamiliar Face," *Nation*, 187 (November 1, 1958), 307–309.

1959

Kazin, Alfred. "The Alone Generation," *Harper's* (Special Supplement), 219 (October, 1959), 127–131.

Lehan, Richard. "Existentialism in Recent American Fiction: The Demonic Quest," *TSLL*, 1 (Summer, 1959), 181–202.

1960

Curley, Thomas F. "The Quarrel with Time in American Fiction," *American Scholar*, 29 (Autumn, 1960), 552, 554, 556, 558, 560.

Davis, Robert Gorham. "Styron and the Students," *Critique*, 3 (Summer, 1960), 37–46.

Fenton, Charles A. "William Styron and the Age of the Slob," *South Atlantic Quarterly*, 59 (Autumn, 1960), 469–476.

Foster, Richard. "An Orgy of Commerce: William Styron's *Set This House on Fire*," *Critique*, 3 (Summer, 1960), 59–70.

Lawson, John H. "Styron: Darkness and Fire in the Modern Novel," *Mainstream*, 13 (October, 1960), 9–18.

Mizener, Arthur. "Some People of our Time," *NYTBR* (June 5, 1960), 5, 26.

Rubin, Louis D., Jr., Katherine Anne Porter, Flannery O'Connor, Caroline Gordon, and Madison Jones. *Recent Southern Fiction*. Macon, Georgia: Wesleyan College, 1960.

Schneider, Harold W. "Two Bibliographies: Saul Bellow, William Styron," *Critique*, 3 (Summer, 1960), 71–91.

Stevenson, David L. "Styron and the Fiction of the Fifties," *Critique*, 3 (Summer, 1960), 47–58. Reprinted in *Recent American Fiction: Some Critical Views*, ed. Joseph J. Waldmeir (New York: Houghton Mifflin, 1963), pp. 265–274.

1961

Friedman, Melvin J. "William Styron: An Interim Appraisal," *English Journal*, 50 (March, 1961), 149–158, 192.

Hassan, Ihab H. "The Avant-Garde: Which Way is Forward?" *Nation*, 193 (November 18, 1961), 396–399.

——. "Encounter with Necessity," *Radical Innocence* (Princeton: Princeton University Press, 1961), pp. 124–133. Reprinted in Richard Kostelanetz (ed.), *On Contemporary Literature* (New York: Avon Books, 1965), pp. 597–606.

Hoffman, Frederick J. "The Sense of Place," *South,* ed. Louis D. Rubin, Jr., and Robert D. Jacobs (Garden City, New York: Doubleday, 1961), pp. 60–75.

Lewis, R. W. B. "American Letters: A Projection," *Yale Review,* 51 (December, 1961), 211–226.

McNamara, Eugene. "Styron's *Long March:* Absurdity and Authority," *WHR,* 15 (Summer, 1961), 267–272.

Nye, Russell B. "Le Roman Américain Contemporain," *Revue des Lettres Modernes,* 8 (Spring, 1961), 3–16.

Roth, Philip. "Writing American Fiction," *Commentary,* 31 (March, 1961), 222–233.

Rubin, Louis D., Jr., and Robert D. Jacobs (eds.). "Introduction: Southern Writing and the Changing South," *South* (Garden City, New York: Doubleday, 1961), pp. 14–25.

Sullivan, Walter. "The Continuing Renascence," *South,* ed. Louis D. Rubin, Jr., and Robert D. Jacobs, pp. 376–391.

Waldmeir, Joseph. "Quest Without Faith," *Nation,* 193 (November 18, 1961), 390–396.

Winner, Arthur. "Adjustment, Tragic Humanism and Italy," *Studi Americani,* 7 (1961), 311–361.

1962

Baudrillard, Jean. "La proie des flammes," *Temps Modernes,* No. 193 (1962), pp. 1928–1937.

Benson, Alice R. "Techniques in the Twentieth-Century Novel for Relating the Particular to the Universal: *Set This House on Fire,*" *Papers of the Michigan Academy of Science,* 47 (1962), 587–594.

Bonnichon, André. "William Styron et le second Oedipe," *Études,* 13 (October, 1962), 94–103.

Brierre, Annie. "La Proie des Critiques," *Nouvelles Littéraires,* 40 (March 22, 1962), 8. Interview with Styron, his translator Maurice Coindreau, and Michel Butor.

Cheyer, A. H. "W. L. B. Biography: William Styron," *Wilson Library Bulletin,* 36 (April, 1962), 691.

Fuller, Edmund. *Books With Men Behind Them* (New York: Random House, 1962), 9–10.

Hassan, Ihab H. "The Character of Post-War Fiction in America," *English Journal,* 51 (January, 1962), 1–8.

Lawson, Lewis. "Cass Kinsolving: Kierkegaardian Man of Despair," *WSCL,* 3 (Fall, 1962), 54–66.

LaMaire, Marcel. "Some Recent American Novels and Essays," *Revue des Langues Vivantes*, 28 (January–February, 1962), 70–78.

Ludwig, Jack. *Recent American Novelists* (Minneapolis: University of Minnesota Press, 1962), 31–33.

McNamara, Eugene. "The Post-Modern American Novel," *Queen's Quarterly*, 69 (Summer, 1962), 265–275.

Rubin, Louis D., Jr. "The South and the Faraway Country," *Virginia Quarterly Review*, 38 (Summer, 1962), 444–459.

Slavitt, David R. "Poetry, Novels, and Critics: A Reply," *Yale Review*, 51 (March, 1962), 502–504.

1963

Arnavon, Cyrille. "Les romans de William Styron," *Europe*, 41 (September, 1963), 54–66.

Bryant, Jerry H. "The Hopeful Stoicism of William Styron," *South Atlantic Quarterly*, 62 (Autumn, 1963), 539–550.

Davis, Robert Gorham. "The American Individualist Tradition: Bellow and Styron," *The Creative Present*, ed. Norma Balakian and Charles Simmons (New York: Doubleday, 1963), pp. 111–141.

Hartt, Julian. *The Lost Image of Man* (Baton Rouge: Louisiana State University Press, 1963), pp. 60–63, 130.

Mailer, Norman. "Norman Mailer vs. Nine Writers," *Esquire*, 60 (July, 1963), 63–69, 105.

Rubin, Louis D., Jr. "William Styron: Notes on a Southern Writer in our Time," *The Faraway Country* (Seattle: University of Washington Press, 1963), pp. 185–230.

Stevenson, David L. "The Activists," *Daedalus*, 92 (Spring, 1963), 238–249.

———. "Novelists of Distinction," *The Creative Present*, ed. Norma Balakian and Charles Simmons, pp. 195–212.

1964

Baumbach, Jonathan. "Paradise Lost: The Novels of William Styron," *South Atlantic Quarterly*, 63 (Spring, 1964), 207–217. Collected in *The Landscape of Nightmare* (New York: New York University Press, 1965), pp. 123–137.

Detweiler, Robert. "William Styron and the Courage To Be," *Four Spiritual Crises in Mid-Century American Fiction* (Gainesville: University of Florida Press, 1964), pp. 6–13.

Doar, Harriet. "Interview with William Styron," *Red Clay Reader, 1964,* pp. 26–30.

Geismar, Maxwell. "The Contemporary American Short Story," *Studies on the Left,* 4 (Spring, 1964), 21–27.

Gresset, Michel. "Sur William Styron," *Mercure de France,* 350 (February, 1964), 297–303.

Klotz, Marvin. "The Triumph over Time: Narrative Form in William Faulkner and William Styron," *Mississippi Quarterly,* 17 (Winter, 1963–1964), 9–20.

Kostelanetz, Richard. "The Bad Criticism of this Age," *Minnesota Review,* 4 (Spring, 1964), 389–414.

Mudrick, Marvin. "Mailer and Styron: Guests of the Establishment," *Hudson Review,* 17 (Autumn, 1964), 346–366.

Noggle, Burl. "Variety and Ambiguity," *Mississippi Quarterly,* 17 (Winter, 1963–1964), 33.

Nyren, Dorothy (ed.). "William Styron," *A Library of Literary Criticism* (New York: Frederick Ungar, 1964), pp. 473–476.

O'Connor, William Van. "John Updike and William Styron: The Burden of Talent," *Contemporary American Novelists,* ed. Harry T. Moore (Carbondale: Southern Illinois University Press, 1964), pp. 205–220.

Podhoretz, Norman. "The Gloom of Philip Roth," *Doings and Undoings* (New York: Farrar, Strauss, 1964), pp. 236–243.

Schickel, Richard. "The Old Criticism and the New Novel," *WSCL,* 5 (Winter–Spring, 1964), 30–31.

Thorp, Willard. "The Southern Mode," *South Atlantic Quarterly,* 63 (Autumn, 1964), 576–582.

1965

Finkelstein, Sidney. "Cold War, Religious Revival and Family Alienation: William Styron, J. D. Salinger and Edward Albee," *Existentialism and Alienation in American Literature* (New York: International, 1965), pp. 211–242.

Galloway, David D. "The Absurd Man as Tragic Hero: The Novels of William Styron," *TSLL,* 6 (Winter, 1965), 512–534.

Gossett, Louise Y. "The Cost of Freedom: William Styron," *Violence in Recent Southern Fiction* (Durham, North Carolina: Duke University Press, 1965), pp. 117–131.

Hassan Ihab. "The Novel of Outrage: A Minority Voice in Postwar American Fiction," *American Scholar,* 34 (Spring, 1965), 239–253.

Rubin, Louis D., Jr. "Notes on the Literary Scene: Their Own Language," *Harper's,* 230 (April, 1965), 173–174.

1966

Aldridge, J. W. "William Styron and the Derivative Imagination," *Time to Murder and Create* (New York: D. McKay Co, 1966), pp. 30–51.

Canzoneri, Robert, and Page Stegner. "An Interview with William Styron," *Per/Se*, 1, no. B (1966), 37–44.

Carver, Wayne. "The Grand Inquisitor's Long March," *University of Denver Quarterly*, 1, no. 2 (1966), 37–64.

Hays, Peter L. "The Nature of Rebellion in *The Long March*," *Critique*, 8 (Winter, 1966), 70–74.

Moore, L. Hugh. "Robert Penn Warren, William Styron, and the Use of Greek Myth," *Critique*, 8 (Winter, 1966), 75–87.

O'Connell, Shaun. "Expense of Spirit: The Vision of William Styron," *Critique*, 8 (Winter, 1966), 20–33.

Robb, Kenneth A. "William Styron's Don Juan," *Critique*, 8 (Winter, 1966), 34–46.

Urang, Gunnar. "The Broader Vision: William Styron's *Set This House On Fire*," *Critque*, 8 (Winter, 1966), 47–69.

1967

Brandriff, Welles T. "The Role of Order and Disorder in *The Long March*," *English Journal*, 56 (January, 1967), 54–59.

Friedman, Melvin J. "*The Confessions of Nat Turner*: The Convergence of 'Nonfiction Novel' and 'Meditation on History,' " *Journal of Popular Culture* (Fall, 1967), 166–175.

Meras, Phyllis. "The Author," *SRL*, 50 (October 7, 1967), 30. Interview.

Nigro, Augustine. "*The Long March*: The Expansive Hero in a Closed World," *Critique*, 9 (Autumn, 1967), 103–112.

Phillips, J. "Styron Unlocked," *Vogue*, 150 (December, 1967), 216, 267–270, 278.

Plimpton, George. "William Styron: A Shared Ordeal," *NYTBR* (October 8, 1967), 2–3, 30, 32, 34.

Rubin, Louis D., Jr. "William Styron and Human Bondage: *The Confessions of Nat Turner*," *Hollins Critic*, 4 (December, 1967), 1–12.

1968

Borzelay, Douglas, and Robert M. Sussman. "William Styron on *The Confessions of Nat Turner*: A Yale Literary Interview," *Yale Literary Magazine*, 137 (September, 1968), 24–35.

Clarke, John Henrik (ed). *William Styron's Nat Turner: Ten Black Writers Respond*. Boston: Beacon Press, 1968.

Newcomb, Horace. "William Styron and the Act of Memory," *Chicago Review*, 20, no. 1 (1968), 86–94.

Sussman, Robert M. "The Case Against William Styron's Nat Turner," *Yale Literary Magazine*, 137 (September, 1968), 20–23.

Thelwell, Mike. "William Styron and the Reverend Turner," *Massachusetts Review*, 9 (Winter, 1968), 7–29. Reprinted, condensed, in *William Styron's Nat Turner: Ten Black Writers Respond*, ed. John Henrik Clarke.

A SAUL BELLOW CHECKLIST

I. PRIMARY SOURCES

A. Books

Dangling Man. New York: Vanguard, 1944.
 Reviews:
  Chamberlain, John. *NYT* (March 25, 1944), 13.
  De Vries, Peter. *Chicago Sun Bookweek* (April 9, 1944), 3.
  Fearing, Kenneth. *NYTBR* (March 26, 1944), 5, 15.
  Hale, Lionel. *Observer* (January 12, 1947), 3.
  Heppenstall, Rayner. *New Statesman and Nation*, n.s. 42 (December 28, 1946), 488–489.
  Kirkus, 12 (February 1, 1944), 48.
  Kristol, Irving. *Politics*, 1 (June, 1944), 156.
  Kupferberg, Herbert. *NYHTBR* (April 9, 1944), 11.
  Mayberry, George. *New Republic*, 110 (April 3, 1944), 473–474.
  O'Brien, Kate. *Spectator* (January 3, 1947), 26.
  Rothman, N. L. *SRL*, 27 (April 15, 1944), 27.
  Straus, Ralph. *Sunday Times* (London), (January 26, 1947), 3.
  Time, 43 (May 8, 1944), 104.
  Trilling, Diana. *Nation*, 163 (April 15, 1944), 455.
  Wilson, Edmund. *NY*, 20 (April 1, 1944), 78, 81.

The Victim. New York: Vanguard, 1947.
 Reviews:
  Cross, Jesse E. *Library Journal*, 72 (November 15, 1947), 1610.

Downer, A. S. *NYTBR* (November 30, 1947), 29.
Farrelly, John. *New Republic*, 117 (December 8, 1947), 27–28.
Hale, Lionel. *Observer* (June 13, 1948), 3.
Kirkus, 15 (November 1, 1947), 10.
Match, Richard. *NYHTBR* (November 23, 1947), 10.
Millar, Ruby. *New English Review*, 15 (July, 1948), 89.
NY, 23 (December 13, 1947), 139.
Poore, Charles. *NYT* (November 22, 1947), 13.
Smith, R. D. *Spectator* (June 4, 1948), 686, 688.
Straus, Ralph. *Sunday Times* (London), (June 6, 1948), 3.
Time, 50 (December 1, 1947), 111–112.
Trilling, Diana. *Nation*, 166 (January 3, 1948), 24–25.
Gibbs, Wolcott. *NY*, 28 (May 10, 1952), 54. Review of Leonard
  Lesley's dramatization of *The Victim*.

The Adventures of Augie March. New York: Viking Press, 1953.

Reviews:

American Scholar, 23 (Winter, 1953–1954), 126.
Amis, Kingsley. *Spectator* (May 21, 1954), 626.
Booklist, 50 (September 1, 1953), 1.
Cassidy, T. E. *Commonweal*, 58 (October 2, 1953), 636.
Crane, Milton. Chicago *Sunday Tribune* (September 20, 1953), 4.
Davis, Robert Gorham. *NYTBR* (September 20, 1953), 1, 36.
Finn, James. *Chicago Review*, 8 (Spring–Summer, 1954), 104–111.
Geismar, Maxwell. *Nation*, 177 (November 14, 1953), 404.
Harwell, Meade. *Southwest Review*, 39 (Summer, 1954), 273–276.
Hicks, Granville. *New Leader* (September 21, 1953), 23–24.
Hopkinson, Tom. *London Magazine*, 1 (June, 1954), 82, 84, 86.
Hughes, Riley. *Catholic World*, 178 (December, 1953), 233–234.
Kirkus, 21 (July 1, 1953), 395.
Kristol, Irving. *Encounter*, 3 (July, 1954), 74–75.
Mizener, Arthur. *NYHTBR* (September 20, 1953), 2.
Newsweek, 42 (September 21, 1953), 102, 104.
Pickrel, Paul. *Yale Review*, 43 (Autumn, 1953), x.
Prescott, Orville. *NYT* (September 18, 1953), 21.
Priestley, J. B. *Sunday Times* (London), (May 9, 1954), 5.
Pritchett, V. S. *New Statesman and Nation*, n.s. 47 (June 19, 1954),
  803.
Rolo, Charles J. *Atlantic*, 192 (October, 1953), 86–87.

Rosenberg, Dorothy. San Francisco *Sunday Chronicle* (October 25, 1953), 136–141.

Shorer, Mark. *Hudson Review,* 7 (Spring, 1954), 136–141.

Time, 62 (September 21, 1953), 114, 117.

TLS (June 4, 1954), 357.

Walbridge, Earle F. *Library Journal,* 78 (September 15, 1953), 1529–1530.

Warren, Robert Penn. *New Republic,* 129 (November 2, 1953), 22–23.

Webster, Harvey Curtis. *SRL,* 36 (September 19, 1953), 13–14.

West, Anthony. *NY,* 29 (September 26, 1953), 140, 142, 145.

West, Ray B. *Shenandoah,* 5 (Winter, 1953), 85–90.

Wilson, Angus. *Observer* (May 9, 1954), 9.

Seize the Day. New York: Viking Press, 1956. Contents: "Seize the Day," "A Father-to-Be," "Looking for Mr. Green," "The Gonzaga Manuscripts," "The Wrecker."

Reviews:

Allen, Walter. *New Statesman and Nation,* n.s. 53 (April 27, 1957), 548.

Alpert, Hollis. *SRL,* 39 (November 24, 1956), 18, 34.

Baker, Robert. *Chicago Review,* 2 (Spring, 1957), 107–110.

Bayley, John. *Spectator* (June 7, 1957), 758.

Booklist, 53 (December 1, 1956), 174.

Bowen, Robert O. *Northwest Review,* 1 (Spring, 1957), 52–56.

Crane, Milton. Chicago *Sunday Tribune* (December 30, 1956), 46.

Fiedler, Leslie. *Reporter,* 15 (December 13, 1956), 46.

Gill, Brendan. *NY,* 32 (January 5, 1957), 69–70.

Gold, Herbert. *Nation,* 183 (November 17, 1956), 435–436.

Hicks, Granville. *New Leader* (November 26, 1956), 24–25.

Hogan, William. San Francisco *Chronicle* (November 15, 1956), 27.

Hopkinson, Tom. *Observer* (April 21, 1957), 11.

Kazin, Alfred. *NYTBR* (November 18, 1956), 5, 36.

Kirkus, 24 (October 1, 1956), 763.

Lynch, John A. *Commonweal,* 65 (November 30, 1956), 238–239.

Newsweek, 48 (November 19, 1956), 142–143.

Pickrel, Paul. *Harper's,* 213 (December, 1956), 100.

Rolo, Charles J. *Atlantic,* 199 (January, 1957), 86–87.

Rugoff, Milton. *NYTBR* (November 18, 1956), 3.

Schwartz, Edward. *New Republic,* 135 (December 3, 1956), 20–21.

Smith, T. Francis. *Library Journal*, 81 (November 1, 1956), 2548.
Stern, Richard G. *Kenyon Review*, 21 (Autumn, 1959), 655–661.
Swados, Harvey. New York *Post Week-End Magazine* (November 18, 1956), 11.
Swan, Michael. *Sunday Times* (London), (April 21, 1957), 7.
Time, 68 (November 19, 1956), 122.
West, Ray B., Jr. *Sewanee Review*, 64 (Summer, 1957), 498–508.
Wyndham, Francis. *London Magazine*, 4 (August, 1957), 66.

Henderson the Rain King. New York: Viking Press, 1959.

Reviews:

Atlantic, 203 (March, 1959), 88.
Baker, Carlos. *NYTBR* (February 22, 1959), 4–5.
Booklist, 55 (December 15, 1958), 202.
Curley, T. F. *Commonweal*, 70 (April 17, 1959), 84.
Friedman, Joseph J. *Venture*, 3 (1959), 71–73.
Gold, Herbert. *Nation*, 188 (February 21, 1959), 169, 170, 171, 172.
Hardwick, Elizabeth. *Partisan Review*, 26 (Spring, 1959), 299–300, 302–303.
Hicks, Granville. *SRL*, 42 (February 21, 1959), 20.
Hogan, William. San Francisco *Chronicle* (February 23, 1959), 25.
Jacobson, Dan. *Spectator* (May 22, 1959), 735.
Kirkus, 27 (January 1, 1959), 16.
Kogan, Herman. Chicago *Sunday Tribune* (February 22, 1959), 3.
Leach, Elsie. *Western Humanities Review*, 14 (Spring, 1961), 223–224.
Levine, Paul. *Georgia Review* (Summer, 1960), 218.
Maddocks, Melvin. *Christian Science Monitor* (February 26, 1959), 11.
Malcolm, Donald. *NY*, 35 (March 14, 1959), 171, 172, 173.
Maud, Ralph. *Audit*, 1 (February 22, 1960), 17–18.
Miller, Karl. *Listener*, 61 (June 25, 1959), 1099–1100.
Perrott, Roy. *Manchester Guardian* (May 29, 1959), 6.
Pickrel, Paul. *Harper's*, 218 (March, 1959), 104.
Podhoretz, Norman. *NYHTBR* (February 22, 1959), 3.
Prescott, Orville. *NYT* (February 23, 1959), 21.
Price, Martin. *Yale Review*, 48 (March, 1959), 453–456.
Scott, J. D. *Sunday Times* (London), (May 24, 1959), 15.
Stern, Richard G. *Kenyon Review*, 21 (Autumn, 1959), 655–661.
Swados, Harvey. *New Leader* (March 23, 1959), 23–24.

Tanasoca, Donald. *Library Journal,* 84 (January, 1959), 118.
Thompson, Frank H. *Prairie Schooner,* 34 (Summer, 1960), 174–175.
Time, 73 (February 23, 1959), 102.
TLS (January 12, 1959), 352.
Wain, John. *Observer* (May 24, 1959), 21.
Waterhouse, Keith. *New Statesman and Nation,* n.s. 57 (June 6, 1959), 805–806.
Weales, Gerald. *Reporter,* 20 (March 19, 1959), 46–47.
Whittemore, Reed. *New Republic,* 140 (March 16, 1959), 17–18.
Wilson, Angus. *Observer* (December 27, 1959), 8.

Herzog. New York: Viking Press, 1964.
Reviews:

Barrett, William. *Atlantic,* 61 (November, 1964), 192.
Burns, R. K. *Library Journal,* 89 (September 1, 1964), 3182.
Curley, Thomas. *Commonweal,* 81 (October 23, 1964), 137–139.
Davenport, Guy. *National Review* (November 3, 1964), 978.
Dolbier, M. *NYHTBR* (September 21, 1964), 23.
Elliott, George P. *Nation,* 199 (October 19, 1964), 252–254.
Fadiman, Clifton. *Book of the Month Club News* (October, 1964), 12.
Fronek, Tom. *Tablet* (February 6, 1965), 154.
Goran, L. Chicago *Sunday Tribune: Books Today* (Sept. 1964), 1.
Gross, Beverly. *Chicago Review,* 17, nos. 2–3 (1964), 217.
Hicks, Granville. *SRL,* 47 (September 19, 1964), 37–38.
Howe, Irving. *New Republic,* 151 (September 19, 1964), 21–24.
Hyman, Stanley Edgar. *New Leader,* 47 (September, 1964), 16.
Lamont, Rosette. *Massachusetts Review* (Spring–Summer, 1965), 630.
Klein, Marcus. *Reporter,* 31 (October 22, 1964), 53–54.
Lamott, Kenneth. *Show,* 4 (December, 1964), 80.
Ludwig, Jack. *Holiday,* 37 (February, 1965), 16.
Maddocks, Melvin. *Christian Science Monitor* (Sept. 24, 1964), 7.
Moynahan, Julian. *NYTBR* (September 20, 1964), 1.
Muggeridge, Malcolm. *Esquire,* 63 (January, 1965), 24.
Newsweek, 64 (September 21, 1964), 114.
Pickrel, Paul. *Harper's,* 229 (October, 1964), 128.
Poirier, Richard. *Partisan Review,* 32 (Spring, 1965), 264.
Prescott, Orville. *NYT* (September 21, 1964), 29.
———. San Francisco *Sunday Chronicle: This World Magazine* (September 27, 1964), 39.
Pritchett, V. S. *NYRB,* 3 (October 22, 1964), 4–5.

Rahv, Philip. *Book Week* (September 20, 1964), 1.
Read, Forrest. *Epoch*, 13 (Winter, 1964), 81–96.
Richler, Mordecai. *Spectator* (January 29, 1965), 139.
Rovit, Earl. *American Scholar*, 34 (Spring, 1965), 292, 294, 296, 298.
Sale, Roger. *Hudson Review*, 17 (Winter, 1964–1965), 608.
Scott, N. *Christian Century* (December 16, 1964), 1562.
Solotaroff, Theodore. *Commentary*, 38 (December, 1964), 63–66.
Steiner, George. *Sunday Times* (London) (January 31, 1965), 48.
Tanner, Tony. *Encounter*, 24 (February, 1965), 58–70.
Time, 84 (September 25, 1964), 105.
TLS (February 4, 1965), 81.
Trachtman, Paul. *Progressive* (November, 1964), 608.
Toynbee, Philip. *Observer* (January 31, 1965), 37.
Trevor, William. *Listener*, 73 (February 4, 1965), 201.
Virginia Quarterly Review, 41 (Winter, 1965), ix.

Mosby's Memoirs, and Other Stories. New York: Viking Press, 1968.
Reviews:
Axthelm, Pete. *Newsweek*, 72 (October 26, 1968), 122.
Dalton, Elizabeth. *Commentary*, 47 (April, 1969), 69–70.
Katz, Bill. *Library Journal*, 93 (October 15, 1968), 3797.
Lasson, Robert. *Book World* (October 20, 1968), 6.
Samuels, C. T. *Atlantic*, 222 (November, 1968), 126.

B. BRIEFER WRITINGS

1. *Short Fiction*

1941
"Two Morning Monologues," *Partisan Review*, 8 (May–June, 1941), 230–236. Reprinted in *Partisan Reader* (New York: Dial Press, 1946), pp. 91–96.

1942
"The Mexican General," *Partisan Review*, 9 (May–June, 1942), 178–194. Reprinted in *More Stories in the Modern Manner* (New York: Avon Publications, Inc., 1954), pp. 235–252.

1943
"Notes of a Dangling Man," *Partisan Review*, 10 (September–October, 1943), 402–409, 429–438. Reprinted in *Best American Short Stories, 1944*, ed. Martha Foley (Boston: Houghton Mifflin Co., 1950), pp. 21–40.

1949

"Dora," *Harper's Bazaar*, 83 (November, 1949), 118, 188–190, 198–199.

"From the Life of Augie March," *Partisan Review*, 16 (November, 1949), 1077–1089. Chapter 1 of *Augie March*, with a few changes in the first paragraphs.

"Sermon by Doctor Pep," *Partisan Review*, 23 (Summer, 1956), 455–462. Reprinted in *Best American Short Stories, 1950*, ed. Martha Foley (Boston: Houghton Mifflin, 1950), pp. 59–66; in *The New Partisan Reader, 1945–1953* (New York: Harcourt, Brace, 1953), pp. 99–105; in *Fiction of the Fifties*, ed. Herbert Gold (New York: Doubleday, 1959), pp. 66–73.

1950

"Trip to Galena," *Partisan Review*, 17 (November–December, 1950), 779–794.

1951

"Address by Gooley MacDowell to the Hasbeens Club of Chicago," *Hudson Review*, 4 (Summer, 1951), 222–227. Reprinted in *Nelson Algren's Book of Lonesome Monsters*, ed. with an introduction by Nelson Algren (New York: Lancer Books, 1962), pp. 147–153.

"By the Rock Wall," *Harper's Bazaar*, 85 (April, 1951), 135–205, 207–208, 214–216.

"The Coblins," *Sewanee Review*, 59 (Autumn, 1951), 635–653. Chapter 2 of *Augie March*, with slight changes.

"The Einhorns," *Partisan Review*, 18 (November–December, 1951), 619–645. Reprinted in *Perspectives, U.S.A.*, 2 (Winter, 1953), 101–129. Chapter 5 of *Augie March*.

"Looking for Mr. Green," *Commentary*, 11 (March, 1951), 251–261. Collected in *Seize the Day*.

1952

"Interval in a Lifeboat," *NY*, 28 (December 27, 1952), 24–28, 33–39. Chapter 25 of *Augie March*, omitting the first pages about Augie and Stella's wedding, and with numerous differences in the texts.

1953

"The Eagle," *Harper's Bazaar*, 87 (February, 1953), 126–127, 196, 203–204, 206. This story, considerably expanded, forms Chapters 15 and 16 of *Augie March*.

"Mintouchian," *Hudson Review*, 6 (Summer, 1953), 239–249. Chapter 24 of *Augie March*, with slight changes.

1955
"A Father-to-be," *NY*, 30 (February 5, 1955), 26–30. Collected in *Seize the Day*.

1956
"The Gonzaga Manuscripts," *discovery*, IV, ed. Vance Bourjaily (New York: Pocket Books, 1956). Collected in *Seize the Day*. Reprinted in *Prize Stories, 1956: The O. Henry Awards* (Garden City: Doubleday and Co., 1956), pp. 76–102.
"Seize the Day," *Partisan Review*, 23 (Summer, 1956), 295–319, 376–424, 426–428, 431–432. This novella became the title work of the later collection.

1958
"Henderson the Rain King," *Hudson Review*, 11 (Spring, 1958), 11–28. Chapters 1–4 of the novel, shortened and otherwise somewhat changed.

1961
"Herzog," *Esquire*, 56 (July, 1961), 115–130. From an early draft of *Herzog*; some sections of the story were abandoned entirely, others incorporated into the first three chapters of the novel, with numerous important alterations in plot, dialogue, and names of characters.

1963
"Letter to Doctor Edvig," *Esquire*, 60 (July, 1963), 61–62, 103–105. An early version of the final section, Chapter 2, of *Herzog*, in which Madeleine is called Juliana and Valentine's last name is given as Grenzbach; extensively rewritten in the novel itself.

1964
"Herzog Visits Chicago," *Saturday Evening Post*, 237 (August 8, 1964), 44–45, 48–49, 51–52, 55–60, 62–64, 66–69. A summary of Herzog's life, followed by the concluding section of Chapter 4; Chapters 7 and 8, with some condensation and elimination of the letters; and passages from the first section of Chapter 9.
"Napoleon Street," *Commentary*, 38 (July, 1964), 30–38. The concluding section of Chapter 4 of *Herzog*, with omission of the opening paragraphs.

2. *Articles and Reviews*

1948

"Spanish Letter," *Partisan Review*, 15 (February, 1948), 217–230.

1949

"The Jewish Writer and the English Literary Tradition," *Commentary*, 8 (October, 1949), 366–367.

1950

"Dreiser and the Triumph of Art," *Commentary*, 11 (May, 1951), 502–503. Review of F. O. Matthiessen's *Theodore Dreiser*. Reprinted in *The Stature of Theodore Dreiser*, ed. Alfred Kazin and Carl Shapiro (Bloomington: Indiana University Press, 1955), pp. 146–148.

"Gide as Autobiographer," *New Leader* (June 4, 1951), 24. Review of Andre Gide's *The Counterfeiters*, with "Journal of *The Counterfeiters*."

"Italian Fiction: Without Hope," *New Leader* (December 11, 1950), 21–22. Review of *The New Italian Writers: An Anthology from Botteghe Obscure*, ed. Marguerite Caetani.

1953

"Hemingway and the Image of Man," *Partisan Review*, 20 (May–June, 1953), 338–342. Review of Philip Young's *Ernest Hemingway*.

"How I Wrote Augie March's Story," *NYTBR* (January 31, 1954), 3, 17.

"Laughter in the Ghetto," *SRL*, 36 (May 30, 1953), 15. Review of Sholom Aleichem's *The Adventures of Gimpel the Fool*.

"A Personal Record," *New Republic*, 130 (February 22, 1954), 20. Review of Joyce Cary's *Except the Lord*.

"Pleasure and Pains of Playgoing," *Partisan Review*, 21 (May, 1954), 312–317. Informal reviews of four plays, including Eliot's *Confidential Clerk* and Sartre's *No Exit*.

Translation of I. B. Singer's "Gimpel the Fool," *Partisan Review*, 20 (May–June, 1953), 300–313. Reprinted in *A Treasury of Yiddish Stories*, ed. Irving Howe and Eliezer Greenberg (New York: Viking Press, 1954), pp. 401–414. Collected in Isaac Bashevis Singer's *Gimpel the Fool and Other Stories* (New York: Noonday Press, 1957), pp. 3–21.

"The Writer and the Audience," *Perspectives U.S.A.*, 9 (Autumn, 1954), 99–102.

1955

Foreword to F. M. Dostoievski's *Winter Notes on Summer Impressions*, trans. Richard Lee Renfield (New York: Criterion Books, 1955), pp. 9–27.

"The French as Dostoievski Saw Them," *New Republic*, 132 (May 23, 1955), 17–20.

1956

"Isaac Rosenfeld," *Partisan Review*, 23 (Fall, 1956), 565–567.

"Rabbi's Boy in Edinburgh," *SRL*, 39 (March 24, 1956), 19. Review of David Daiches' autobiography, *Two Worlds*.

"A Talk with the Yellow Kid," *The Reporter*, 15 (September 6, 1956), 41–44.

1957

"Distractions of a Fiction Writer," *New World Writing*, 12 (New York: New American Library, 1957), 229–243. Also in *The Living Novel*, ed. Granville Hicks (New York: Macmillan, 1957), pp. 1–20.

"The University as a Villain," *Nation*, 185 (November 16, 1957), 361–363.

1959

"Deep Readers of the World, Beware!" *NYTBR* (February 15, 1959), 1, 34. Reprinted in *Opinions and Perspectives from* THE NEW YORK TIMES BOOK REVIEW, ed. Francis Brown (Boston: Houghton Mifflin, 1964), pp. 24–28.

"Illinois Journey," *Holiday*, 22 (September, 1959), 62, 102–107.

"The Swamp of Prosperity," *Commentary*, 28 (July, 1959), 77–79. Review of Philip Roth's *Goodbye, Columbus*.

"The Uses of Adversity," *Reporter*, 21 (October 1, 1959), 42–44. Review of Oscar Lewis's *Five Families*.

1960

"The Sealed Treasure," *TLS* (July 1, 1960), 414. Reprinted in *The Open Form*, ed. Alfred Kazin (New York: Harcourt, Brace, 1961), pp. 3–9.

1961

"Literary Notes on Khruschev," *Esquire*, 55 (March, 1961), 106–107. Reprinted in *First Person Singular*, ed. Herbert Gold (New York: Dial Press, 1963), pp. 46–54.

1962

"Facts That Put Fancy to Flight," *NYTBR* (February 11, 1962), 1, 28. Reprinted in *Opinions and Perspectives from* THE NEW YORK TIMES BOOK REVIEW, ed. Francis Brown, pp. 235–240.

"Movies: Art of Going It Alone," *Horizon*, 5 (September, 1962), 108–
110. Discussion of the work of Morris Engel, including *The Little
Fugitive, Lovers and Lollipops,* and *Weddings and Babies.*

"Movies: Buñel's Unsparing Vision," *Horizon*, 5 (November, 1962),
110–112.

"Where Do We Go from Here: The Future of Fiction," *Michigan Quarterly Review*, 1 (Winter, 1962), 27–33.

1963

"Beatrice Webb's America," *Nation*, 197 (September 7, 1963), 116.

"Literature," *The Great Ideas Today*, ed. Mortimer Adler and Robert
M. Hutchins (Chicago: The Encyclopedia Britannica, 1963), pp.
135–179.

"Movies," *Horizon*, 5 (March, 1963), 109–111.

"Some Notes on Recent American Fiction," *Encounter*, 21 (November,
1963), 22–29. Reprinted, with minor changes in wording and para-
graphing, as *Recent American Fiction*. Washington: The Library of
Congress, 1963.

"The Writer as Moralist," *Atlantic Monthly*, 211 (March, 1963), 58–62.

1964

"A Comment on 'Form and Despair'," *Location*, 1 (Summer, 1964), 10–
12.

1965

"Thinking Man's Waste Land," *SRL*, 48 (April 3, 1965), 20. Excerpt
from Bellow's speech in acceptance of the National Book Award for
Herzog.

1966

"The Enemy Is Academe," *Publishers Weekly*, 190 (July 18, 1966), 34.

3. *Plays*

1954

"The Wrecker," *New World Writing*, 6 (1954), 271–287. Collected in
Seize the Day.

1962

"Scenes from Humanitis—A Farce," *Partisan Review*, 29 (Summer,
1962), 327–349. Excerpts from an early version of *Last Analysis* (unpublished), produced in October, 1964; revised and published in full
by Viking Press, 1965.

Reviews of the production of *Last Analysis:*
  Hudson Review, 17 (Winter, 1964–1965), 556–557.
  Life, 57 (December 30, 1964), 17.
  Nation, 199 (October 19, 1964), 256–257.
  New Republic, 151 (October 24, 1964), 25–26.
  Newsweek, 64 (October 12, 1964), 105.
  SRL, 47 (October 9, 1964), 29.
  Time, 84 (October 9, 1964), 92.
  Vogue, 144 (November 15, 1964), 110–111.

1965
The Last Analysis. New York: Viking Press, 1965. See entry under
  Plays, 1962.
"Orange Soufflé," *Esquire*, 64 (October, 1965), 130–131.
"Wen," *Esquire*, 63 (January, 1965), 72–74, 111.

1966
Under the Weather. A production of three one-act plays: "The Wen,"
  "Orange Soufflé," and "Out from Under" (unpublished).
Reviews:
  Clurman, Harold. *Nation*, 203 (November 18, 1966), 523–524.
  Commonweal, 85 (November 18, 1966), 199–201.
  Gilman, Richard. *Newsweek*, 68 (November 7, 1966), 96.
  Hewes, Henry. *SRL*, 49 (November 12, 1966), 34.
  McCarten, John. *NY*, 42 (November 5, 1966), 127–128.
  Time, 88 (November 4, 1966), 85.

II. SECONDARY SOURCES (biographical and critical)

1951
Warfel, Harry R. (ed.) *American Novelists of Today* (New York:
  American Book Company, 1951), pp. 32–33.

1953
Breit, Harvey. "Talk with Saul Bellow," *NYTBR* (September 20, 1953),
  22.
Hobson, Laura. "Trade Winds," *SRL*, 36 (August 22, 1953), 6.
Hutchens, J. K. "On an Author," *NYHTBR* (October 4, 1953), 2.
Kalb, Beatrice. "Biographical Sketch," *SRL* (September 19, 1953), 13.
"Some Important Fall Authors Speak for Themselves," *NYHTBR*
  (October 11, 1953), 18.

1954

Cowley, Malcolm. "Naturalism: No Teacup Tragedies," *The Literary Situation* (New York: Viking Press, 1954), pp. 74–95.

Frank, Reuben. "Saul Bellow: The Evolution of a Contemporary Novelist," *Western Review*, 18 (Winter, 1954), 101–112.

1955

Duesberg, Jacques C. "Un jeune romancier américain: Saul Bellow," *Synthesis*, 10 (May–June, 1955), 149–150.

Kunitz, Stanley J. (ed.) *Twentieth Century Authors—First Supplement* (New York: H. W. Wilson Co., 1955), pp. 72–73.

Lewis, R. W. B. *The American Adam* (Chicago: University of Chicago Press, 1955), pp. 199–200.

1956

Aldridge, John W. "The Society of Three Novels," *In Search of Heresy* (New York: McGraw Hill Book Co., 1956), pp. 126–148.

Breit, Harvey. *Writer Observed* (New York: World Publishing Company, 1956), pp. 271–274.

Clay, George R. "The Jewish Hero in American Fiction," *The Reporter*, 17 (September 19, 1956), 43–46.

Hoffman, Frederick J. *The Modern Novel in America* (Chicago: Henry Regenery Co., 1951), pp. 188–189.

Sanavio, Piero. "Il Romanzo di Saul Bellow," *Studi Americani*, No. 2 (1956), 261–284.

1957

Bergler, Edmund. "Writers of Half-Talent," *American Imago*, 14 (Summer, 1957), 155–164.

Fiedler, Leslie. "The Breakthrough: The American Jewish Novelist and the Fictional Image of the Jew," *Midstream*, 4 (1957), 15–35.

———. "Saul Bellow," *Prairie Schooner*, 31 (Summer, 1957), 103–110. Reprinted in Gerald J. and Nancy M. Goldberg (eds.), *The Modern Critical Spectrum* (New York: Prentice Hall, 1962), pp. 155–161; and in Richard Kostelanetz (ed.), *On Contemporary Literature* (New York: Avon Books, 1965), pp. 286–295.

Glicksberg, Charles I. "The Theme of Alienation in the American Jewish Novel," *Reconstructionist*, 23 (November 29, 1957), 8–13.

Lombardo, Agostino. "L'arte di Saul Bellow," *Realismo e Simbolismo: Saggi di Letteratura Americana Contemporanea* (Roma: Edizioni di Storia e Letteratura, 1957), 245–254.

1958

Davis, Robert G. "Readers and Writers Face to Face," *NYTBR* (November 9, 1958), 4, 40–41.

Eisenger, Chester E. "Saul Bellow: Love and Identity," *Accent*, 18 (Summer, 1958), 179–203.

Geismar, Maxwell. "Saul Bellow: Novelist of the Intellectuals," *American Moderns: From Rebellion to Conformity* (New York: Hill and Wang, 1958), pp. 210–224.

Praz, Mario. "Impressioni italiane di Americani dell' Ottocento," *Studi Americani*, 4 (1958), 85–108.

Raes, Hugo. "Amerikaanse Literatuur: Saul Bellow," *Vlaamse Gids*, 42 (December, 1958), 283–284.

Stevenson, David L. "Fiction's Unfamiliar Face," *Nation*, 187 (November 1, 1958), 307–309.

1959

Cambon, Glauco. "Il nuovo romanzo di Saul Bellow," *Aut Aut*, No. 53 (September, 1959), 318–320.

Chase, Richard. "The Adventures of Saul Bellow," *Commentary*, 27 (April, 1959), 323–330.

Gold, Herbert. "Fiction of the Fifties," *Hudson Review*, 12 (Summer, 1959), 192–201. Reprinted in *Fiction of the Fifties: A Decade of American Writing*, edited with an introduction by Gold (New York: Doubleday and Co., 1959).

Howe, Irving. "Mass Society and Post-Modern Fiction," *Partisan Review*, 26 (Summer, 1959), 420–436.

Kazin, Alfred. "The Alone Generation," *Harper's*, 219 (October, 1959), 127–131.

————. "The World of Saul Bellow," *Griffin* (June, 1959), 4–9.

Lehan, Richard. "Existentialism in Recent American Fiction: The Demonic Quest," *TSLL*, 1 (Summer, 1959), 181–192.

Levine, Paul. "Saul Bellow: The Affirmation of the Philosophical Fool," *Perspective*, 10 (Winter, 1959), 163–176.

"A Place in the Sun," *TLS* (June 12, 1959), 352.

Quinton, Anthony. "The Adventures of Saul Bellow," *The London Magazine*, 6 (December, 1959), 55–59.

Ross, Theodore J. "Notes on Saul Bellow," *Chicago Jewish Forum*, 18 (Winter, 1959), 21–27.

Solotaroff, Theodore. "Philip Roth and the Jewish Moralists," *Chicago Review*, 13 (Winter, 1959), 87–99.

"A Vocal Group: The Jewish Part in American Letters," *TLS* (November 6, 1959), 35. (In a special number called *The American Imagination*.)

Widmer, Kingsley. "Poetic Naturalism in the Contemporary Novel," *Partisan Review*, 26 (Summer, 1959), 467–472.

1960

Demott, Benjamin. "Jewish Writers in America: A Place in the Establishment," *Commentary*, 30 (November, 1960), 127–134.

Freedman, Ralph. "Saul Bellow: The Illusion of Environment," *WSCL*, 1 (Winter, 1960), 50–65.

Goldberg, Gerald J. "Life's Customer, Augie March," *Critique*, 3 (Summer, 1960), 15–27.

Hassan, Ihab H. "Saul Bellow: Five Faces of a Hero," *Critique*, 3 (Summer, 1960), 28–36.

Leach, Elsie. "From Ritual to Romance Again: *Henderson the Rain King*," *WHR*, 14 (Spring, 1960), 223–224.

Levenson, J. C. "Bellow's Dangling Men," *Critique*, 3 (Summer, 1960), 3–14.

Schneider, Harold W. "Two Bibliographies: Saul Bellow, William Styron," *Critique*, 3 (Summer, 1961), 71–91.

1961

Arnavon, Cyrille. "Le Roman Africain de Saul Bellow: *Henderson the Rain King*," *Études anglaises*, 14 (January–March, 1961), 25–35.

Hasenclever, Walter. "Grosse Menschen und kleine Wirklichkeit," *Monat*, 13 (February, 1961), 71–75.

Hughes, Daniel. "Reality and the Hero: *Lolita* and *Henderson the Rain King*," *MFS*, 6 (Winter, 1960–1961), 345–364.

Roth, Philip. "Writing American Fiction," *Commentary*, 21 (March, 1961), 223–233.

1962

Goldfinch, Michael A. "A Journey to the Interior," *English Studies*, 43 (October, 1962), 439–443.

Gross, John. "Marjorie Morningstar, PhD," *New Statesman* (November 30, 1962), 784.

Kazin, Alfred. "The World of Saul Bellow," *Contemporaries* (Boston: Little, Brown, 1962), pp. 217–223.

Klein, Marcus. "A Discipline of Nobility: Saul Bellow's Fiction," *Kenyon Review*, 24 (Spring, 1962), 203–226. Reprinted in Joseph J.

Waldmeir (ed.), *Recent American Fiction: Some Critical Views* (New York: Houghton Mifflin, 1963), pp. 121–138; and in Marcus Klein, *After Alienation* (Cleveland: World Publishing Co., 1964), pp. 33–70.

Lemaire, Marcel. "Some Recent American Novels and Essays," *Revue des Langues Vivantes*, 18 (January–February, 1962), 70–78.

Ludwig, Jack. *Recent American Novelists* (Minneapolis: University of Minnesota Press, 1962), pp. 7–18. Reprinted in Richard Kostelanetz (ed.), *On Contemporary Literature* (New York: Avon Books, 1964), pp. 296–299.

Opdahl, Keith M. "The Crab and the Butterfly," *Dissertation Abstracts*, 24 (1962), 203–226.

Pritchett, V. S. "That Time and That Wilderness," *New Statesman* (September 28, 1962), 405–406.

Weiss, Daniel. "Caliban on Prospero: A Psychoanalytic Study of the Novel *Seize the Day* by Saul Bellow," *American Imago*, 19 (Fall, 1962), 277–306.

1963

Bradbury, Malcolm. "Saul Bellow's *The Victim*," *Critical Quarterly*, 5 (Summer, 1963), 119–128.

——. "Saul Bellow and the Naturalist Tradition," *Review of English Literature*, 4 (October, 1963), 80–92.

Cook, Bruce. "Saul Bellow: A Mood of Protest," *Perspectives on Ideas and the Arts*, 12 (February, 1963), 46–50.

Davis, Robert Gorham. "The American Individualist Tradition: Bellow and Styron," *The Creative Present*, ed. Norma Balakian and Charles Simmons (New York: Doubleday, 1963), 111–141.

Fiedler, Leslie. "The Jew as Mythic American," *Ramparts*, 2 (Autumn, 1963), 32–48.

Galloway, David D. "An Interview with Saul Bellow," *Audit*, 3 (Spring, 1963), 19–23.

Geismar, Maxwell. "The Jewish Heritage in Contemporary American Fiction," *Ramparts*, 2 (Autumn, 1963), 5–13.

Jensen, Emily. "Saul Bellow's *The Victim*: A View of Modern Man," *Literature*, No. 4 (1963), 38–44.

Mailer, Norman. "Norman Mailer vs. Nine Writers," *Esquire*, 60 (July, 1963), 63–69, 105.

Rans, Geoffrey. "The Novels of Saul Bellow," *REL*, 4 (October, 1963), 18–30.

Stevenson, David L. "The Activists," *Daedalus,* 92 (Spring, 1963), 238–249.

1964

Alter, Robert. "Heirs of the Tradition," *Rogue's Progress* (Cambridge: Harvard University Press, 1964), pp. 106–132.

Boroff, David. "Saul Bellow," *SRL,* 47 (September 19, 1964), 38–39, 77.

Chametsky, Jules. "Notes on the Assimilation of the American Jewish Writer: Abraham Cahan to Saul Bellow," *Jahrbuch für Amerikastudien,* No. 9 (1964), 172–180.

Donoghue, Denis. "Commitment and the Dangling Man," *Studies: An Irish Quarterly Review* (1964), 174–187.

Galloway, David D. "The Absurd Man as Picaro: The Novels of Saul Bellow," *TSLL,* 6 (Summer, 1964), 226–254.

Geismar, Maxwell. "The American Short Story Today," *Studies on the Left,* 4 (Spring, 1964), 21–27.

Handy, W. J. "Saul Bellow and the Naturalistic Hero," *TSLL,* 5 (Winter, 1964), 538–545.

Hoffman, Frederick J. "The Fool of Experience: Saul Bellow's Fiction." *Contemporary American Novelists,* ed. Harry T. Moore (Carbondale: Southern Illinois University Press, 1964), pp. 80–94.

Nyren, Dorothy. "Saul Bellow," *A Library of Literary Criticism* (New York: Frederick Ungar, 1964), pp. 42–47.

Pearce, Richard. "The Walker: Modern American Hero," *Massachusetts Review,* 5 (Summer, 1964), 761–764.

"People Are Talking About . . . ," *Vogue,* 144 (November 15, 1964), 63–66.

Podhoretz, Norman. "The Adventures of Saul Bellow," *Doings and Undoings* (New York: Farrar, Straus and Giroux, 1964), pp. 205–227.

Read, Forrest. [untitled] *Epoch,* 13 (Winter, 1964), 81–96.

Way, Brian. "Character and Society in *The Adventures of Augie March,*" *British Association for American Studies Bulletin,* No. 8 (1964), 36–44.

1965

Baumbach, Jonathan. "The Double Vision: The Victim by Saul Bellow," *The Landscape of Nightmare* (New York: New York University Press, 1965), pp. 35–54.

Bernstein, Melvin H. "Jewishness, Judaism, and the American-Jewish Novelist," *Chicago Jewish Forum,* 23 (Summer, 1965).

Bradbury, Malcolm. "Saul Bellow's *Herzog*," *Critical Quarterly*, 7 (Autumn, 1965), 425–427.

Capon, Robert F. "Herzog and the Passion," *America*, 112 (March 27, 1965), 18–32.

Crozier, Robert D. "Theme in *Augie March*," *Critique*, 7 (Spring, 1965), 18–32.

Enck, John. "Saul Bellow: An Interview," *WSCL*, 7 (Summer, 1965), 156–160.

Fiedler, Leslie. *Waiting for the End* (New York: Stein and Day, 1965), pp. 61–64, 85–86, 88, 98–100.

Finkelstein, Sidney. "Lost Convictions and Existentialism: Arthur Miller and Saul Bellow," *Existentialism and Alienation in American Literature* (New York: International Publishers, 1965), pp. 252–269.

Garrett, George. "To Do Right in a Bad World: Saul Bellow's *Herzog*," *Hollins Critic*, 2 (April, 1965), 1–12.

Guttmann, Allen. "Bellow's *Henderson*," *Critique*, 7 (Spring–Summer, 1965), 33–45.

Kazin, Alfred. "My Friend Saul Bellow," *Atlantic*, 215 (January, 1965), 51–54.

Lombardo, Agostino. "La Narrativa di Saul Bellow," *Studi Americani*, 2 (1965), 309–344.

Malin, Irving. *Jews and Americans*. Carbondale: Southern Illinois University Press, 1965.

———. "Reputations—XIV: Saul Bellow," *London Magazine*, 4 (January, 1965), 43–54.

Raines, Cathleen. "The Writer and the Common World," *Library Journal*, 90 (April 1, 1965), 1622.

Rovit, Earl. "Bellow in Occupancy," *American Scholar*, 34 (Spring, 1965), 292, 294, 296, 298.

Tanner, Tony. *Saul Bellow*. Edinburgh: Oliver and Boyd, 1965.

———. "Saul Bellow: The Flight from Monologue," *Encounter*, 24 (February, 1965), 58–70.

Young, James Dean. "Bellow's View of the Heart," *Critique*, 7 (Spring, 1965), 5–17.

1966

Binni, Francesco. "Percorso Narrativo di Saul Bellow," *Ponte*, 22 (June, 1966), 831–842.

Casty, A. "Post-Loverly Love: A Comparative Report," *Antioch Review*, 26 (Fall, 1966), 399–411. Comparison of *Herzog*, Miller's *After the Fall*, and Fellini's 8½.

Coren, Alan. "Displaced Persons," *Punch*, 251 (October 19, 1966), 603. Review of collected edition of Bellow's works.

Dickstein, Morris. "For Art's Sake," *Partisan Review*, 33 (Fall, 1966), 617–621.

Fossum, Robert H. "The Devil and Saul Bellow," *Comparative Literature Studies*, 3, no. 2 (1966), 197–206.

Gallo, Louis. *Like You're Nobody: Letters to Saul Bellow, 1961–62.* New York: Dimensions Press, 1966.

Galloway, David. "Moses-Bloom-Herzog: Bellow's Everyman," *Southern Review*, 2 (January, 1966), 61–76.

Harper, Gordon Lloyd. "The Art of Fiction XXXVII: Saul Bellow/An Interview," *Paris Review* (Winter, 1966), 49–73.

Kazin, Alfred. "Imagination and the Age," *Reporter*, 34 (May 5, 1966), 32–35.

Mudrick, Marvin. "Who Killed Herzog? or, Three American Novelists," *University of Denver Quarterly*, 1, no. 1 (1966), 61–97.

Nathan, Monique. "Saul Bellow," *Esprit*, 34 (September, 1966), 363–370.

Popescu, Petru. "Omul oscilant: Debutal lui Saul Bellow," *Luc*, 9 (March 19, 1966), 1.

Uphaus, Suzanne. "From Innocence to Experience: A Study of *Herzog*," *Dalhousie Review*, 46 (Spring, 1966), 67–78.

1967

Allen, Michael. "Idiomatic Language in Two Novels by Saul Bellow," *Journal of American Studies*, 1 (October, 1967), 275–280.

Baker, Sheridan. "Saul Bellow's Bout with Chivalry," *Criticism*, 9 (Spring, 1967), 109–122.

Baruch, Franklin R. "Bellow and Milton: Professor Herzog in His Garden," *Critique*, 9, no. 3 (1967), 74–83.

Chapman, Abraham. "The Image of Man as Portrayed by Saul Bellow," *College Language Association Journal*, 10 (1967), 285–298.

Cixioux, Hélène. "Situation de Saul Bellow," *Lettres Nouvelles* (March–April, 1967), 130–145.

Detweiler, Robert. "Patterns of Rebirth in *Henderson the Rain King*," *MFS*, 12 (Winter, 1967), 405–414.

———. *Saul Bellow: A Critical Essay.* Grand Rapids: Eerdmans, 1967.

Dommergues, Pierre. "Rencontre avec Saul Bellow," *Preuves*, 191 (January, 1967), 38–47.

Malin, Irving (ed.). *Saul Bellow and the Critics.* New York: New York University Press, 1967.

Morrow, Patrick. "Threat and Accommodation: The Novels of Saul Bellow," *Midwest Quarterly*, 8 (Summer, 1967), 389–411.

Opdahl, Keith M. *The Novels of Saul Bellow: An Introduction*. University Park: Pennsylvania State University Press, 1967.

Rovit, Earl. *Saul Bellow*. Minneapolis: University of Minnesota Press, 1967.

Schulman, Robert. "Myth, Mr. Eliot, and the Comic Novel," *MFS*, 12 (Winter, 1967), 395–403.

Stock, Irvin. "The Novels of Saul Bellow," *Southern Review*, 3 (January, 1967), 13–47.

Trachtenberg, Stanley. "Saul Bellow's *Luftmenschen*: The Compromise with Reality," *Critique*, 9 (Summer, 1967), 62–73.

1968

Clayton, John. *Saul Bellow: In Defense of Man*. Bloomington: Indiana University Press, 1968.

Frohock, W. M. "Saul Bellow and His Penitent Picaro," *Southwest Review*, 53 (Winter, 1968), 36–44.

Schulman, Robert. "The Style of Bellow's Comedy," *Publications of the Modern Language Association*, 83 (March, 1968), 109–117.

Weber, Ronald. "Bellow's Thinkers," *Western Humanities Review*, 22 (Autumn, 1968), 305–313.

1969

Bezanker, Abraham. "The Odyssey of Saul Bellow," *Yale Review*, 58 (Spring, 1969), 359–371.

Hoffman, Michael. "From Cohn to Herzog," *Yale Review*, 58 (Spring, 1969), 342–358.

Malin, Irving. *Saul Bellow's Fiction*. Carbondale: Southern Illinois University Press, 1969.

A J. D. SALINGER CHECKLIST

Note: For economy of space the following shortcut versions of authors and editors and titles of anthologies in which short fiction by Salinger and critical articles on Salinger have been republished are used in the Salinger Checklist after the first full listing:

Belcher and Lee, *J. D. Salinger and the Critics*

William F. Belcher and James W. Lee (eds.). *J. D. Salinger and the Critics.* Belmont, California: Wadsworth, 1962.

Grunwald, *Salinger: A Portrait*

Harvey A. Grunwald (ed.). *Salinger*: A *Critical and Personal Portrait.* New York: Harper, 1962.

Laser and Fruman, *Studies in J. D. Salinger*

Marvin Laser and Norman Fruman (eds.). *Studies in J. D. Salinger: Reviews, Essays and Critiques of* THE CATCHER IN THE RYE *and Other Fiction.* New York: Odyssey, 1963.

Marsden, *If You Really Want To Know*

Malcolm M. Marsden (ed.). *If You Really Want to Know: A Catcher Casebook.* Chicago: Scott, Foresman, 1963.

Simonson and Hager, *Salinger's* CATCHER IN THE RYE

Harold P. Simonson and E. P. Hager (eds.). *Salinger's* CATCHER IN THE RYE: *Clamor vs. Criticism.* New York: D. C. Heath, 1963.

I. PRIMARY SOURCES

A. BOOKS

The Catcher in the Rye. Boston: Little, Brown, 1951.
  Reviews:
      Behrman, S. N. *NY,* 27 (August 11, 1951), 71.
      Booklist, 47 (July 15, 1951), 401.
      Breit, Harvey. *Atlantic,* 188 (August, 1951), 82.
      Brooke, Jocelyn. *New Statesman and Nation,* n.s. 42 (August 18, 1951), 185.
      Charques, R. D. *Spectator,* 187 (August 17, 1951), 227.
      Engle, Paul. *Chicago Sunday Tribune* (July 15, 1951), 3.
      Goodman, Anne L. "Mad About Children," *New Republic,* 125 (July 16, 1951), 20. Reprinted in *Salinger's* CATCHER IN THE RYE: *Clamor vs. Criticism,* ed. Harold P. Simonson and E. P. Hager (New York: D. C. Heath, 1963), 3–4.

Hughes, Riley. *Catholic World*, 174 (November, 1951), 154.
Jones, Ernest. *Nation*, 173 (September 1, 1951), 176.
Kirkus, 19 (May 15, 1951), 247.
Longstreth, T. M. *Christian Science Monitor* (July 19, 1951), 7.
Neal, S. M. *Springfield Republican* (July 22, 1951), 5.
Newsweek, 38 (July 16, 1951), 89–90.
Peterson, Virgilia. *NYHTBR* (July 15, 1951), 3.
Poster, William. *Commentary*, 13 (January, 1952), 90–92.
Ritt, Thomas Francis. *America*, 85 (August 11, 1951), 463–464.
Roth, H. L. *Library Journal*, 76 (July, 1951), 1125.
Shrapel, Norman. *Manchester Guardian* (August 10, 1951), 4.
Smith, Harrison, "Manhattan Ulysses, Junior," *SRL*, 34 (July 14, 1951), 12. Reprinted in Simonson and Hager, *Salinger's* Catcher in the Rye, pp. 2–3.
Stern, James, *NYTBR* (July 15, 1951), 11.
Time, 58 (July 16, 1951), 96.
TLS (September 7, 1951), 60.
Vogler, Lewis. San Francisco *Sunday Chronicle* (July 15, 1951), 17.
Yaffe, James. *Yale Review*, 41 (Autumn, 1951), viii.

Nine Stories. Boston: Little, Brown, 1953.
  Reviews:
    Baro, Gene. *NYHTBR* (April 12, 1953), 6.
    Booklist, 49 (May 1, 1953), 286.
    Butcher, Fanny. Chicago *Sunday Tribune Magazine of Books* (April 26, 1953).
    Highet, Gilbert. *Harper's*, 206 (June, 1953), 104.
    Hughes, Riley. *Catholic World*, 178 (June, 1953), 233.
    Kirkus, 21 (February 1, 1953), 80.
    Krim, Seymour. *Commonweal*, 58 (April 24, 1953), 78. Reprinted in *Salinger: A Critical and Personal Portrait*, ed. Harvey A. Grunwald (New York: Harper, 1962), pp. 64–66.
    Larrabee, C. X. San Francisco *Chronicle* (May 3, 1953), 13.
    Martin, Hansford. *Western Review*, 18 (Winter, 1954), 172–174.
    Mizener, Arthur. *New Republic*, 128 (May 25, 1953), 19–20.
    Monas, Sidney. *Hudson Review*, 6 (Autumn, 1953), 466–470.
    Nation, 176 (April 18, 1953), 332.
    Newsweek, 41 (April 6, 1953), 98.
    Peden, William. *SRL*, 36 (April 11, 1953), 43.
    Pickrel, Paul. *Yale Review*, 42 (Summer, 1953), 12.

Poore, Charles. *NYT* (April 9, 1953), 166.
U.S. Quarterly Book Review, 9 (June, 1953), 166.
Welty, Eudora. *NYTBR* (April 5, 1953), 1.
Wisconsin Library Bulletin, 49 (July, 1953), 175.

Franny and Zooey. Boston: Little, Brown, 1961.
Reviews:
Bode, Carl. *John O'London's*, 6 (June 7, 1962), 140.
——. *WSCL*, 3 (Winter, 1961–1962), 65–71.
Booklist, 58 (September 15, 1961), 64.
Bradbury, Malcolm. *Punch*, 242 (June 27, 1962), 989.
Bryden, Ronald. *Spectator*, 208 (June 8, 1962), 755.
Daniels, Sally. *Minnesota Review*, 11 (Summer, 1962), 553–557.
Didion, Joan. "Finally (Fashionably) Spurious," *National Review*, 11 (August 12, 1961), 341–342. Reprinted in Grunwald, *Salinger: A Portrait*, pp. 77–79; and in *Studies in J. D. Salinger: Reviews, Essays and Critiques of* THE CATCHER IN THE RYE *and Other Fiction*, ed. Marvin Laser and Norman Fruman (New York: Odyssey, 1963), pp. 232–234.
Dolbier, Joan. *NYHT* (September 14, 1961), 19.
Engle, Paul. *Chicago Sunday Tribune Magazine of Books* (September 24, 1961), 3.
Fiedler, Leslie. "Up from Adolescence," *Partisan Review*, 29 (Winter, 1962), 127. Reprinted in Grunwald, *Salinger: A Portrait*, pp. 56–62; and in Laser and Fruman, *Studies in J. D. Salinger*, pp. 235–240.
Fremont-Smith, Eliot. *Village Voice*, 7 (March 8, 1962), 5–6.
Gallagher, Patricia. *Tamarack Review*, 21 (Autumn, 1961), 26.
Gardiner, H. C. *America*, 105 (September 30, 1961), 832.
Hartt, J. N. *Yale Review*, 51 (December, 1961), 307–308.
Hicks, Granville. *SRL*, 44 (September 16, 1961), 26.
Hogan, William. *San Francisco Chronicle* (September 5, 1961), 33.
Jackson, Robert B. *Library Journal*, 86 (October 1, 1961), 3303.
Kapp, Isa. "Salinger's Easy Victory," *New Leader*, 45 (January 8, 1962), 27. Reprinted in Grunwald, *Salinger: A Portrait*, pp. 79–82.
Kermode, Frank. "One Hand Clapping," *New Statesman*, 63 (June 8, 1962), 831–832. Collected in Frank Kermode, *Puzzles and Epiphanies—Essays and Reviews* (London: Routledge and Kegan Paul, 1962), pp. 188–192. Reprinted in *J. D. Salinger and the Critics*, ed. William F. Belcher and James W. Lee (Belmont, Cali-

fornia: Wadsworth Press, 1962), pp. 40–43; and in Laser and Fruman, *Studies in J. D. Salinger,* pp. 172–176.

Kirkus, 29 (June 15, 1961), 512.

Kirkwood, Hilda. *Canadian Forum,* 41 (November, 1961), 189.

Lerman, Leo. *Mademoiselle,* 53 (October, 1961), 108–111.

Maitland, Zane. *Time and Tide,* 43 (June 7, 1962), 30.

Marple, Anne. "Salinger's Oasis of Innocence," *New Republic,* 145 (September 18, 1961), 22–23. Reprinted in Laser and Fruman, *Studies in J. D. Salinger,* pp. 241–244.

Mayhew, A. E. *Commonweal,* 75 (October 6, 1961), 48.

McCarthy, Mary. "J. D. Salinger's Closed Circuit," *Observer* (June 3, 1962), 46–48. Reprinted in *Harper's,* 225 (October, 1962), 46–48; in *If You Really Want to Know: A Catcher Casebook,* ed. Malcolm M. Marsden (Chicago: Scott, Foresman, 1963), pp. 84–85; and in Laser and Fruman, *Studies in J. D. Salinger,* pp. 245–250.

Murray, James G. *Critic,* 20 (November, 1961), 72.

Nordell, Rod. *Christian Science Monitor* (September 14, 1961), 7.

Phelps, Robert. *NYHTBR* (September 17, 1961), 17.

Phillips, Paul. *Mainstream,* 15 (January, 1962), 32–39.

Poore, Charles. *NYT* (September 14, 1961), 29.

Pugh, Griffith. *English Journal,* 51 (May, 1962), 32–39.

Rowland, Stanley J. *Christian Century,* 78 (December 6, 1961), 1464.

Sullivan, Walter. *Modern Age: A Conservative Review,* 6 (Spring, 1962), 211–212.

Time, 78 (September 15, 1961), 84.

TLS (June 8, 1962), 425.

Updike, John. "Anxious Days for the Glass Family," *NYTBR* (September 17, 1961), 1, 52. Collected in John Updike, *Assorted Prose* (New York: Knopf, 1965), pp. 234–239. Reprinted in Grunwald, *Salinger: A Portrait,* pp. 53–56; and in Laser and Fruman, *Studies in J. D. Salinger,* pp. 227–231.

Virginia Quarterly, 38 (Winter, 1962), viii.

Walker, Gerald. *Cosmopolitan,* 151 (September, 1961), 36.

Wisconsin Library Bulletin, 57 (September, 1961), 307.

Raise High the Roof Beam, Carpenters, and Seymour: An Introduction. Boston: Little, Brown, 1963.

Reviews:

Barrett, William. *Atlantic,* 211 (February, 1963), 128, 130.

Fry, J. R. *Christian Century*, 80 (February 6, 1963), 175–176.
Gold, A. R. *NYHTBR* (April 7, 1963), 8.
Hassan, Ihab. "The Casino of Silence," *SRL*, 46 (January 26, 1963), 38.
Hicks, Granville. *SRL*, 46 (January 26, 1963), 37–38.
Hill, W. B. *America*, 108 (May 11, 1963), 678.
Holzhauer, Jean. *Commonweal*, 77 (February 22, 1963), 575.
Howe, Irving. *NYTBR* (April 7, 1963), 4.
Jackson, R. B. *Library Journal*, 88 (April 15, 1963), 1787.
Kermode, Frank. *New Statesman*, 65 (March 15, 1963), 388.
Kirkwood, Hilda. *Canadian Forum*, 43 (April, 1963), 19.
Library Journal, 88 (April 15, 1963), 1787.
Marcus, Stephen. *NYTBR* (Special Issue, 1963), 18.
McGovern, Hugh. *America*, 108 (February 2, 1963), 174–175.
Newsweek, 61 (January 28, 1963), 90, 92.
Nott, Kathleen. *Encounter*, 20 (June, 1963), 80–81.
Quinn, J. J. *Best Sellers*, 22 (February 1, 1963), 408.
Sheed, Wilfred. *Jubilee*, 10 (April, 1963), 48–54.
Smith, Laurence. *Critic* (February, 1963), 73.
Time, 81 (February 8, 1963), 86.
TLS (March 8, 1963), 165.
Wain, John. *New Republic*, 48 (February 16, 1963), 21–22.

B. Briefer Writings

1. *Short Fiction*

1940
"The Young Folks," *Story*, 16 (March–April, 1940), 26–30.

1941
"The Hang of It," *Collier's*, 108 (July 12, 1941), 22.
"The Heart of a Broken Story," *Esquire*, 16 (September, 1941), 32, 131–133.

1942
"The Long Debut of Lois Taggett," *Story*, 21 (September–October, 1942), 28–34. Reprinted in *Story: Fiction of the Forties*, ed. Whit Burnett and Hallie S. Burnett (New York: Dutton, 1949), pp. 153–162.
"Personal Notes on an Infantryman," *Collier's*, 110 (December 12, 1942), 96.

1944

"Both Parties Concerned," *Saturday Evening Post,* 216 (February 26, 1944), 47–48.

"Last Day of the Furlough," *Saturday Evening Post,* 217 (July 15, 1944), 26–27, 61–62, 64.

"Once a Week Won't Kill You," *Story,* 25 (November–December, 1944), 23–27.

"Soft-Boiled Sergeant," *Saturday Evening Post,* 216 (April 15, 1944), 18, 82, 84–85.

"The Varioni Brothers," *Saturday Evening Post,* 216 (February 26, 1944), 12–13, 76–77.

1945

"A Boy in France," *Saturday Evening Post,* 217 (March 31, 1945), 21, 92. Reprinted in *Saturday Evening Post Stories, 1942–1945,* ed. Ben Hibbs (New York: Random House, 1946), pp. 314–320.

"I'm Crazy," *Collier's,* 116 (December 22, 1945), 36, 48, 51. Portions of this story were used in Chapters 1, 2, and 22 of *The Catcher in the Rye.*

"The Stranger," *Collier's,* 116 (December 1, 1945), 18, 77.

"This Sandwich Has No Mayonnaise," *Esquire,* 24 (October, 1945), 54–56, 147–149. Reprinted in *The Armchair Esquire,* ed. Arnold Gingrich and L. Rust Hills (New York: Putnam's, 1958), 187–197.

1946

"Slight Rebellion Off Madison," *NY,* 22 (December 21, 1946), 82–86. With slight changes, this story became Chapter 17 of *The Catcher in the Rye.*

1947

"The Inverted Forest," *Cosmopolitan,* 113 (December, 1947), 73–80, 85–86, 88, 90, 92, 95–96, 98, 100, 102, 104. Reprinted in *Cosmopolitan,* 123 (March, 1961), 111–132.

"A Young Girl in 1941 with No Waist at All," *Mademoiselle,* 25 (May, 1947), 222–223, 292–302.

1948

"Blue Melody," *Cosmopolitan,* 125 (September, 1948), 51–55, 112–119.

"A Girl I Knew," *Good Housekeeping,* 126 (February, 1948), 37, 186, 188, 191–196. Reprinted in *Best American Short Stories of 1949,* ed. Martha Foley (Boston: Houghton Mifflin, 1949), pp. 248–260.

"Just Before the War with the Eskimos," *NY*, 24 (June 5, 1948), 37–40. Reprinted in *Prize Stories of 1949: The O. Henry Awards*, ed. Herschell Brickell (Garden City, New York: Doubleday, 1949), pp. 249–261; and in *Manhattan: Stories from the Heart of a Great City* (New York: Bantam, 1954), pp. 22–35. Collected in *Nine Stories*.

"A Perfect Day for Bananafish," *NY*, 23 (January 31, 1948), 21–25. Reprinted in *Fifty-Five Short Stories from the New Yorker* (New York: Simon and Schuster, 1949), pp. 144–155. Collected in *Nine Stories*.

"Uncle Wiggily in Connecticut," *NY*, 24 (March 20, 1948), 30–36. Reprinted in *Short Story Masterpieces*, ed. Robert Penn Warren and Albert Erskine (New York: Dell Books, 1954), pp. 408–423. Collected in *Nine Stories*.

1949

"Down at the Dinghy," *Harper's*, 198 (April, 1949), 87–91. Collected in *Nine Stories*.

"The Laughing Man," *NY*, 25 (March 19, 1949), 27–32. Collected in *Nine Stories*.

1950

"For Esmé—with Love and Squalor," *NY*, 26 (April 8, 1950), 28–36. Reprinted in *World Review*, No. 18 (August, 1950), 44–59; in *Prize Stories of 1950: The O. Henry Awards*, ed. Herschel Brickell (Garden City, New York: Doubleday, 1950), pp. 244–264; in *Better Reading Two: Literature*, ed. Walter Blair and John C. Gerber (Chicago: Scott, Foresman, 1954), pp. 436–453; in *Interpreting Literature*, ed. K. L. Knickerbocker and H. Willard Reninger (New York: Henry Holt, 1955), pp. 274–285; and in *Fifty Great Short Stories*, ed. Milton Crane (New York: Bantam Books, 1952), pp. 252–275. Collected in *Nine Stories*.

1951

"Pretty Mouth and Green My Eyes," *NY*, 27 (July 14, 1951), 20–24. Reprinted in *An Anthology of Famous American Stories*, ed. J. A. Burrell and Bennett Cerf (New York: Modern Library, 1953), pp. 1297–1306. Collected in *Nine Stories*.

1952

"De Daumier-Smith's Blue Period," *World Review*, No. 39 (May, 1952), 33–48. Collected in *Nine Stories*.

1953

"Teddy," *NY*, 28 (January 31, 1953), 26–34. Collected in *Nine Stories.*

1955

"Franny," *NY*, 30 (January 29, 1955), 24–32, 35–43. Collected in *Franny and Zooey.*

"Raise High the Roof Beam, Carpenters," *NY*, 31 (November 19, 1955), 51–58, 60, 62, 65–66, 68, 70, 72–74, 76, 78–80, 83–84, 86–92, 95–98, 100–105, 107–110. Reprinted in *Stories from The New Yorker 1950–1960* (New York: Simon and Schuster, 1960), pp. 46–95. Collected in *Raise High the Roof Beam, Carpenters, and Seymour: An Introduction.*

1957

"Zooey," *NY*, 33 (May 4, 1957), 32–42, 44, 47–48, 52, 54, 57–59, 62, 64, 67–68, 70, 73–74, 76–78, 86–88, 91–94, 97–98, 100–104, 107–114, 117–135. Collected in *Franny and Zooey.*

1959

"Seymour: An Introduction," *NY*, 35 (June 6, 1959), 42–52, 54, 57–58, 60–61, 64–66, 68, 71–78, 83–84, 86–90, 93–104, 107–111. Collected in *Raise High the Roof Beam, Carpenters, and Seymour: An Introduction.*

1965

"Hapworth 16, 1924," *NY*, 41 (June 19, 1965), 32–40, 42, 44, 49–50, 52, 55–56, 58, 60–62, 67–68, 70, 72–74, 77–78, 80, 85–86, 88, 90, 92–96, 98, 100, 102–108, 111–113.

2. *Letters*

1942

"Contributors," *Story*, 21 (September–October, 1942), 2.

1944

"Biographical Notes," *Story*, 25 (November–December, 1944), 1.

1955

"Letter to the Editor," *Twentieth Century Authors* (First Supplement) (New York: H. W. Wilson, 1955), pp. 859–860.

1959

"Man-Forsaken Men," *New York Post Magazine* (December 9, 1959), 49.

II. SECONDARY SOURCES (biographical and critical)

1951

Hutchens, John K. "On an Author," *NYHTBR* (August 19, 1951), 2.

"J. D. Salinger," *Glamour*, 26 (September, 1951), 205.

Maxwell, William. "J. D. Salinger," *Book-of-the-Month-Club News* (July 1951), 5–6.

Sproul, Kathleen. "The Author," *SRL*, 34 (July 14, 1951), 12.

1952

Hazard, Eloise Perry. "Eight Fiction Finds," *SRL*, 35 (February 16, 1952), 16–17.

Martin, Hansforth. "The American Problem of Direct Address," *Western Review*, 16 (Winter, 1952), 101–114.

1954

Maclean, Hugh. "Conservatism in Modern American Fiction," *College English*, 15 (March, 1954), 315–325. Reprinted (abridged) in *J. D. Salinger and the Critics,* ed. William F. Belcher and James W. Lee (Belmont, California: Wadsworth, 1962), pp. 11–14; (abridged) in *If You Really Want To Know: A Catcher Casebook,* ed. Malcolm M. Marsden (New York: William R. Scott, 1963), pp. 14–16; and in *Salinger's* CATCHER IN THE RYE: *Clamor vs. Criticism,* ed. Harold P. Simonson and E. P. Hager (New York: D. C. Heath, 1963), 101–102.

1956

Aldridge, John W. "The Society of Three Novels," *In Search of Heresy* (New York: McGraw-Hill, 1956), pp. 124–128. Reprinted (abridged) in Marsden, *If You Really Want To Know,* pp. 126–127; (abridged) in Simonson and Hager, *Salinger's* CATCHER IN THE RYE, 80–81; and (abridged) in *Studies in J. D. Salinger: Reviews, Essays and Critiques of* THE CATCHER IN THE RYE *and Other Fiction,* ed. Marvin Laser and Norman Fruman (New York: Odyssey, 1963), pp. 50–52.

Heiserman, Arthur, and James E. Miller, Jr. "J. D. Salinger: Some Crazy Cliff," *WHR*, 10 (Spring, 1956), 129–137. Reprinted in *Salinger: A Portrait,* pp. 196–205; (abridged) in Belcher and Lee, *J. D. Salinger and The Critics,* pp. 14–17; in Marsden, *If You Really Want to Know,* pp. 16–21; in Laser and Fruman, *Studies in J. D. Salinger,* 23–30; and in Simonson and Hager, *Salinger's* CATCHER IN THE RYE, pp. 74–80.

Kaplan, Charles. "Holden and Huck: The Odysseys of Youth," *College English*, 18 (November, 1956), 76–80. Reprinted in Marsden, *If You Really Want To Know*, pp. 127–131; and in Laser and Fruman, *Studies in J. D. Salinger*, pp. 31–38.

Lipton, Lawrence. "Disaffiliation and the Art of Poverty," *Chicago Review*, 10 (Spring, 1956), 53–79.

Matthews, James F. "J. D. Salinger: An Appraisal," *University of Virginia Magazine*, 1 (Spring, 1956), 52–60.

1957

Barr, Donald. "Saints, Pilgrims and Artists," *Commonweal*, 67 (October 25, 1957), 88–90. Reprinted (abridged) in *Commonweal*, 71 (October 30, 1959), 165; in Grunwald, *Salinger: A Portrait*, pp. 170–176; (abridged) in Marsden, *If You Really Want To Know*, pp. 39–40; in Simonson and Hager, *Salinger's* CATCHER IN THE RYE, pp. 102–106; and in *On Contemporary Literature*, ed. Richard Kostelanetz (New York: Avon, 1965), pp. 537–543.

Bonheim, Helmut W. "An Introduction to J. D. Salinger's *The Catcher in the Rye*," *Exercise Exchange*, 4 (April, 1957), 144–158. Reprinted (abridged) in Grunwald, *Salinger: A Portrait*, pp. 205–217; in Belcher and Lee, *J. D. Salinger and the Critics*, pp. 20–34; in Marsden, *If You Really Want To Know*, pp. 132–143; and in Laser and Fruman, *Studies in J. D. Salinger*, pp. 39–49.

Carpenter, Frederic I. "The Adolescent in American Fiction," *English Journal*, 46 (September, 1957), 313–319. Reprinted (abridged) in Simonson and Hager, *Salinger's* CATCHER IN THE RYE, pp. 92–93.

Dodge, Stewart. "In Search of the Fat Lady," *English Record* (New York State English Council), 8 (Winter, 1957), 10–13. Reprinted (abridged) in Marsden, *If You Really Want To Know*, pp. 40–42.

Fowler, Albert. "Alien in the Rye," *Modern Age*, 1 (Fall, 1957), 193–197. Reprinted in Belcher and Lee, *J. D. Salinger and the Critics*, pp. 34–40; and in Marsden, *If You Really Want To Know*, pp. 34–48.

Hassan, Ihab. "Rare Quixotic Gesture: The Fiction of J. D. Salinger," *Western Review*, 21 (Summer, 1957), 261–280. Expanded and collected in *Radical Innocence: Studies in the Contemporary American Novel* (Princeton: Princeton University Press, 1961), pp. 259–289. Reprinted in Grunwald, *Salinger: A Portrait*, pp. 138–163; (abridged) in Belcher and Lee, *J. D. Salinger and the Critics*, pp. 115–120; (abridged) in Marsden, *If You Really Want to Know*, pp. 29–34; and (abridged) in Laser and Fruman, *Studies in J. D. Salinger*, pp. 57–71.

Kegel, Charles H. "Incommunicability in Salinger, *The Catcher in the Rye*," *WHR*, 11 (Spring, 1957), 188–190. Reprinted in Belcher and Lee, *J. D. Salinger and the Critics*, pp. 17–20; in Marsden, 25–28; in Simonson and Hager, *Salinger's* CATCHER IN THE RYE, pp. 63–65; and in Laser and Fruman, *Studies in J. D. Salinger*, pp. 53–55.

"The No-Nonsense Kids," *Time*, 20 (November 18, 1957), 51–54.

Stevenson, David L. "J. D. Salinger: The Mirror of Crisis," *Nation*, 184 (March 9, 1957), 215–217. Reprinted in *A View of the Nation—An Anthology: 1955–1959*, ed. Harvey M. Christman (New York: Grove Press, 1960), pp. 56–61; in Grunwald, *Salinger: A Portrait*, pp. 36–41; (abridged) in Belcher and Lee, *J. D. Salinger and the Critics*, pp. 137–141; and (abridged) in Marsden, *If You Really Want To Know*, pp. 22–24.

Weals, Gerald. "The Not So Modern Temper," *Antioch Review*, 17 (December, 1957), 510–515.

1958

Boyle, S. J. "Teaching 'Dirty Books' in College," *America*, 100 (December 13, 1958), 337–339.

Camerino, Aldo. "Adolescente Americano," *Fiera Letteraria*, 13 (November 16, 1958), 5.

Fiedler, Leslie. "Boys Will Be Boys!" *New Leader*, 41 (April, 1958), 23–26. Collected (abridged) in Leslie Fiedler, *Love and Death in the American Novel* (New York: Criterion Books, 1960), p. 271; and in Leslie Fiedler, *No! In Thunder* (Boston: Beacon Press, 1960), pp. 266–274. Reprinted in Grunwald, *Salinger: A Portrait*, pp. 228–233.

———. "Good Good Girl and Good Bad Boy," *New Leader*, 41 (April 14, 1958), 22–25. Collected (abridged) in Fiedler, *Love and Death in the American Novel*, pp. 267–268; and in Fiedler, *No! In Thunder*, pp. 257–265. Reprinted (abridged) in Grunwald, *Salinger: A Portrait*, pp. 223–228.

———. "From Redemption to Initiation," *New Leader*, 41 (June 23, 1958), 26–29. Collected (abridged) in Fiedler, *Love and Death in the American Novel*, p. 324; and in Fiedler, *No! In Thunder*, pp. 282–291. Reprinted (abridged) in Grunwald, *Salinger: A Portrait*, pp. 239–245.

———. "The Invention of the Child," *New Leader*, 41 (March 31, 1958), 22–24. Collected in Fiedler, *No! In Thunder*, pp. 251–257. Reprinted (abridged) in Grunwald, *Salinger: A Portrait*, pp. 218–223.

———. "The Profanation of the Child," *New Leader*, 41 (June 23, 1958), 26–29. Collected (abridged) in Fiedler, *Love and Death in the American Novel,* p. 324; and in Fiedler, *No! In Thunder,* pp. 282–291. Reprinted (abridged) in Grunwald, *Salinger: A Portrait,* pp. 239–245.

———. "The Un-Angry Young Men," *Encounter*, 10 (January, 1958), 3–12. Collected in Fiedler, *No! In Thunder,* pp. 169–187.

Friedrich, Gerhard. "Perspective in the Teaching of American Literature," *College English,* 20 (December, 1958), 122–128.

Geismar, Maxwell. "J. D. Salinger: The Wise Child and the *New Yorker* School of Fiction," *American Moderns: From Rebellion to Conformity* (New York: Hill and Wang, 1958), pp. 195–209. Reprinted (abridged) in Belcher and Lee, *Salinger and the Critics,* pp. 121–129; in Grunwald, *Salinger: A Portrait,* pp. 87–101; (abridged) in Marsden, *If You Really Want To Know,* pp. 42–43; and (abridged) in Laser and Fruman, *Studies in J. D. Salinger,* pp. 72–76.

Green, Martin. "Amis and Salinger: The Latitude of Private Conscience," *Chicago Review,* 11 (Winter, 1958), 20–25.

Gwynn, Frederick L., and Joseph L. Blotner. *The Fiction of J. D. Salinger.* Pittsburgh: University of Pittsburgh Press, 1958. Sections reprinted in Grunwald, *Salinger: A Portrait,* pp. 102–114 and 259–266; (abridged) in Belcher and Lee, *J. D. Salinger and the Critics,* pp. 141–145; (abridged) in Marsden, *If You Really Want To Know,* pp. 45–47; (abridged) in Simonson and Hager, *Salinger's* CATCHER IN THE RYE, pp. 93–94; and in Laser and Fruman, *Studies in J. D. Salinger,* pp. 85–87 and 251–254.

Levine, Paul. "J. D. Salinger: The Development of the Misfit Hero," *Twentieth Century Literature,* 4 (October, 1958), 92–99. Reprinted in Belcher and Lee, *J. D. Salinger and the Critics,* pp. 107–115; and (abridged) in Marsden, *If You Really Want To Know,* pp. 47–48.

Wakefield, Dan. "Salinger and the Search for Love," *New World Writing,* No. 14 (December, 1958), 68–85. Reprinted in *Discussions of the Short Story,* ed. H. S. Summers (Boston: D. C. Heath, 1963), pp. 110–118; in Grunwald, *Salinger: A Portrait,* pp. 176–191; (abridged) in Marsden, *If You Really Want To Know,* pp. 52–55; and (abridged) in Laser and Fruman, *Studies in J. D. Salinger,* pp. 77–84.

Wiegand, William. "J. D. Salinger: Seventy-Eight Bananas," *Chicago Review,* 11 (Winter, 1958), 3–19. Reprinted in *Recent American Fiction: Some Critical Views,* ed. Joseph J. Waldmeir (New York:

Houghton Mifflin, 1963), pp. 252–264; in Grunwald, *Salinger: A Portrait,* pp. 123–136; and (abridged) in Marsden, *If You Really Want To Know,* pp. 48–52.

1959

Barr, Donald. "The Talent of J. D. Salinger," *Commonweal,* 71 (October 30, 1959), 165.

Cahill, Robert. "J. D. Salinger's Tin Bell," *Cadence* (Autumn, 1959), 20–22.

Costello, Donald P. "The Language of *The Catcher in the Rye,*" *American Speech,* 34 (October, 1959), 172–181. Reprinted in Grunwald, *Salinger: A Portrait,* pp. 266–276; (abridged) in Belcher and Lee, *J. D. Salinger and the Critics,* pp. 45–53; in Marsden, *If You Really Want To Know,* pp. 87 94; in Simonson and Hager, *Salinger's* CATCHER IN THE RYE, pp. 32–39; and in Laser and Fruman, *Studies in J. D. Salinger,* pp. 92–104.

Drake, Robert Y., Jr. "Two Old Juveniles," *Georgia Review,* 13 (Winter, 1959), 443–453.

Faulkner, William. "A Word to Young Writers," *Faulkner in the University: Class Conferences at the University of Virginia, 1957–1958,* ed. Frederick L. Gwynn and Joseph L. Blotner (Charlottesville: University of Virginia Press, 1959), pp. 241–245.

Giles, Barbara. "The Lonely War of J. D. Salinger," *Mainstream,* 12 (February, 1959), 2–13.

Hassan, Ihab. "The Idea of Adolescence in American Fiction," *College English,* 21 (December, 1959), 140–146.

Hicks, Granville. "J. D. Salinger: Search for Wisdom," *SRL,* 42 (July 25, 1959), 13, 30. Reprinted in Grunwald, *Salinger: A Portrait,* pp. 191–194; in Simonson and Hager, *Salinger's* CATCHER IN THE RYE, p. 109; and in Laser and Fruman, *Studies in J. D. Salinger,* pp. 88–91.

———. "Quest in a Quiet Time," *SRL,* 42 (November 28, 1959), 20.

Howe, Irving. "Mass Society and Post-Modern Fiction," *Partisan Review,* 26 (Summer, 1959), 420–436.

Jacobs, Robert G. "J. D. Salinger's *Catcher in the Rye*: Holden Caulfield's 'Goddam Autobiography'," *Iowa English Yearbook* (Fall, 1959), 9–14. Reprinted (abridged) in Marsden, *If You Really Want To Know,* pp. 55–61.

"J. D. Salinger—Biographical," *Harper's,* 218 (February, 1959), 87.

Johannson, Ernest J. "Salinger's Seymour," *Carolina Quarterly,* 7 (Winter, 1959), 51–54.

Johnson, James W. "The Adolescent Hero: A Trend in Modern Fiction," *Twentieth Century Literature*, 5 (April, 1959), 3–11.

Kazin, Alfred. "The Alone Generation: A Comment on the Fiction of the 'Fifties'," *Harper's*, 209 (October, 1959), 127–131. Reprinted in *Writing in America*, ed. John Fischer and Robert B. Silvers (New Brunswick, New Jersey: Rutgers University Press, 1960), pp. 14–26; collected in Alfred Kazin, *Contemporaries* (Boston: Little, Brown, 1962), pp. 207–217.

"The Limits of the Possible: Accepting the Reality of the Human Situation," *TLS* (November 6, 1959), xvi.

Lowrey, Burling. "Salinger and the House of Glass," *New Republic*, 141 (October 26, 1959), 23–24. Reply to Wiegand, *New Republic* (October 19, 1959).

Mailer, Norman. "Evaluations: Quick and Expensive Comments on the Talent in the Room," *Advertisements for Myself* (New York: G. P. Putnam's, 1959), pp. 463–473.

Martin, Augustine. "A Note on J. D. Salinger," *Studies: An Irish Quarterly Review*, 48 (Fall, 1959), 336–345.

Mizener, Arthur. "The Love Song of J. D. Salinger," *Harper's*, 218 (February, 1959), 83–90. Reprinted in Grunwald, *Salinger: A Portrait*, pp. 23–36; in Belcher and Lee, *J. D. Salinger and the Critics*, pp. 151–158; in *Off Campus*, 1 (January, 1963), 18–20, 44, 51, 54, 64; and in Laser and Fruman, *Studies in J. D. Salinger*, pp. 202–215.

Schrader, Allen. "Emerson to Salinger to Parker," *SRL*, 42 (April 11, 1959), 52, 58. Reprinted in Simonson and Hager, *Salinger's* CATCHER IN THE RYE, 106–108.

Steiner, George. "The Salinger Industry," *Nation*, 189 (November 14, 1959), 360–363. Reprinted in Grunwald, *Salinger: A Portrait*, pp. 82–85; in Marsden, *If You Really Want To Know*, pp. 62–65; and in Laser and Fruman, *Studies in J. D. Salinger*, pp. 113–118.

Weigel, John. "Teaching the Modern Novel," *College English*, 21 (December, 1959), 172–173.

Wiegand, William. "The Knighthood of J. D. Salinger," *New Republic*, 141 (October 19, 1959), 19–21. Reprinted in Grunwald, *Salinger: A Portrait*, pp. 116–122; and in Laser and Fruman, *Studies in J. D. Salinger*, pp. 105–112.

Wilson, John F. "The Step Beyond," *SRL*, 62 (December, 1959), 19–21. Reply to Hicks, *SRL* (July 25, 1959).

1960

Bungert, Hans. "J. D. Salinger's *The Catcher in the Rye*: An Isolation und Kommunikationsversuch des Jungendlichen," *Die Neuren Sprachen*, 60 (May, 1960), 208–217. Reprinted (abridged) in Laser and Fruman, *Studies in J. D. Salinger*, pp. 177–185 (trans. Wulf Griessbach).

Carpenter, Frederic I. "Fiction and the American College," *American Quarterly*, 12 (Winter, 1960), 443–456.

Davis, Tom. "J. D. Salinger: 'Some Crazy Cliff' Indeed," *WHR*, 14 (Winter, 1960), 97–99. Reply to Heisermann, *WHR* (Spring, 1956). Reprinted in Marsden, *If You Really Want To Know*, pp. 95–97.

Fenton, Charles. "Lost Years of Twentieth-Century American Literature," *South Atlantic Quarterly*, 59 (September, 1960), 332–338.

Fiedler, Leslie. "The Eye of Innocence," *No! In Thunder* (Boston: Beacon Press, 1960), pp. 251–291. Reprinted (abridged) in Grunwald, *Salinger: A Portrait*, pp. 56–62.

Green, Martin. "Cultural Images in England and America," *A Mirror for Anglo-Saxons: A Discovery of America, A Rediscovery of England* (New York: Harper, 1960), pp. 69–88. Reprinted (abridged) in Grunwald, *Salinger: A Portrait*, as "The Image Maker," pp. 247–253.

Jacobsen, Josephine. "Beatific Signals: The Felicity of J. D. Salinger," *Commonweal*, 81 (February 26, 1960), 589–591. Reprinted in Grunwald, *Salinger: A Portrait*, pp. 165–170.

Krassner, Paul. "The Age of Form Letters," *Realist*, No. 15 (February, 1960), 6.

———. "What Makes Critics Happy?" *Realist*, No. 14 (December–January, 1959–1960), 5–6.

Leitch, David. "The Salinger Myth," *Twentieth Century*, 168 (November, 1960), 428–435. Reprinted in *Mademoiselle*, 264 (August, 1961), 264–265, 273, 288; in Grunwald, *Salinger: A Portrait*, pp. 69–77; and (abridged) in Marsden, *If You Really Want To Know*, pp. 66–67.

Leverett, Ernest. "The Virtues of Vulgarity—Russian and American Views," *Carleton Miscellany*, 1 (Spring, 1960), 29–40.

Light, James F. "Salinger's *The Catcher in the Rye*," *Explicator*, 18 (June, 1960), Item 59. Reprinted in Marsden, *If You Really Want To Know*, p. 98; and in Simonson and Hager, *Salinger's* CATCHER IN THE RYE, pp. 39–40.

"The Mysterious J. D. Salinger . . . His Woodsy Secluded Life," *Newsweek*, 55 (May 30, 1960), 92–94.

Nyren, Dorothy (ed.). "J. D. Salinger," *A Library of Literary Criticism* (New York: Frederick Ungar, 1960), pp. 414–416.

Swados, Harvey. "Must Writers Be Characters?" *SRL*, 43 (October 1, 1960), 12–14. Reprinted in Laser and Fruman, *Studies in J. D. Salinger*, pp. 119–121.

Swinton, John. "A Case Study of an 'Academic Bum': Salinger Once Stayed at Ursinus," *Ursinus Weekly*, 60 (December 12, 1960), 2, 4.

Walzer, Michael. "In Place of a Hero," *Dissent*, 7 (Spring, 1960), 156–167. Reprinted in Belcher and Lee, *J. D. Salinger and the Critics*, pp. 99–106.

Wells, Arvin R. "Huck Finn and Holden Caulfield: The Situation of the Hero," *Ohio University Review*, 2 (1960), 31–42. Reprinted in Marsden, *If You Really Want To Know*, pp. 144–152.

Workman, Molly F. "*The Catcher* in the Classroom," *Virginia English Bulletin*, 10 (December 10, 1960), 1–6.

1961

Bowden, Edwin T. "The Frontier Isolation," *The Dungeon of the Heart* (New York: Macmillan, 1961), pp. 20–65. Reprinted (abridged) in Simonson and Hager, *Salinger's* CATCHER IN THE RYE, pp. 94–100.

Browne, Robert M. "In Defense of Esmé," *College English*, 22 (May, 1961), 584–585. Reply to Hermann, *College English* (January, 1961). Reprinted in Belcher and Lee, *J. D. Salinger and the Critics*, pp. 149–150; and in Laser and Fruman, *Studies in J. D. Salinger*, pp. 259–261.

Bryan, James E. "J. D. Salinger: The Fat Lady and the Chicken Sandwich," *College English*, 23 (December, 1961), 226–229.

Corbett, Edward P. J. "Some Thoughts on *The Catcher in the Rye*: Raise High the Barriers, Censors," *America*, 104 (January 7, 1961), 441–443. Reprinted in Belcher and Lee, *J. D. Salinger and the Critics*, pp. 54–59; Marsden, *If You Really Want To Know*, pp. 68–72; in Simonson and Hager, *Salinger's* CATCHER IN THE RYE, pp. 5–9; and in Laser and Fruman, *Studies in J. D. Salinger*, pp. 134–141.

Creeger, George. " 'Treacherous Desertion': Salinger's *The Catcher in the Rye*." Middletown, Connecticut: Wesleyan University Press, 1961. Pamphlet. Reprinted in Belcher and Lee, *J. D. Salinger and the Critics*, pp. 43–54.

Fiene, Donald M. "From a Study of Salinger: Controversy in *The Catcher*," *Realist*, 30 (December, 1961), 1, 23–25. Reprinted in Simonson and Hager, *Salinger's* CATCHER IN THE RYE, pp. 15–21.

Fleischer, Frederic. "J. D. Salinger och hans familj," *Bonniers Litterära Magasin,* 30 (December, 1961), 846–848.

Gilman, Richard. "Salinger Reconsidered," *Jubilee,* 9 (October, 1961), 38–41.

Gutwillig, Robert. "Everybody's Caught *The Catcher in the Rye,*" *NYTBR* (Paperback Book Section, January 15, 1961), 38–39. Reprinted in Laser and Fruman, *Studies in J. D. Salinger,* pp. 1–5.

Hassan, Ihab. "Love in the Modern American Novel: Expense of Spirit and Waste of Shame," *WHR,* 14 (Spring, 1961), 149–161.

Havemann, Ernest. "Search for the Mysterious J. D. Salinger," *Life,* 51 (November 3, 1961), 129–130, 132–144.

Hayman, Jane. "The White Jew," *Dissent,* 8 (Spring, 1961), 191–196.

Hermann, John. "J. D. Salinger: Hello Hello Hello," *College-English,* 22 (January, 1961), 262–264. Reprinted in Belcher and Lee, *J. D. Salinger and the Critics,* pp. 145–149; and in Laser and Fruman, *Studies in J. D. Salinger,* pp. 254–259.

Hicks, Granville. "Another Look at the Deserving," *SRL,* 44 (December 23, 1961), 18.

——. "Sisters, Sons, and Lovers," *SRL,* 44 (September 16, 1961), 26.

——. "These Are Their Lives," *SRL,* 44 (November 4, 1961), 21.

Kanesaki, Hisao. "J. D. Salinger," *Jimbun Kenkyu,* 12 (June, 1961), 123–124.

Kanters, Robert. "Le mystère Salinger—Un Alain Fournier américain?" *Figaro Littéraire,* 16 (November 11, 1961), 2.

Kazin, Alfred. "J. D. Salinger: Everybody's Favorite," *Atlantic,* 158 (August, 1961), 27–31. Collected in Alfred Kazin, *Contemporaries* (Boston: Little, Brown, 1962), pp. 230–240; reprinted in Grunwald, *Salinger: A Portrait,* pp. 43–52; in Belcher and Lee, *J. D. Salinger and the Critics,* pp. 158–166; and in Laser and Fruman, *Studies in J. D. Salinger,* pp. 216–226.

Kosner, Edward. "The Private World of J. D. Salinger," *New York Post Weekend Magazine* (April 30, 1961), 5.

Levin, Beatrice. "Everybody's Favorite: Concepts of Love in the Work of J. D. Salinger," *Motive,* No. 22 (October, 1961), 9–11.

——. "J. D. Salinger in Oklahoma," *Chicago Jewish Forum,* 19 (Spring, 1961), 231–233.

Lyndenberg, John. "American Novelists in Search of a Lost World," *Revue des Langues Vivantes,* 27 (No. 4, 1961), 306–321.

McCarthy, Mary. "Characters in Fiction," *Partisan Review*, 28 (March–April, 1961), 171–191. Collected in Mary McCarthy, *On the Contrary: Articles of Belief* (New York: Farrar, Straus, and Cudahy, 1961), pp. 271–292.

Moore, Everett T. "Catcher and Mice," *American Library Association Bulletin* (March, 1961). Reprinted in Laser and Fruman, *Studies in J. D. Salinger*, pp. 130–134.

Oldsey, Bernard S. "The Movies in the Rye," *College English*, 33 (December, 1961), 209–215. Reprinted in Belcher and Lee, *J. D. Salinger and the Critics*, pp. 68–75; in Marsden, *If You Really Want To Know*, pp. 116–121; and in Simonson and Hager, *Salinger's* CATCHER IN THE RYE, pp. 40–44.

Orel, Harold. "What They Think about Teen-Agers in Books," *College English*, 23 (November, 1961), 147–149.

Phelps, Robert. "Salinger: A Man of Fierce Privacy," *NYHTBR* (September 17, 1961), 3.

Pillsbury, Frederick. "Mysterious J. D. Salinger: The Untold Chapter of the Famous Writer's Years as a Valley Forge Cadet," *Philadelphia Sunday Bulletin Magazine* (October 29, 1961), 23–24.

Romanovna, Elena. "Reviews and News: What American Novels Do Russians Read?" *Soviet Literature*, No. 7 (July, 1961), 178–182.

Roth, Philip. "Writing American Fiction," *Commentary*, 31 (March, 1961), 223–233.

Seng, Peter J. "The Fallen Idol: The Immature World of Holden Caulfield," *College English*, 23 (December, 1961), 203–209. Reprinted in Belcher and Lee, *J. D. Salinger and the Critics*, pp. 60–68; in Marsden, *If You Really Want To Know*, pp. 73–80; and in Simonson and Hager, *Salinger's* CATCHER IN THE RYE, pp. 65–73.

"Sonny," *Time*, 78 (September 15, 1961), 84–90. Reprinted in Grunwald, *Salinger: A Portrait*, pp. 3–18; and (abridged) in Belcher and Lee, *J. D. Salinger and the Critics*, pp. 1–7.

Strauch, Carl I. "Kings in the Back Row: Meaning through Structure—A Reading of Salinger's *The Catcher in the Rye*," *WSCL*, 2 (Winter, 1961), 5–29. Reprinted in Belcher and Lee, *J. D. Salinger and the Critics*, pp. 76–98; (abridged) in Marsden, *If You Really Want To Know*, pp. 99–115; in Simonson and Hager, *Salinger's* CATCHER IN THE RYE, pp. 46–62; and in Laser and Fruman, *Studies in J. D. Salinger*, pp. 143–171.

Tick, Stanley. "Initiation In and Out: The American Novel and the American Dream," *Quadrant* (1961), 63–74.

1962

Antonini, Giacomo. "Il successo di Salinger," *Fiera Letteraria,* 17 (October 28, 1962), 4.

Beaver, Harold. "A Figure in the Carpet: Irony and the American Novel," *Essays and Studies,* 15 (1962), 101–114.

Belcher, William F. and James W. Lee. *J. D. Salinger and the Critics.* Belmont California: Wadsworth Press, 1962.

Bhaerman, Robert D. "Rebuttal: Holden in the Rye," *College English,* 23 (March, 1962), 508. Reply to Oldsey, *College English* (December, 1961). Reprinted in Marsden, *If You Really Want To Know,* pp. 122–123.

Booth, Wayne C. "Distance and Point of View: An Essay in Classification," *Essays in Criticism,* 11 (January, 1961), 60–79. Partly reprinted in Wayne C. Booth's *The Rhetoric of Fiction* (Chicago: University of Chicago Press, 1962), pp. 66, 155, 171, 213, 287.

Bowen, Robert. "The Salinger Syndrome: Character Against Whom?" *Ramparts,* 1 (May, 1962), 52–60. Reprinted in Simonson and Hager, *Salinger's* CATCHER IN THE RYE, pp. 21–30.

Bryan, James E. "Salinger's Seymour's Suicide," *College English,* 24 (December, 1962), 226–229.

Bury, Richard. "Salinger," *Books and Bookmen* (London), 7 (June, 1962), 8.

Cecile, Sister Mary. "J. D. Salinger's Circle of Privacy," *Catholic World,* 194 (February, 1962), 296–301.

Chugunov, Konstantin. "Soviet Critics on J. D. Salinger's Novel *The Catcher in the Rye,*" *Soviet Literature,* No. 5 (1962), 182–185.

Cowley, Malcolm. "American Myth, Old and New," *SRL,* 45 (September 1, 1962), 6–8, 47.

Davis, Tom. "J. D. Salinger: The Identity of Sergeant X," *WHR,* 16 (Spring, 1962), 181–183. Reprinted in Laser and Fruman, *Studies in J. D. Salinger,* pp. 186–189.

Dembo, L. S. "Salinger's Pilgrim Finds His Way," *Uclan,* 7 (Summer, 1962), 19–24.

Dempsey, David. "Secret of Seymour and Esmé," *SRL,* 45 (June 30, 1962), 19.

Franconiere, Francesco. "Jerome David Salinger: Un americano in cerca d'amore," *Vita e Pensiero,* 45 (1962), 394–411.

Grunwald, Harvey A. "He Touches Something Deep in Us," *Horizon*, 4 (May, 1962), 100–107.

——. Introduction to *Salinger: A Critical and Personal Portrait*, ix–xxviii.

——. "The Invisible Man: A Biographical Collage," *Salinger: A Critical and Personal Portrait*, 1–21.

——. (ed.) *Salinger: A Critical and Personal Portrait*. New York: Harper, 1962.

Hassan, Ihab. "The Character of Post-War Fiction in America," *English Journal*, 51 (January, 1962), 1–8.

Hinckle, Warren. "J. D. Salinger's Glass Menagerie," *Ramparts*, 1 (May, 1962), 48–51.

Kanters, Robert. "Salinger, la grosse dame et le bouddha," *Figaro littéraire*, 17 (December 29, 1962), 2.

Keating, Edward. "Salinger: The Murky Glass," *Ramparts*, 1 (May, 1962), 61–66.

Larner, Jeremy. "Salinger's Audience: An Explanation," *Partisan Review*, 29 (Fall, 1962), 594–598.

Laser, Marvin and Norman Fruman (eds.). *Studies in J. D. Salinger: Reviews, Essays and Critiques of* THE CATCHER IN THE RYE *and Other Fiction*. New York: Odyssey, 1963.

Ludwig, Jack. *Recent American Novelists* (Minneapolis: University of Minnesota Press, 1962), 28–30.

Malin, Irving. *New American Gothic* (Carbondale: Southern Illinois University Press, 1962), pp. 26–35, 59–64, 86–90, 117–120, 139–143.

Marks, Barry A. "Rebuttal: Holden in the Rye," *College English*, 23 (March, 1962), 507. Reply to Seng, *College English* (December, 1961). Reprinted in Marsden, *If You Really Want To Know*, p. 81.

Martin, Dexter. "Rebuttal: Holden in the Rye," *College English*, 23 (March, 1962), 507–508. Reply to Seng, *College English* (December, 1961). Reprinted in Marsden, *If You Really Want To Know*, p. 83.

McIntyre, John P. (S.J.). "A Preface for *Franny and Zooey*," *Critic*, 20 (February–March, 1962), 25–28.

Milton, John R. "The American Novel: The Search for Home, Tradition and Identity," *WHR*, 16 (Spring, 1962), 169–180.

Mizener, Arthur. "Defining 'the Good American': J. D. Salinger and the Glass Family," *Listener*, 68 (August 16, 1962), 241–242.

Nathan, Monique. "J. D. Salinger et le rêve américain," *Critique*, 18 (April, 1962), 299–305.

Parker, Christopher. "Why the Hell *Not* Smash All the Windows?" in *Salinger: A Critical and Personal Portrait,* ed. Harvey A. Grunwald, pp. 254–258.

Reiman, Donald H. "Rebuttal: Holden in the Rye," *College English,* 23 (March, 1962), 507. Reply to Seng, *College English* (December, 1961). Reprinted in Marsden, *If You Really Want To Know,* p. 82.

Sadoya, Shigenobu. "The Modern Lonely Catcher: On J. D. Salinger's *The Catcher in the Rye,*" *Studies in English Language and Literature,* 3 (September, 1962), 85–106. In Japanese.

Sato, Hiroko. "The World of J. D. Salinger," *Essays and Studies in British and American Literature,* 10 (Winter, 1962), 43–53. In Japanese.

Slabey, Robert M. "Sergeant X and Seymour Glass," *WHR,* 16 (Autumn, 1962), 376–377. Reply to Davis, *WHR* (Spring, 1962).

Toebosch, Wim. "Revelatie of belofte: De opkomst van J. D. Salinger in de amerikaanse literatur," *De Claasmse Gids,* 46 (1962), 725–735.

Tosta, Michael R. " 'Will the Real Sergeant X Please Stand Up'," *WHR,* 16 (Autumn, 1962), 376. Reply to Davis, *WHR* (Spring, 1962).

Travis, Mildred K. "Salinger's *The Catcher in the Rye,*" *Explicator,* 21 (December, 1962), Item 36.

Wakefield, Dan. "The Heavy Hand of College Humor: Superman, Sex and Salinger," *Mademoiselle,* 55 (August, 1962), 288–289, 341–343.

Way, Brian. " 'Franny and Zooey' and J. D. Salinger," *New Left Review* (May–June, 1962), 72–82. Reprinted (abridged) in Laser and Fruman, *Studies in J. D. Salinger,* pp. 190–201.

Weatherby, W. J. "Rejection World," *Twentieth Century,* 170 (Spring, 1962), 74–75.

Whittemore, Reed. "But Seriously," *Carleton Miscellany,* 3 (Spring, 1962), 58–76.

1963

Barr, Donald. "Ah, Buddy: Salinger," *The Creative Present,* ed. Norma Balakian and Charles Simmons (New York: Doubleday, 1963), pp. 27–62.

Baskett, Sam S. "The Splendid/Squalid World of J. D. Salinger," *WSCL,* 4 (Winter, 1963), 48–61.

Blotner, Joseph L. "Salinger Now: An Appraisal," *WSCL,* 4 (Winter, 1963), 100–108.

Bostwick, Sally. "Reality, Compassion and Mysticism," *Midwest Review,* 5 (1963), 30–43.

Bruccoli, Matthew. "States of Salinger Book," *American Notes and Queries,* 2 (October, 1963), 21–22.

Cagle, Charles. *"The Catcher in the Rye* Revisited," *Midwest Quarterly,* 4 (Summer, 1963), 343–351.

Chester, Alfred. "How to Live Without Love," *Commentary,* 35 (June, 1963), 467–474.

Costello, Donald P. "Salinger and His Critics: Autopsy of a Faded Romance," *Commonweal,* 79 (October 25, 1963), 132–135.

Davis, Tom. "J. D. Salinger: 'The Sound of One Hand Clapping'," *WSCL,* 4 (Winter, 1963), 41–47.

Fiene, Donald M. "J. D. Salinger: A Biography," *WSCL,* 4 (Winter, 1963), 109–149.

French, Warren. *J. D. Salinger.* New York: Twayne, 1963.

——. "The Phony World and the Nice World," *WSCL,* 4 (Winter, 1963), 21–30.

——. "Salinger's Seymour: Another Autopsy," *College English,* 24 (April, 1963), 563.

Gale, Robert L. "Redburn and Holden—Half-Brothers One Century Removed," *Forum H,* 3 (Winter, 1963), 32–36.

Hassan, Ihab. "Almost the Voice of Silence: The Later Novelettes of J. D. Salinger," *WSCL,* 4 (Winter, 1963), 5–20.

——. "The Dismembering of Orpheus: Reflections on Modern Culture, Language, and Literature," *American Scholar,* 32 (Summer, 1963), 463–464, 466, 468, 470, 472, 474, 476, 478, 480, 482, 484.

Hayes, Ann L. "J. D. Salinger: A Reputation and a Promise," *Carnegie Institute of Technology Department of English Lectures on Modern Novelists* (1963), 15–24.

Jesse, Cornelia. "Creative Fulfillment," *Critic,* 12 (October–November, 1963), 24–31.

Kearns, F. E. "Salinger and Golding: Conflict on Campus," *America,* 108 (January 26, 1963), 136–139.

Kinney, Arthur F. "J. D. Salinger and the Search for Love," *TSLL,* 5 (Spring, 1963), 111–126.

——. "The Theme of Charity in *The Catcher in the Rye,*" *Papers of the Michigan Academy of Science, Arts, and Letters,* 48 (1963), 691–702.

Lakin, R. D. "D. W.'s: The Displaced Writer in America," *Midwest Quarterly,* 4 (1963), 295–303.

Laser, Marvin, and Norman Fruman. "Not Suitable for Temple City," *Studies in J. D. Salinger,* pp. 124–129.

——. "Salinger: The Early Reviews," *Studies in J. D. Salinger,* pp. 6–22.

—— (eds.). *Studies in J. D. Salinger: Reviews, Essays and Critiques of* THE CATCHER IN THE RYE *and Other Fiction*. New York: Odyssey, 1963.

Little, Gail B. "Three Novels for Comparative Study in the Twelfth Grade," *English Journal*, 52 (September, 1963), 501–505.

Lyons, John O. "The Romantic Style of Salinger's 'Seymour: An Introduction'," *WSCL*, 4 (Winter, 1963), 62–69.

Mailer, Norman. "Norman Mailer vs. Nine Writers," *Esquire*, 60 (July, 1963), 63–69, 105.

Marcus, Fred H. "*The Catcher in the Rye*: A Live Circuit," *English Journal*, 52 (January, 1963), 1–8.

Margolis, John D. "Salinger's *The Catcher in the Rye*," *Explicator*, 21 (November, 1963), Item 23.

Marsden, Malcolm M. (ed.). *If You Really Want To Know: A Catcher Casebook*. Chicago: Scott, Foresman, 1963.

Noon, William T. "Three Young Men in Rebellion," *Thought*, 38 (Winter, 1963), 559–577.

Olan, Levi A. "The Voice of the Lonesome: Alienation from Huck Finn to Holden Caulfield," *Southwest Review*, 48 (Spring, 1963), 143–150.

Panichas, George A. "J. D. Salinger and the Russian Pilgrim," *Greek Orthodox Theological Review*, 8 (Summer, 1962–Winter, 1962–1963), 111–126.

Parrish, M. E. *Commonweal*, 25 (November, 1963), 350. Reply to Chester, *Commonweal* (June, 1963).

Réda, Jacques. "Franny and Zooey," *Cahiers du Sud*, 55 (April–May, 1963), 151.

Reiman, Donald H. "Salinger's *The Catcher in the Rye*, Chapters 22–26," *Explicator*, 21 (March, 1963), Item 58.

Rosenthal, Jean. "J. D. Salinger," *Informations et Documents*, No. 175 (February, 1963), 24–28.

Russell, John. "Salinger: From Daumier to Smith," *WSCL*, 4 (Winter, 1963), 70–87.

Saha, Winifred M. "The Story of Holden Caulfield," *If You Really Want To Know: A Catcher Casebook*, ed. Malcolm M. Marsden, pp. 28–29.

"Salinger: An Introduction," *Christian Century*, 80 (February 27, 1963), 287.

Schwartz, Arthur. "For Seymour—With Love and Judgment," *WSCL*, 4 (Winter, 1963), 88–99.

Shigeo, Hisash. "The Genealogical Record of the Glasses," *Hiyoshi Ronbunshu* (September, 1963), 14–28. In Japanese.

Simonson, Harold P., and Philip E. Hager (eds.). *Salinger's* CATCHER IN THE RYE: *Clamor vs. Criticism.* Boston: D. C. Heath, 1963.

Slabey, Robert M. *"The Catcher in the Rye:* Christian Theme and Symbol," *College Language Association Journal,* 6 (March, 1963), 170–183.

Strauch, Carl F. "Salinger: The Romantic Background," *WSCL,* 4 (Winter, 1963), 31–40.

Turner, Decherd. "The Salinger Pilgrim," *Seventeenth Annual Conference: American Theological Library Association* (Austin, Texas: Episcopal Theological Seminary of the Southwest, 1963), 59–69.

Vanderbilt, Kermit. "Symbolic Resolution in *The Catcher in the Rye:* The Cap, the Carousel, and the American West," *WHR,* 17 (Summer, 1963), 271–277.

Vogel, A. W. "J. D. Salinger on Education," *School and Society,* 91 (Summer, 1963), 240–242.

1964

Baumbach, Jonathan. "The Saint as a Young Man: A Reappraisal of *The Catcher in the Rye," Modern Language Quarterly,* 25 (December, 1964), 461–472. Collected in *The Landscape of Nightmare* (New York: New York University Press, 1965), pp. 55–67.

Brown, Robert McAfee. "The Theme of Waiting in Modern Literature," *Ramparts,* 5 (Spring, 1964), 68–75.

Costello, Patrick. "Salinger and 'Honest Iago'," *Renascence,* 16 (Summer, 1964), 176–187.

Detweiler, Robert. "J. D. Salinger and the Quest for Sainthood," *Four Spiritual Crises in Mid-Century American Fiction* (Gainesville: University of Florida Press, 1964), pp. 36–43.

Hamilton, Kenneth. "J. D. Salinger's Happy Family," *Queen's Quarterly,* 71 (Summer, 1964), 176–187.

———. "One Way to Use the Bible," *Christian Scholar,* 47 (Fall, 1964), 243–251.

Howell, John Michael. "The Waste Land Tradition in the American Novel," *Dissertation Abstracts,* 24 (1964), 3337.

Kranidas, Thomas. "Point of View in Salinger's 'Teddy'," *Studies in Short Fiction,* 2 (Autumn, 1964), 89–91.

Mannoni, O. "Le masque et le parole," *Les Temps Modernes,* 20 (November, 1964), 930–942.

Mizener, Arthur. "The American Hero as Poet: Seymour Glass," *The Sense of Life in the Modern Novel* (Boston: Houghton Mifflin, 1964), pp. 227–246.

Murphy, Carol. "Some Last Puritans," *Approach*, No. 53 (Fall, 1964), 38–43.

O'Hara, J. D. "No Catcher in the Rye," *MFS*, 9 (Winter, 1963–1964), 370–376.

Rees, Richard. "The Salinger Situation," *Contemporary American Novelists*, ed. Harry T. Moore (Carbondale: Southern Illinois University Press, 1964), pp. 95–105.

Ross, Theodore J. "Notes on J. D. Salinger," *Chicago Jewish Forum*, 22 (Winter, 1963–1964), 149–153.

Slabey, Robert M. "Salinger's 'Casino': Wayfarers and Spiritual Acrobats," *English Record*, 14 (February, 1964), 16–20.

Tirumali, Candadai K. "Salinger's *The Catcher in the Rye*," *Explicator*, 22 (March, 1964), Item 56.

Uchiyama, Miyazo. "Salinger's Religious Phases in Their Development," *Eigo Eibungako Ronso* (January, 1964), 115–126. In Japanese.

Wiebe, Dallas E. "Salinger's 'A Perfect Day for Bananafish'," *Explicator*, 23 (September, 1964), Item 3.

Yamaya, Saburo. "J. D. Salinger's Quest of 'The Valley of the Sick'," *Studies in English Literature*, 40 (March, 1964), 215–243.

1965

Bode, Carl. "Mr. Salinger's *Franny and Zooey*," *The Half-World of American Culture: A Miscellany* (Carbondale: Southern Illinois University Press, 1965), pp. 212–220.

Finkelstein, Sidney. "Cold War, Religious Revival, and Family Alienation: William Styron, J. D. Salinger and Edward Albee," *Existentialism and Alienation in American Literature* (New York: International Publishers, 1965), pp. 211–242.

French, Warren. "Holden's Fall," *MFS*, 10 (Winter, 1965), 389.

——. "An Unnoticed Salinger Story," *College English*, 26 (February, 1965), 394–395.

Genthe, Charles V. "Six, Sex, Sick: Seymour, Some Comments," *Twentieth Century Literature*, 10 (January, 1965), 170–171.

Glazier, Lyle. "The Glass Family Saga: Argument and Epiphany," *College English*, 27 (December, 1965), 248–251.

Green, Martin. "*Franny and Zooey*," *Re-Appraisals: Some Commonsense Readings in American Literature* (New York: W. W. Norton, 1965), pp. 197–230.

Laser, Marvin. "Character Names in *The Catcher in the Rye*," *California English Journal*, 1, no. 1 (1965), 29–40.

McNamara, Eugene. "Holden as Novelist," *English Journal*, 54 (March, 1965), 166–170.

Miller, James E., Jr. *J. D. Salinger*. Minneapolis: University of Minnesota Press, 1965.

Moore, Robert P. "The World of Holden," *English Journal*, 54 (March, 1965), 159–165.

Peavy, Charles D. "Holden's Courage Again," *CEA Critic*, 28, no. 1 (1965), 1.

Seitzman, Daniel. "Salinger's 'Franny': Homoerotic Imagery," *American Imago*, 22 (Spring–Summer, 1965), 57–76.

Tanner, Tony. *The Reign of Wonder: Naivity and Reality in American Literature* (New York: Cambridge University Press, 1965), pp. 339–349.

Warner, Deane M. "Huck and Holden," *CEA Critic*, 27, no. 6 (1965), 4a–4b.

Weber, Ronald. "Narrative Method in *A Separate Peace*," *Studies in Short Fiction*, 3 (1965), 63–72. Comparison with *Catcher in the Rye*.

Wiegland, William. "Salinger and Kierkegaard," *Minnesota Review*, 5 (1965), 137–156.

1966

Antico, John. "The Parody of J. D. Salinger: Esmé and the Fat Lady Exposed," *MFS*, 12 (Autumn, 1966), 325–340.

Beebe, Maurice, and Sperry, Jennifer. "Criticism of J. D. Salinger: A Selected Checklist," *MFS*, 12 (Autumn, 1966), 377–390.

Bellman, Samuel I. "New Light on Seymour's Suicide: Salinger's 'Hapworth 16, 1924,' " *Studies in Short Fiction*, 3 (1966), 348–351.

Brother Fidelian Burke, F.S.C. "Salinger's 'Esmé': Some Matters of Balance," *MFS*, 12 (Autumn, 1966), 341–347.

Cohen, Hubert I. " 'A Woeful Agony Which Forced Me to Begin My Tale': *The Catcher in the Rye*," *MFS*, 12 (Autumn, 1966), 355–366.

Ely, M. "A Cup of Consecrated Chicken Soup," *Catholic World*, 202 (February, 1966), 298–301.

Goldstein, Bernice and Sanford. "Zen and Salinger," *MFS*, 12 (Autumn, 1966), 313–324.

Hagopian, John V. " 'Pretty Mouth and Green My Eyes': Salinger's Paolo and Francesca in New York," *MFS*, 12 (Autumn, 1966), 349–354.

Hainsworth, J. D. "J. D. Salinger," *Hibbert Journal*, 64 (Winter, 1966), 63–64.

Howell, John M. "Salinger in the Waste Land," *MFS*, 12 (Autumn, 1966), 367–375.

Noland, Richard W. "The Novel of Personal Formula: J. D. Salinger," *University Review*, 32 (1966), 19–24.

Pilkington, John. "About This Madman Stuff," *University of Mississippi Studies in English*, 7 (1966), 65–75. The question of sanity in *The Catcher in the Rye* and *Huckleberry Finn.*

Russell, John. "Salinger's Feat," *MFS*, 12 (Autumn, 1966), 299–311.

Sherr, Paul C. *"The Catcher in the Rye* and the Boarding School," *Independent School Bulletin*, 26, no. 2 (1966), 42–54.

Trowbridge, Clinton. "The Symbolic Structure of *The Catcher in the Rye*," *Sewanee Review*, 74 (Summer, 1966), 681–693.

Walcutt, Charles Child. "Anatomy of Alienation," *Man's Changing Mask: Modes and Methods of Characterization in Fiction* (Minneapolis: University of Minnesota Press, 1966), pp. 317–326.

1967

Bryan, James. "A Reading of Salinger's 'For Esmé–with Love and Squalor,' " *Criticism*, 9 (Summer, 1967), 275–288.

D'Avanzo, Mario L. "Gatsby and Holden Caulfield," *Fitzgerald Newsletter*, 38 (1967), 4–6.

Delpech, Jeanine. "Un Kennedyste s'explique," *Nouvelles Littéraires* (February 16, 1967), 3.

Hainsworth, J. D. "Maturity in Salinger's *The Catcher in the Rye*," *English Studies*, 48 (October, 1967), 426–431.

Hamilton, Kenneth. *J. D. Salinger: A Critical Essay.* Grand Rapids: Eerdmans, 1967.

Perrine, Laurence. "Teddy? Booper? Or Blooper?" *Studies in Short Fiction*, 4 (1967), 217–224.

1968

Balke, Betty T. "Some Judeo-Christian Themes Seen Through the Eyes of J. D. Salinger and Nathanael West," *Cresset*, 31, no. 7 (1968), 14–18.

Bryan, James. "A Reading of Salinger's 'Teddy,' " *American Literature*, 40 (November, 1968), 352–369.

Foran, D. J. "Doubletake on Holden Caulfield," *English Journal*, 54 (October, 1968), 977–979.

Freese, Peter. "Jerome David Salinger: *The Catcher in the Rye*," *Literatur in Wissenschaft und Unterricht* (1968), 123–152.

Schulz, Max. "Epilogue to *Seymour: An Introduction,*" *Studies in Short Fiction,* 5 (1968), 128–138.

Seitzman, Daniel. "Therapy and Antitherapy in Salinger's 'Zooey,'" *American Imago,* 25 (Summer, 1968), 140–162.

Trowbridge, Clinton. "Hamlet and Holden," *English Journal,* 57 (January, 1968), 26–29.

INDEX